Persuasive Copywriting

Second Edition

Persuasive Copywriting

Cut through the noise
and communicate with impact

Andy Maslen

KoganPage

First published in Great Britain and the United States in 2015 by Kogan Page Limited
Second edition 2019

2nd Floor, 45 Gee Street	c/o Martin P Hill Consulting	4737/23 Ansari Road
London	122 W 27th Street	Daryaganj
EC1V 3RS	New York, NY 10001	New Delhi 110002
United Kingdom	USA	India

© Andy Maslen 2019

The right of Andy Maslen to be identified as the author of this work has been asserted by him in accordance with the Copyright, Designs and Patents Act 1988.

Hardback   978 0 7494 9773 6
Paperback 978 0 7494 8366 1
Ebook   978 0 7494 8367 8

British Library Cataloguing-in-Publication Data

A CIP record for this book is available from the British Library.

Library of Congress Cataloging-in-Publication Data

A CIP record for this title is available from the Library of Congress.

Typeset by Integra Software Services Pvt. Ltd., Pondicherry
Print production managed by Jellyfish
Printed and bound in Great Britain by CPI Group (UK) Ltd, Croydon CR0 4YY

I dedicate this book, first to my wife, Jo,
a talented writer and marketeer in her own right
and the even keel of my occasionally storm-tossed ship;
and second to you, dear reader, because without
readers, books are meaningless.

CONTENTS

06   Three big ideas you should use for copy before highlighting the 'benefits' 76

07   A powerful process for developing customer empathy through copy 102

08   Copywriting hacks: Flattery will get you everywhere 121

09   The Ancient Greek secret of emotionally engaging copy 132

INTERVIEW
What does a global top 50 copywriter think about the world of copy?

Steve Harrison was a European Creative Director (OgilvyOne) and Global Creative Director (Wunderman) either side of starting his own agency, HTW. At HTW he won more Cannes Lions in his discipline than any creative director in the world.

I asked Steve the following question, which, with his customary generosity and good humour, he answered in a lucid and engaging article that I have left untouched.

You've said that the job of the copywriter being to solve the customer's problem, not the client's. Could you expand on that a little? What sort of problems do clients have that they mistake for those of their customers? And how does that affect the way they judge copy?

The creative departments I ran at Ogilvy and HTW were regarded as the best in the business. This, however, had little to do with my brilliance or that of the art directors and copywriters I worked with. The secret of our success lay in something I called the 'Problem/Solution Dynamic'.

At both Ogilvy and HTW, I insisted that all the briefs began with a statement of *a*) the problem being faced by the prospect and *b*) the solution being offered by the product or service we were selling. This led to a single-minded customer-focused proposition, which, in turn, told the creatives exactly what their ad should be about.

When we pitched a new client, we'd tell them about the Problem/Solution dynamic and why it was central to everything we did. Most would nod receptively. But some misinterpreted what we'd said and, instead of doing ads that focused on the prospect's problems, wanted us to do creative that dealt with the problems that *they* were having.

For example, a widget manufacturer might tell us that they'd introduced a new line but that like-for-like sales were down 3% that quarter.

Or a management consultant might say that their approach to the market was markedly different to that of their competitors but that potential customers were failing to see the benefit.

Or an airline might complain it was not being recognized as the aspirational brand that the client insisted it most definitely was.

At which, we'd tell them that while they were awake at 4.00am worrying about these things, their prospect couldn't care less. Other troubles were ruining their sleep, and these problems had to be our focus.

Yes, we'd address the 3% sales shortfall, the lack of awareness about the consultancy's different approach to the market, or the need to boost the aspirational appeal of the airline client's brand. But we would only get there by first showing how the attributes of the products and services we were selling could solve the prospects' problems.

Unfortunately most agencies, then and now, do not explain the distinction between the problems faced by the client and the prospect. Instead they ignore the latter and produce work that panders to the client's desire to see their concerns being addressed directly in the advertising.

So the widget client with the failing new product line might be presented with an ad that announces: 'The best just got better' or 'Tomorrow's technology today'.

The one with the different approach to consultancy will be presented with 'Business as unusual' or, if that get the thumbs down, 'Expect the unexpected'.

And as for the airline that seeks to raise its aspirational profile – well, the chances are that amidst the pile of self-referential clichés will be the classic: 'The Art of Flight'.

Clients love this kind of thing because it looks like it's talking about the benefits of doing business with them. But actually the only people who will notice this work are the clients themselves. Because this advertising is all about them.

The worrying thing is that most agencies don't know any better. They don't realize that their prospects' problems and the products' solutions should be at the forefront of all their thinking.

It seems there's little interest in actually crafting a message that addresses a prospect's problems when there's more fun to had adapting the latest digital innovation as the means by which it is transmitted.

Typically the fickle judges at the major award shows are dazzled by such novelty. Patrick Collister who for years has tracked the trends at these shows for The Directory Big Won rankings told me: 'Out of 27 Grand Prix at Cannes in 2017, only three of them were for work with an overtly commercial purpose. In other words, only three campaigns were trying to sell stuff.'

PREFACE
Copywriting and its place in business and marketing today

Although there is a lot of talk about the basics of copywriting being ever-green, our world does not stand still, any more than does the world of our clients. New products come along all the time, new ways of communicating with customers, new ways of understanding how people make decisions. So when my editor at Kogan Page asked me to revise this book for a second edition, I was delighted.

Our goals in producing this new edition for you were threefold.

First, to further build your confidence in your writing abilities. That's equally true whether you regard yourself as a copywriter, as someone who has copywriting as part of their broader marketing role, or as neither of those, but a generalist who still has to write copy from time to time. You may be working in advertising, marketing or PR. Or running a department, a business unit or your own company. All that matters is that you want to write copy that influences, persuades or sells.

Second, to give you even more useful content. In particular, I have written four brand-new chapters looking at content marketing, social media, creativity and the right (and wrong) way to judge copy.

Third, to make the book even more useful to you by focusing on the fast-changing demands of modern, digital, global communications.

But first, how about a question: what do we mean by 'copywriting'?

Copywriting used to be an easy word to define. It was the text you saw in press advertisements, direct mail, brochures, posters and catalogues, and saw or heard on TV and radio ads. Words that sold. There are other definitions: some circular – copywriting is the writing done by copywriters; some utilitarian – copywriting is any writing designed to get a result; some conceptual – copywriting is behaviour modification. But none, I think, comes close to encompassing the sheer variety of channels, approaches and purposes involved in contemporary copywriting.

How should we define an activity that includes the algorithmically driven process of attracting software robots ('bots') to ensure a high-scoring web page on search engines? The relationship-building inherent in blogging and social media updates? The writing of scripts for webinars and in-app videos? And, of course, the always-with-us, hardnosed selling using the written word in mailshots, email marketing and long-form landing pages?

To arrive at a workable definition, we should avoid rigid thinking about the range of channels and media open to us today, the sorts of people who carry out the trade (of which more in a moment), and the narrow objectives of particular sub-activities or campaigns. Instead, we should focus on the underlying benefit that copywriting alone provides.

Key takeaway: Copywriting is the commercial activity of creating, maintaining and deepening profitable relationships using the written word.

Can we parse this statement to test whether it holds up?

- 'Commercial activity' – this places copywriting within an environment of trading and exchange, the fundamental principle of business the world over.

- 'Creating, maintaining and deepening' – this covers the phases of customer acquisition, retention and up-selling common to many if not all businesses.

- 'Profitable' – because without their being profitable, the resulting relationships would be worthless.

- 'Relationships' – more than at any time since the invention of the telegraph, we live in an age where commerce is personal. Yes, we have a multitude of communications channels available to us, but the defining medium of our time is email, with social media close behind: both defined in terms of personal, one-to-one relationships.

- 'Using' – copywriting is merely a tool, a means to an end. Unlike journalism, fiction or reference works, the words we write are not of intrinsic value. (With a possible Get-out-of-jail-free card for content, although even here, organizations would, I am sure, stop paying to produce it if its impact on the bottom line turned out to be zero.)

- 'The written word' – copywriting is subject to the rules of composition, in whatever language it is written, and it relies for its emotional and intellectual impact on subtleties of phrasing, punctuation and syntax, not on body language, prosody or eye contact.

That will do as a definition. But what about copywriting's place in contemporary business?

How the internet changed copywriting

Here, we should review the impact of the internet on our trade. There are essentially three philosophical positions available to us in considering how the internet altered the world for copywriters:

1 It turned everything upside down, revolutionized it, in fact. Nothing is the same. Everything that we used to know is irrelevant. This is a brave new world.

2 It altered nothing. People are the same. The human brain is the same. The products we are promoting are the same. This is the comfortable old world.

3 It altered a few things that affect the presentation and consumption of copy, but left the underlying psychological principles of influence untouched. This is the old world wearing some snappy new clothes.

I cleave to this last position. To modify someone's behaviour, causing them to think, feel or act differently, by writing to them is still our goal. And that calls for traditional strengths including the ability to empathize, influence and persuade. But the new technologies have brought additional benefits.

Hypertext is genuinely exciting, allowing us to present the reader of our copy with options for how much and in what order they want to read – *without seeing what they don't*. Leave out that final clause and you might as well be describing a catalogue. Search changed the way people could find their way to our sales copy, and, for a while, it seemed as though attracting search engines was going to be the main goal of copy. Multimedia allowed us to enhance or present our copy via audio, video or animation as well as in textual form. *But it still needed writing.*

Who is the consumer of web or mobile copywriting?

Do we need to write differently for the web and other digital channels, such as mobile? Or are the ideas in this book universally applicable? Well, it depends on your view of human nature.

If you believe that there are two distinct species on Planet Earth – humans and 'web users' – then yes, for all I know, you probably do have to write differently for the web. If, on the other hand, you believe, as I do, that there is only one species, then no, you don't.

Your Auntie Sarah may be surfing at this very moment, so I suppose we could call her a 'web user'. But when she logs off and goes shopping in the high street, does she stop being a 'web user' and become a 'shop user'? I think not.

Her needs don't change the moment she goes online or swipes a finger across her tablet's screen. In fact nobody's needs do that. The only reliable and unchallenged model of human motivation is that devised by Abraham Maslow.

Maslow's 'Hierarchy of Needs' includes physiological needs, such as food, air and sleep; security needs, such as shelter and law and order; love needs, such as belongingness and relationships; esteem needs, both of the self and others; and the grandly monickered self-actualization needs, such as living a moral life and finding personal fulfilment.

None of these needs is met by the channel through which one searches but only by the object of one's search.

So, Sarah may have moved to a new town and be looking for a dance class to join. In the old days she might have looked at the noticeboard in her local library. Now she is just as likely to Google 'salsa class Newtown'. But my point is, she's looking for dance classes that will meet her need to make new friends, belong to a group and feel healthy and happy. All these needs existed before the internet.

How about her reading behaviour online? Does she read differently or need different triggers? Some say yes. Web users scan, we are told, so use headings. Well, that's not bad advice but which of these scenarios is more likely?

- After the invention of the internet in the mid-1990s, people developed a *new* reading strategy called scanning to cope with screen-based information.

- After the invention of the internet in the mid-1990s, people used an *existing* reading strategy called scanning to cope with screen-based information.

Scanning probably has its roots in the evolutionary advantage conferred on those individuals within a species able to look at their immediate environment and register threats. If you were better than your neighbours at spotting things that were going to eat you, you probably passed your genes into the next generation.

Collapsing human history down into a sentence: that primeval ability evolved into a strategy for picking out what was relevant from sheets of type.

No. Far more important is to write words that readers find *relevant*. As long as we continue to be relevant to our reader, they will favour us with their attention. How else to explain the continuing popularity of novels, which, to my certain knowledge, tend not to contain headings – even <gasp> in e-book form.

I have written this book on the assumption that you are selling to, or seeking to persuade, human beings. Human beings like stories. They are driven by their emotions. They like patterns. They are curious. These are the levers we must pull, and the techniques presented here will help you to do it. Where you deploy your words is up to you. It will make very little difference to your customer.

The rise of content marketing

At the time of writing, there is a great deal of interest in the subject of content marketing. Put simply, content marketing means providing useful information for nothing in the hope that people will search it out, consume it and trust the provider sufficiently to place their next order with them. It is of course entirely possible that we are training our potential customers to come to us for free information *and nothing else.*

However, organizations of every size and shape are churning out blog posts, reports, presentations, videos and podcasts with the zeal of a Soviet-era Russian tractor factory trying to meet its production quotas. And much of this content is written by people who call themselves copywriters (though content specialists, often with a background in editorial or journalistic work, ply their trade in these waters, too).

Is content the same as copy? The consensus seems to be that, no, it isn't, even when it's produced by copywriters. In much the same way, I suppose, that a flower bed planted by your decorator isn't a spare bedroom. But how clear is this distinction, really? Would content marketing exist if it were persistently and measurably unprofitable? From conversations with finance directors, I suspect not. In fact, content seems to fit into my definition of copywriting rather well. Its goal is the same as its more, shall we say, predatory sibling: that of creating, maintaining and deepening profitable relationships. The only real difference between copywriting and content is the subject matter. The intent, the outcome and the commercial rationale are identical.

Non-direct copywriting

Those of us who were schooled in direct marketing had it drummed into us that measurable and directly attributable results were everything. My own training as a copywriter included helping to open the mail every morning and counting order forms: that's about as direct as it gets. Measuring results has never been easier, thanks to the analytical tools available to us all for pennies, if not outright free.

But what about those forms of copywriting that we might call indirect? All those places where words appear in front of prospects and customers but there is no call to action? Packaging. Petrol pumps. Posters. Bus-sides. Bar towels. Beach umbrellas. I am sure one could argue that a strategically placed QR code would render every piece of copy trackable, but in reality that isn't happening. Or not yet. But this kind of copywriting still matters. I am inclined to believe that companies take it on faith that if there is a chance to talk to their customers, it's a chance worth taking, even if its impact can't be measured but only imagined.

What we do when we talk to employees

Whether specialist or generalist, many copywriters from time to time write copy designed to be read by a company's employees rather than its customers. This is not sales copywriting. But we are trying to increase the strength of the relationship between employer and employee. If that results in higher productivity, lower staff turnover and greater creativity at work then, surely, it fits the bill?

Employee handbooks, contracts of employment, maternity guidelines, staff handbooks, training manuals: handled well, all these communications have the ability to tap into the reader's motivations and influence their behaviour.

Then there are those communications directed towards potential employees. Another piece of HR–marketing crossover jargon is 'the employer brand'. Put simply, this just means how we talk to people who might want to work for us. As such it includes everything from recruitment advertising to job descriptions and application forms. All of which, again, fit reasonably neatly into the definition of copywriting.

CASE STUDY Lidl – press advertisement

This press ad for Lidl, a discount supermarket chain, relies for its power on two things: the research that clearly went into discovering just how the price-matching process worked at their rival; and the cheeky tone of voice employed in the body copy.

Morrisons have found a way to match Lidl's prices.*

* –– Go to the Morrisons website
– Find the new Loyalty Card Scheme page
– Set up your online account
– Create memorable password
– Confirm memorable password
– Hand over some 'minor details' about yourself such as name, last name, email and post code
– Remember to un-tick the 'Would you like to receive spam?' box
– Hand over some more 'minor details' about yourself such as post code (again), DOB, mobile number and double check you're definitely the gender you think you are
– Tell them how many people live in your household and choose from an endless list of dietary requirements
– Request a card
– Wait around for the card to turn up
– Sign back in to your account
– Try to remember your memorable password
– Enter your 19 digit card number onto the website
– Then enter the CORRECT 19 digit card number
– Realise the price match difference is given to you in points
– Learn that 1p = 10 points
– Then realise you can only start saving when you have your first 5,000 points
– Practise your mental arithmetic and work out that 5,000 points is £5
– Go into your M local store and discover you can't use your loyalty card here
– Head to a big Morrisons
– Find out your basket must include one product that is comparable to another supermarket's to make a saving
– Pick up some beans and realise they aren't part of the deal
– Try and find the beans that are part of the deal
– Wonder if that applies to beans with sausages?
– Search for other applicable items so your shop exceeds the £15 required spend
– Finally, receive your £5 voucher after you've paid for your stuff
– Get told you can only spend the £5 voucher on your next shop

Or you could just go to Lidl.

Anyone reading the ad, whether a customer of either supermarket or not, would recognize the frustration of trying to get through the maze of requirements to qualify for a discount or offer. And laugh.

Though they may have embroidered the truth a little, the writers have simply written down a list of steps you have to go through to get the price match deal. It's not a complicated idea, just a brilliant one.

Executive Creative Director: Jeremy Carr
Creative Team: Dan Kenny, Matt Deacon, Ben Fallows
All at TBWA London

Globalization and the decline of advertising copywriting

The one area where copywriting is less visible than ever before is above-the-line, or brand, advertising. Despite the halcyon glow that still emanates from the former global hubs of copywriting talent – Madison Avenue in New York and Charlotte Street in London – advertising as a medium for writers, as opposed to 'creatives', is in terminal decline. In part this has been driven by globalization. As multinational corporations strive to cut costs they begin producing international or global advertising campaigns. At a stroke, all national or even regional cultural references are *verboten*. Too much work for the different national audiences to get them.

In place of copy comes the high-concept visual and bland corporate strapline. Or the packshot and the pun. The car industry is one of my favourite exemplars of this style of advertising; not really very surprising, given the eye-watering capital costs of producing automobiles, the furious competition from new market entrants, and the long dusty highway stretching into history littered with the rusted, burned-out wrecks of brands such as Packard, Saab, Pierce-Arrow, Hummer, Rover, Geo, Sunbeam, British Leyland and DeLorean (which at least achieved immortality through its starring role in the Back to the Future films).

This may be a slightly gloomy prognosis. After all, open any magazine or newspaper and you will, still, find advertisements full of copy. I have tried to include some in this book as a reminder to ourselves that sweeping generalizations about the death of advertising copywriting are, as Mark Twain might have said, 'greatly exaggerated'.

The heart that keeps beating

Yet despite this perceived and very specific decline, the art and science of copywriting is in rude health. When every window cleaner, yoga teacher, tattoo parlour and provincial solicitor has a website, copywriting will be there to fill its pages. When giant corporations set up 20-person content marketing teams, copywriting will be there to create those blog posts, tweets and infographics. When charities launch appeals for funds to counter this disease or that natural disaster, copywriting will be the difference between empty coffers and full ones.

Why? Why is the often written-off craft of persuasive writing still with us? Can it be because it is efficient? Able to convey complex propositions succinctly for people to read on their smartphones. Can it be because it is effective? Able to open wallets and purses over thousands of miles. Can it be because, compared to the eventual rewards, it is remarkably good value for money? I suspect it is all these things and more.

At its heart, copywriting is about understanding how other people feel and showing them alternatives to the lives they lead. Better, richer, more fulfilling lives; lives free from anxiety, doubt and insecurity; lives with problems minimized or solved altogether.

Now, how to do it better.

ACKNOWLEDGEMENTS

Anybody who claims to be a copywriter should thank the people who make their job possible. In my case that means an inspiring, challenging and above all smart group of people I am proud to call my clients. Thank you all. Jo Kelly is my long-time collaborator as well as the creative director at Sunfish. To her I owe a debt of gratitude I may never be able to repay, but I try.

No book on copywriting is *sui generis* so I humbly offer my thanks to the writers whose books have inspired me over the years. They are too many to mention individually, but the works of David Ogilvy, John Caples, Drayton Bird, Phil Barden, Richard Shotton, Antonio Damasio and Steven King have been particularly close friends.

I'd also like to thank the people who graciously granted or arranged permission for me to feature their campaigns in the book. They are Vanessa Armstrong, David Bateman, Mark Beard, Bill Brand, Dave Cates, Jason Coles, Mark Dibden, Neda Hashemi, Henrik Knutssen, Sophie Lambert-Russell, Natalie Mueller, Gerard O'Brien, Charlotte Poh (who also contributed a great idea for the book itself), Ryan Wallman and Gabrielle de Wardener.

When I set out to write this book I asked the members of my Copywriting Academy for ideas about how to make it more useful to readers. Many took the time to suggest ideas and to all of them I offer my thanks. Those whose ideas made the cut and who deserve to be singled out for special thanks are Mary Clarke, Derek Etherton, Elizabeth Harrin, Matthew McMillion, Dale Moore, Les Pickford and Gary Spinks.

Also, huge thanks to Helen Kogan, Melody Dawes, Géraldine Collard, Jenny Volich, Jasmin Naim, Katleen Richardson, Stefan Leszczuk, Megan Mondi and their colleagues at Kogan Page.

Finally, I would like to offer my deepest gratitude to my family, for their support, patience and love.

HOW TO USE THIS BOOK

Each chapter in this book blends theory and practice. I introduce new techniques and ideas. Give you examples of good and bad copy. And share interviews and case studies from real-world marketing campaigns. You'll see exactly what good copywriting looks like across different roles and functions, particularly marketing. Where I can, I've included indicators of what worked and why. As you can imagine, many companies are reluctant to share sensitive sales and other performance data.

Features include:
From theory to profit…
Workshop…
Putting it into action…
Try this…
Key takeaway…
Download…
Engage…
Good/Bad…

> **From theory to profit:** inviting you to consider how, specifically, to apply the ideas in the chapter to your own business, your own copywriting.

> **Test your knowledge:** a quiz to see how much you have retained. Your chance to review and to double-check key points. All the answers are given at the back of the book.

> practical copywriting exercises you can use to practise what I've preached. Why not integrate them into your current work to make the most of your time?

Features

Throughout the book you'll see additional features:

> **Try this.** A practical idea you can experiment with right now.

> **Lightbulb moment.** If you take nothing else away from this section, take this.

> **Download.** Worksheet templates you can download at **www.sunfish. co.uk/downloads-for-persuasive-copywriting**. Or use this shortened version: **tinyurl.com/nzed99x**.

Engage. Psychology techniques and pointers to help you engage, influence and sell to your customer

Good/bad. Examples of both bad and good copywriting. For obvious reasons, the bad examples are hypothetical (though often based on real copy received by the author).

Glossary: If you come upon an unfamiliar word it's probably in the glossary. If it's not, tweet me! @Andy_Maslen

Index: If you want to find something in a hurry, flip to the index and find your keyword then turn to the relevant page(s).

From: Andy Maslen
To: You
Subject: Thank you for buying this book

Like me, you have realized that there is more to copywriting than listing benefits. More, even, than getting to the heart of what it is that your prospect really wants.

I think we must, as writers, accept that the moment we begin a new piece of work, we are connecting to a tradition of storytelling that goes back to the days of pre-history. It follows that we must also accept that there is a rich seam of writing we can learn from that doesn't have its roots in marketing 'best practice'.

So when I wrote this book my aim was to look deeper into the psychology of influence. Deeper into the rhythms and cadences of storytelling. Deeper into the influence that the world's greatest-ever communicators have wielded over their audiences.

This book is not a copywriting primer. It rests on the assumption that you already know the difference between a feature and a benefit. That you are aware of the desirability of the active voice. That you believe testimonials are important in sales copy. (And that, if you don't, you will be looking elsewhere for guidance on those basic technical points.)

It takes as its starting point the idea that psychology has more to teach us about copywriting than literature. During the course of my career as a copywriter I have observed the focus of my own interest shift from an interest in the mechanics of language to the mechanics of motivation and influence. Yes, I still care deeply about getting each word, sentence and paragraph just right, but that ability is more or less innate now and I don't believe it makes the difference between 'meh' and 'wow'.

However, this book doesn't replace anything you have already learned, from me or any of your other teachers. I have devised a completely new set of exercises to give you practice in using, playing with and modifying the techniques I discuss.

As usual, you can post your comments and questions on our LinkedIn Group – The Andy Maslen Copywriting Academy. Tweet me at @Andy_Maslen using the hashtag #HeyAndy. Or even drop me a line.

So. To work.

Yours for more profitable copywriting,

Andy Maslen F IDM

Introduction: How to write like an angel and sell like a demon

Yes, that's the worst of it. It's a desperately vexatious thing that, after all one's reflections and quiet determinations, we should be ruled by moods.

GEORGE ELIOT, *ADAM BEDE*

You are a copywriter. Writing words, and using formats, that virtually every single recipient will immediately react to with indifference, apathy or downright hostility. Your aim is to change the way they think, feel and act. You are asking them, usually, to spend money.

If that weren't a tough enough challenge, it gets worse. Because most of us have been taught to write the wrong way. All through further and higher education, and into our professional lives, our instructors, tutors, mentors and managers have insisted we stick to the facts. Nothing persuades better than the relentless piling up of evidence. Make the logical case with enough force and your reader is powerless to do anything other than comply.

Yet even the most fleeting consideration of our efforts to date would suggest that this approach is way off beam. How often have you felt like screaming, 'What do you mean you don't agree with me'? Your arguments were impregnable, your logic impeccable, your suggestion... resistible. Something was missing. And that something was emotion.

I have always felt that emotions and feelings play an important part in the way people make decisions. Over the years, I have had my suspicions confirmed by, variously, economists, scientists and strategy consultants. So I wanted to investigate further to understand not just *what* happens but *why* it happens.

Decision-making, motivation and emotion

It feels natural to attribute our decision-making ability to rationality. After all, humans are the most highly evolved form of life on Earth and have developed the greatest capacity for reason and logical thought. Our lives are awash with data – with information – from the Mozart our ambitious mothers play us while we're still swimming around in the amniotic fluid, to the endless reviews we search out and devour before buying even the cheapest item from a website. So surely we construct a mental pro/con chart using that information before we decide to do something? Well, yes. After a fashion. Our decisions are in fact powered by our motivations, which themselves are a blend of cognitive and emotional components. We may well have weighed up the pros and cons of a particular gym, but our motivation is underpinned by unhappiness with our physical body. Or a desire to get fit because we are frightened of having a heart attack.

Consumer copywriters (often but not exclusively working in advertising agencies) have long known about and played on the power of motivation. Telling a young mother in 1950s America, 'This brand of talcum powder is 30 per cent finer' might have made the logical case for buying. But, 'You'll be a good Mom when you powder junior's butt with our talcum powder' connect to her motivation to be 'a good mom'. Guess which way Mom's going to jump?

The best copywriters have always combined rational and emotional arguments. Most do it intuitively. Neuroscientists have offered reassuring evidence that it's a sound approach. For example, if your reader engages with your copy emotionally, as well as rationally, they will spend longer reading, and also remember more of it. It's a powerful approach to persuasion. And the roots of its power are twined deeply into the anatomical structure of our own brains.

The brain bits that matter

First, a disclaimer. I am not a neuroscientist (oh, you already knew that?). Research into the brain, is continuous. Whether we can map *precisely* emotions and specific brain structures is still hotly debated by scientists. But for us, as copywriters, there are two structures that help us to understand the way our brains deal with relationships between emotions and decision-making.

The limbic system is also called the palaeomammalian brain. To save you from reaching for your dictionary, that means 'old mammal' brain. Some people even call it the lizard brain to further indicate its position in the evolution of the nervous system. The limbic system is the seat of our emotions. If you have ever felt worried or anxious, happy or sad, angry or optimistic, that was your limbic system doing its job.

Were you to remove your own brain, or that of a friend, and dissect it, looking for the limbic system, where would you find it? Well, here's a clue. It isn't the furled, grey convolutions on the surface. The classic image of the brain always shows these squirming ridges, demarcated by the deep crevices, or *sulci*, running between them. This is the Cray supercomputer of the neurological world – the part of our brain that deals with higher functions such as abstract thought, logical reasoning and moral analysis. No. The limbic system is of such ancient provenance that it sits *inside* the brain, atop the brain stem, where the spinal cord emerges from the spine and joins the brain proper.

The limbic system comprises a series of discrete, yet linked structures. These include the amygdala, a tiny, almond-shaped organ involved in memory, emotional processing, especially anxiety, and social relationships; and the olfactory bulbs, which allow us to smell, considered by many psychologists to be the most powerful sense, and linked, once more, to memory.

Figure 0.1   The limbic system and the orbitofrontal cortex (OFC)

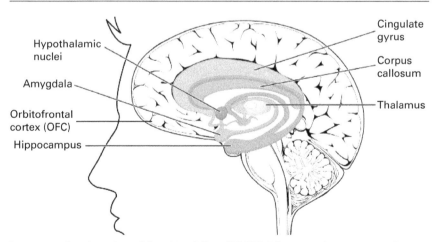

The difference between emotions and feelings

Happiness. Sadness. Fear. Anger. Disgust. Surprise. These are the six primary emotions. They cross cultural, national, racial, gender, age and intellectual boundaries. To the layperson, which I would suggest includes virtually every copywriter, advertising executive, marketeer and entrepreneur, 'emotion' is synonymous with 'feeling'. We *feel* sad and we *are* sad. But neuroscientists such as Antonio Damasio draw a clear distinction between the two words.

Emotions are bodily states that are visible to an external observer. Visual cues give away the emotion, from a drooping mouth, puffy eyes, crumpled forehead and, possibly, tears for sadness, to pallor, lips drawn back, staring eyes and heightened muscle tone for anger. Feelings are internal 'maps' of those emotions that are experienced mentally by the person 'having' the emotion, but are invisible to the external observer. Important though this distinction is, we can leave it to one side because for us, the key is understanding the role that emotions play in human motivation and decision-making.

Engage: Identify the primary emotion that best fits the sales pitch you are making. Find a way to tap into that primitive driver in your copy.

Why do we have emotions at all? Out of the six primary emotions I have listed above, four are unpleasant. In each case there is a direct evolutionary advantage in being able to experience those emotions. Take disgust, for example. Without the emotional response we label 'disgust' the prospect of eating rotten food would not appal us – with obvious and probably lethal consequences.

As far as decision-making goes, emotions also play the role of a feedback mechanism. To stick with our example of somebody considering which gym to join, they are motivated to get fit but they have also heard horror stories of people being soaked for extortionate membership fees and punitive clauses for cancelling membership. They review four or five local gyms and find one that seems to offer the best blend of equipment, trainers and reasonable fees. They join, and the positive emotions they experience say to them, Yes, you made the right decision.

Key takeaway: Motivation drives action. Information drives analysis. We want our reader to act.

Using a sophisticated form of brain scanning called fMRI – functional magnetic resonance imaging – researchers have shown how the limbic system is the primary part of the brain to fire when subjects are experiencing emotions. And when listening to stories. The part of the brain that lights up when subjects are making decisions is the orbitofrontal cortex (OFC). Put these two parts of the brain together and you have a powerful neurological nexus that we can try to affect.

The importance of information

So where does information come into the picture? Surely, we aren't all blindly being led by our hypothalamus or amygdala to select a car insurance policy or dining table? Of course not! Our motivations – to get a promotion, to find a mate, to impress our friends – drive our decision-making. And in making that decision, we rely on information to assess the fit between product X and our motivation. Emotions inform our motivations and help us measure whether our decision 'feels right'.

Towards an empathetic approach to copywriting

In this book I have assembled and explained a group of related techniques that go beyond the differentiation of features and benefits. You can group them roughly in two: those that talk about the psychology of influence, especially the role played by motivation and the emotions; and those that talk about the psychological impact of your style and tone of voice.

The second group, though more inward-looking than the first, still have an impact on your reader's emotions, since by making your copy easier and more pleasurable to read, they should decrease resistance to reading.

Throughout, I have used the words 'customer', 'prospect' and 'reader' more or less interchangeably. This was not a random act on my part, more an attempt to reflect the way all of us tend to conflate these categories. Additionally, each word brings a slightly different shade of meaning. 'Customer' suggests the transactional nature of our relationship. 'Prospect' reminds us that, as yet, we have not persuaded them. 'Reader' emphasizes the fact that we are using the written word to do our selling for us.

You can use all of the techniques across all communications channels that call for copywriting, though some may feel more appropriate for web or print or mobile. My company is not a print copywriting agency, or a new media copywriting agency: it is a *writing* agency. (That is, in fact, our slogan.) We use the techniques in this book every day when writing multi-channel campaigns for our clients, who include consumer goods companies, retailers, media companies, industrial companies, technology providers, manufacturers, professional service firms and everything in between.'

The trick is to know the techniques and be able to practise them effortlessly, but always to exercise judgement. That's not something I believe you can gain from a book – or even a training course. You have to learn it the old-fashioned way, by doing the job and working it out as you go.

Thinking about customer emotions

This book is about how to engage your reader's emotions so that they will listen to and believe your message. It is not about mind control or manipulation. I have too much trust in human nature and too much belief that my reader is not an idiot, to believe I can force them to do something they don't want to. But if they *are* considering doing it, then I strongly believe that we must get them to *feel* it's a good idea, not just think it is.

Many copywriters, both amateur and professional, do believe that it is necessary to engage their readers' emotions. So far, so good. But then comes the difficult bit. How, precisely, to do that. This is where it gets a bit messy. Here is a typical passage written by someone with good intentions and bad style. I have lightly paraphrased from an email I received while writing this chapter.

Bad: We are delighted to announce that you have been specially selected to receive a fantastic discount off our amazing new range of office furniture.

Spot the problem? Of course you do. This style of writing clogs up our inboxes every day of the year. The writer may or may not be delighted to make me the offer (I suspect they are not). But this is beside the point.

I, the reader, don't care how *they* are feeling. Their emotions are of no interest to me. They are emoting, when they should be evoking.

When I run copywriting workshops, and we fall to discussing emotional copywriting, the question is always the same.

'Well then, how *do* I convey my emotions, if I can't describe them?'

And my answer is always the same. You don't. Your reader isn't interested. Funnily enough, they are not really interested in their own emotions. They just have them. The difference is that their emotions move them to action, whereas yours don't.

So, our first commitment is to stop even attempting to describe our emotions. Every time we do, we intrude our character onto the page, where it has no business being. That solves a big problem. Now, onto the really hard work: evoking an emotional response in our reader.

Believe it or not, using adjectives, as our writer above did, doesn't really help either.

Leaving aside the question of whether a discount of 10 per cent off a filing cabinet is, in reality, fantastic (it isn't), will sticking the F-word onto the beginning of the noun it qualifies make our reader feel something that they wouldn't feel if we left it out?

Will it leave them wide-eyed and open-mouthed? No. It will not. Except, possibly, at the naïveté of a salesperson still believing that this kind of stuff works.

The true meaning of superlatives

Words such as fantastic, amazing, exciting and incredible, do, still, have meanings that aren't transferable.

I saw Led Zeppelin live at the Knebworth Festival in 1979. It was fantastic.

My first date with the woman who became my wife was exciting (and, if I am honest, just a little nerve-racking). I have had dinner with her under the stars at Uluru. That was incredible.

I was present at the births of both my children. Those experiences were amazing.

I do not find I experience those emotions when selecting accounting software, pencils, car shampoo or dog treats.

Aside from the fact that simply larding your writing with superlatives doesn't work as a sales tactic, it has a far more damaging effect.

If we describe mundane objects as breathtaking, what word do we use when writing about Niagara Falls? If everyday sales promotions are fantastic, how do we describe a new piece of music or painting that truly moves us?

This book is about persuasive writing, but the language we write in, as I said in my book, *Write to Sell*, is the English language. The commercial pool in which we swim is fed by the clear stream of writing flowing from Chaucer to the present day. Pollute it and the effluent eventually seeps into the main channel.

Let's agree to use adjectives for their intended purpose, which is to add information, not emphasis. We will talk of a limited-time offer. A one-off opportunity. A members-only discount. These phrases suggest scarcity or exclusivity, and will start our reader's emotional brain firing.

Writing that respects the reader

So back to our core question. How do we evoke an emotional response in our reader? There are a number of tools we can use. None is particularly difficult to understand or even to employ.

Once you understand how to use them, the trick is to make your effort (and they do take effort) invisible to your reader.

'Why should I?' That is what the person you are trying to persuade is thinking. They don't necessarily know you. They don't necessarily trust you. (They almost certainly *don't* trust you.)

So why *should* they? You want them to do something, or feel something, or think something that they weren't planning on doing, feeling or thinking before you wrote to them. And your challenge goes deeper than simply giving them an answer to that question.

Why? Because it masks a deeper, unspoken question that, unless you answer it first, will wreck your chances before you've got halfway through your opening sentence.

That question is, 'Why should I *read* this?' And it goes to the heart of the whole issue of persuasive writing. Before your reader grants you a moment of their time to ask for something, you have to give them a reason to start reading.

Four facts about every reader

Let's remind ourselves of four facts about our reader. About any reader:

1 They are not idiots.
2 They are under no compulsion to read what you have written, still less to keep reading it once they have started.
3 They have other things to do besides reading emails, letters, adverts or websites.
4 They have other things that matter to them a great deal more than whatever it is you want to talk about.

Does this hold true even when they have sought out your website to research a holiday perhaps, an accountancy firm, or a new car? Well, yes. It does. Here's why.

You are not the only game in town. So even if your website ranks first on Google, once your reader clicks through, you are in exactly the same position as a website that ranks 17th. If the writing is boring, or just plain bad, there are hundreds of other sites they can click away to instead of yours.

So you need to do two things if you are to have a chance of persuading your reader to adopt your preferred course of action. Firstly, make your writing persuasive. Secondly, make the experience of reading it pleasurable.

Should copywriting be pleasurable?

By 'pleasurable' I don't mean that they sit there staring at your email or sales letter smiling and making marginal notes about your expressive way with metaphors. I mean that it hooks deeply into their brains and meets the basic human need for a good story. It should be at once invisible stylistically and yet so engrossing that they cannot but help reading on.

In this regard, our writing – persuasive writing – may borrow all sorts of approaches from novelists, playwrights and journalists, but it must avoid at all costs any of their flashier devices. We do not want to draw attention to our writing. (Or do we? More in Part Two.)

For a novelist, a reader momentarily conscious that they are reading a novel is not that much of a problem. The reader has already bought the book, for one thing. For another, the writer's reputation as a turner of fabulous sentences may have been part of the appeal of the book.

For you and me, people writing to persuade, that awareness of the reading process is fatal. Once our reader becomes aware, however briefly, that they are reading junk mail, advertising, spam, marketing-speak, or just plain business writing, they lose interest both in the writing and the pitch we are making.

What are we to do then? Novelists may have to think up characters, plots and all the paraphernalia of human relationships, but at least they have willing, eager readers.

We face a reader who is, at best, merely tolerant of our writing or, and much more likely, actively hostile to it. They know they are being sold to, even as they seek out our website for information. Yet sell we must, or fail not just as writers but as business owners or managers.

My new copywriting formula that makes AIDA look tired

Let's try a little word association game. I'm going to give you a word and I want you to say the first thing that comes into your head:

AIDA

If you said 'opera', leave the room. If you said, 'Copywriting formula popularized in the mid-Twentieth Century and adapted to AIDCA (the C standing for Conviction) in the 1970s', you can stay. (And here's a gold star.)

Attention. Interest. Desire. Conviction. Action. Not bad, is it. I teach it. I've written about it. And I use it. But now there's a new way to get people round to your way of thinking. It's based on ideas drawn from psychology and neuroscience, specifically the prime role played in decision-making by your emotions.

TIPS

TIPS takes your prospect from apathy to zeal by playing on their desire to be entertained, connected, valued, recognized and satisfied.

It works by engaging your prospect's emotions progressively more deeply, without their noticing.

T is for Tempt

Before you can interest your prospect in your selling copy, you have to give them a reason to read your copy *at all*. At this point in the history of human culture, it's fairly hard to find somebody who can't recognize an ad, whether it's on social media, their favourite magazine or the side of a bus. That means we might as well recognize the fact that they know we're trying to sell to them.

Advertising copywriters and their colleagues in the art and TV departments have always known that a bright idea will catch the punter's eye. The prerequisite for making a sales pitch and the A in AIDA. Their problem has often been that laughter, tears, or 'OMG you have to see this' became the goal. The means became the end. For us, this is not enough. We want them to pay attention so that we can move to the next step. So how do we tempt our prospect to read on?

I think the strongest approach is one that connects deeply with the prospect's emotions. So a headline reading, 'The ultimate for your Porsche', typical of many I see in car magazines, is unlikely to be enough.

Sure there's a picture of a shiny 911 underneath it, but the magazine I saw it in is full of such pictures, often better shot and of the car in motion. So what connects with our prospect's emotions? How about something that makes them happy, makes them sad, or disgusts, angers, surprises or frightens them?

Here are three alternative headlines for our Porsche parts dealer:

> 'I loved that car, until this happened.'
>
> She looks beautiful, doesn't she?
>
> Keyed, crashed and left to rot in a barn. Then one man did something amazing.

Note that at this point we are really more concerned with trying to arrest our prospect in the act of turning, clicking or swiping away to something else. The pitch comes later.

Another form of temptation to read advertising copy is the clickbait headline. They are all but irresistible, until you start to notice the formula peeking out from under the copy. Generally they rely on our desire to be made happy by experiencing a positive emotion such as joy or wonder; or on our curiosity, frequently to witness somebody else's discomfort or something vaguely 'naughty'.

This type of thing:

> 31 people who wished they'd stayed in bed. Number 19 will make you blush to your boots.
>
> The hottest boyband stars hit the Oscars after party. Who is that with the First Lady?
>
> Literally THE cutest animal pictures on the Internet. I cried at the baby lemur in the teacup.

I is for Influence

Now they've been tempted, you do two things. First of all you deliver the satisfaction you promised when you tempted them. Then you start to work on their deeper motivations. Please note: you are still not going to pitch to them. It's too early to switch to a list of benefits – they're still in 'entertain me' mode. What you can do, though, is weave a story that draws them deeper into your world.

Let's say you are writing copy to promote a new private gym. You tempted them with a photograph of a man and a woman doing weights together. Your headline reads:

> One of these people weighed 17 stone just a year ago.

A fairly simple puzzle story headline and damn hard to resist. Your prospect thinks, 'Well, I definitely want to know who it was and I can just read long enough to get the answer then I'm outta here.'

But they aren't, are they. Because you're not going to make it that easy. Here's what you do. You write:

> Hello, I'm Chris. That's me in the picture. I look pretty good, I think. But you'd be shocked if you could see a selfie I took just 12 months ago.
> Fat, out of condition and heading for a heart attack. (That's what my doctor said, by the way.)

Ah, Jeez. I really do need to know which of these two is Chris. It's probably the woman. Maybe I'll just read a couple more sentences.

Let's put our prospect out of their misery.

> The first thing I decided to do was start exercising. My wife advised me to join a gym so I'd have support and all the right equipment. And guess what? I lost so much weight they asked me to be a fitness adviser for Sarah. That's her with the weights.

Oh my God! It's the guy!

Now, at this point in the story, our prospect could just leave. After all, they've got the information they needed. But it's too late. Because we have, subtly, started to influence their emotions.

Bear in mind that the people we are ultimately pitching to are those who feel they ought to join a gym. People who don't want to join a gym may still be reading the ad, perhaps because they are waiting for a dentist's appointment, but they aren't going to buy. So our prospect, who wants to join a gym, has just read one headline and eight sentences of body copy. They have committed to reading our copy. Which is about somebody they can identify with.

P is for Persuade

Now, when your prospect is lapping up your copy, you turn from a story about somebody like them, to a story about them, themselves. You are going to persuade them with arguments, proof, examples and further emotional rapport building that your gym is good for them. Like this:

> I didn't know where to start. So I did a Google search. The Lawns came up and what I liked about them was the way they talked about exercise.
>
> They made it sound like fun. Not some sweaty session trying to look like a weightlifter, just normal people trying to keep fit and healthy. And they have free advice from their fitness advisers (like I am now).
>
> I gave Sarah a simple, seven-point plan to shed her weight and get stronger too.
>
> We worked together once a week for the first six weeks and I couldn't believe how fast everything changed for Sarah. Just like it had for me.

This is where you can talk about the benefits, but remember, most people have a vague idea that joining a gym helps you lose weight and get fit, so you'd better have something better than that to talk about. Pretty much the entire content of an old-style ad would fit into this part of your thinking.

The evidence, the special offers, the testimonials, the money-back guarantees, the descriptions of the luxury changing rooms, state-of-the-art equipment and vanilla-scented towels. The thing is, most private gyms will have all of this, so it's not much of a point of difference. Your storytelling ability, on the other hand, is.

S is for Sell

Well, you didn't think we were just going to let it all end on persuasion, did you? At some point, your client or your finance director or your investor is going to look you straight in the eye and ask you one, simple question about your copy: 'Are we making any money from it?'

And you are going to look them straight back and say, 'Yes, tons'.

Because you are going to finish your ad with the deepest and most forceful level of emotional engagement of all. You are going to modify your prospect's behaviour to the point that they take out membership – by selling to them. No, let's be more specific. By closing the sale.

Those prospects who are still with you at this stage are convinced. They just need you to nudge them to find their credit card and pick up the phone, or fill out the online membership application.

The four Rs

The best way to close the sale is to use my four Rs sub-formula. *Repeat* your story from the beginning. *Remind* them of the reason they stayed with you (the benefits, in other words). *Reassure* them that they are making the right decision. Then *relieve* them of their money.

It's as powerful as you can get without holding a gun to their head and believe it or not they will be glad you did. Because deep down they want to join. You gave them all the reasons why it was a good idea and removed all their doubts. What's left but to say 'Yes'? Here's how we might do it:

> Join Chris and our other members at The Lawns and say 'Hi' to the new you.
>
> Remember, your trial membership comes complete with our 'Fit, fun and fabulous' money-back guarantee so you have nothing to lose (except those pesky pounds).
>
> Call Julie our friendly New Member Team Leader now on 0800 555 1253 or join here on our secure New Member Welcome Page.

Out with the old, in with the new?

Is this a call for the head of AIDA? Of course not! It's served me faithfully since I started writing copy for a living. But it's mechanistic and focuses too much on the need of the copywriter to have an easy way to write copy.

I like TIPS (and I developed it) because it's all about the customer and their emotions.

And that's where selling really happens.

Figure 0.2 The four Rs

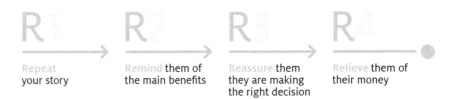

| Repeat your story | Remind them of the main benefits | Reassure them they are making the right decision | Relieve them of their money |

The important thing to remember as you work through this book is that everything you have learned so far about copywriting is still true. *In principle*. It's just that there is a richer seam of language you can mine once you start to understand how the world looks from your customer's perspective. One of the techniques that definitely applies is keeping things as simple as you can manage. Flashy language that demonstrates your towering command of the English language is unlikely to possess the qualities needed to engage your reader's emotions, namely rapid understanding, resonance, sensory qualities and everyday tone of voice.

PART ONE
Copywriting in a 21st-century context: What now, where next?

Creativity 01

All shall win prizes or a genuinely marketable skill?

Of all the terms flying about in the world of copywriting, the one that gives me the greatest pause is 'creativity'. I think that's because it promises so much and yet delivers so little. Everyone has an idea that creativity is a good thing. There are even categories of advertising folk called, simply, 'creatives'. In this section, I want to explore what the word means for us, as copywriters, and whether and how we can exploit, connect with or otherwise develop our own creativity. But first, a definition.

What is creativity?

What is creativity? And while we're about it, why are we here, is there a God and what is art? In researching this chapter I did what everyone does and turned to Google. Then I turned away. There are gazillions of attempts to define creativity. Most focus on a few core ideas having to do with problem-solving, originality, newness and non-obviousness.

'Given time, the brain and the subconscious are able to deliver real magic.'

VIKKI ROSS

Yet I worry that in our industry, the term is defined much more narrowly. You have your new-business people, who bring in the clients. Your account people, who lunch the clients and sell the ads in. Your planners and strategists who come up with insights. And your creatives who do one of two things. Write or design ads. Increasingly now, we are seeing the rise of the 'hybrid creative' who does a bit of writing and a bit of art direction.

There's another word that gives me the creeps. 'Art'. The day ad agencies decided that graphic designers were 'art directors' was the day commerce was shoved to the back of the room and given a horrible nylon-covered chair with chewing gum stuck to the seat.

A hint of the mystery attached to the word comes from its dictionary definition. The first four words of the definition of 'create' in my *Shorter Oxford English Dictionary* are these:

'Of a divine being...'

In the Renaissance, the idea of creativity was bound up entirely with the idea of a human being as a vessel for a divine spark of creation. It wasn't until the Enlightenment that the word began to take on connotations of human cognition and imagination.

In layperson's language, 'creative' means 'arty' or possibly 'crafty'. They would not, generally, consider engineers, soldiers or urban planners to be creative, even though these three, and many other, jobs involve a huge amount of problem-solving, imagination, non-obvious thinking and improvization. Whereas a man painting the same landscape over and over again for his entire adult life, as does the father of Henning Mankell's fictional Swedish detective Wallander, would receive the designation 'creative'.

I find Graham Wallas's five-stage model of the creative process useful in mapping the way copywriters (and designers) solve problems using creativity.

1 **Preparation** (preparatory work on a problem that focuses the individual's mind on the problem and explores the problem's dimensions).

2 **Incubation** (where the problem is internalized into the unconscious mind and nothing appears externally to be happening).

3 **Intimation** (the creative person gets a 'feeling' that a solution is on its way).

4 **Illumination** or insight (where the creative idea bursts forth from its preconscious processing into conscious awareness).

5 **Verification** (where the idea is consciously verified, elaborated, and then applied).

Graham Wallas, *The Art of Thought* (Solis Press, 2014)

Let's map these stages onto the copywriting process and look for some inspiration along the way.

Preparation

The problem a copywriter faces is, 'How do I sell product X to prospect Y?' (I could add, while staying inside the brand voice, assuming there is one.) I touch on this aspect of our job in the section on *The right and the wrong way to judge copy* on page XX. Our start point should be the brief, and all the background material – customer profiles, research, earlier ads and marketing materials, competitor advertising and so on – that they provide. Or should. But there are many more activities we can engage in to immerse ourselves fully in the world of our client and their customers.

- We could visit the client's factory, offices, call centre, trading floor or retail outlets.
- We could spend some time on their social media feeds.
- We could interview a bunch of their customer service people, or their sales team.
- We could spend some time using their product for ourselves. (I am, at the time of writing, still waiting for a call from Maserati.)

Incubation

Beyond all of these activities, I would also recommend some of those I talk about in the chapter *How to engage your imagination and free your creativity* on page 188. I have many of my best ideas while walking with my dog in the fields near my home. It's equally likely that an idea will bubble into your unconscious mind while you are sleeping or doing some non-writing-related activity. When I picture young copywriters playing pinball or table football in the rec rooms so thoughtfully provided by their agencies, this is what's happening. I hope.

Intimation

I get the feeling of an idea's arriving as I sit at my desk, staring at an empty screen, fingers hovering over the keyboard. It's on the tip of my tongue. I try to look the other way so that the idea can complete its journey from my subconscious to my conscious mind. At this point I can almost hear competing voices in my head, all clamouring to be heard with their version of 'the line'. This leads to…

Illumination or insight

Yes! That's it! I just know that this is the way to go. I'm willing to trust this moment and then try to write the idea down as fast and as furiously as I can before the spark dims.

Verification

I start typing, hesitantly at first, then with growing speed and confidence. Critically, I do not look up from the keyboard. Never having learned to touch-type, I find this very easy. I don't want to see what's appearing on screen, lest I be tempted to backspace over it, judging the writing before it's even finished. Instead I bash away as fast as I can, trying to capture those elusive few lines that will open the way to the rest of the copy. From there on, it's a process of finishing the execution (the first draft), then leaving it for a while before returning to redraft, polish edit, check and show it to our creative director for her opinion.

How a top copywriter 'does' creativity

Vikki Ross is one of the UK's leading independent copywriters. She has worked with major brands including Adidas, The Body Shop, Crew Clothing, Habitat, ITV, Paperchase, Philips, Sainsbury's, Sky and Virgin. She was so sure she wanted to be a copywriter that, rather than going to university, she headed straight for her chosen career. She is now one of the most sought-after copywriters in the country. She's a friend and a very creative writer, so I asked her a couple of questions about creativity.

How do you feed that part of you that has to be creative on demand?
It's so unfortunate that our business is so demanding of instant wins because given time, the brain and the subconscious are able to deliver real magic. To find the magic on demand, I often have to flick through magazines to get words going around my head. I don't read them page by page – the headlines are often enough to spark something, especially if the magazine is relevant to the subject I'm working on (my house is filled with old December issues for when I need Christmas copy inspiration, usually around May each year!).

Sometimes just going for a short walk straight after reading the brief will reward me with ideas. If it's a really great brief, full of insight and inspiration, I'll have the line or an idea before I've even finished reading it.

You often have to encapsulate an entire TV show in a very short line. How do you go about it?
I'm very lucky because I get to read whole scripts or watch episodes before a series goes live, so at first I let go and immerse myself

in the story – just as the audience would. Then I read it again but with my laptop or pen and paper to hand to note any elements or characters that are key to the overall theme. Those notes become the brief to myself and then I get to work, writing words and phrases any which way until I crack 'the line'.

When should we apply creativity?

There are two answers to this question. The first answer, the principled, high-toned answer, is 'All the time'. It matters not whether you are writing about AI-based HR software, organic soya yoghurt or Kevlar body armour, you should be searching out that elusive, non-obvious, novel way of explaining their benefits. The second answer, which is rather more pragmatic, is, 'Well, it depends'.

Is creative copywriting a red herring?

If you have been asked to write product copy for 137 different types of stationery for a website, frankly you don't need creativity so much as caffeine and a big gob of self-discipline. Over the thirty or so years I've been writing copy, there have been projects where, if I'm honest, the client didn't need a novel or innovative approach. They had a tried and tested formula for promoting their products and services, and it worked just fine. What they lacked was either the time to write the copy themselves, or a large enough stable of external writers whom they could call up on to write it for them. In circumstances like these, you may find yourself asking, 'Is creative copywriting a red herring?'

Again, the non-definitive answer is, 'It might be'. Too much of the copy I see, either in above-the-line campaigns or direct response applications, reveals nothing more than the copywriter's obvious desperation and/or delight in creating punning headlines and 'cute' body copy. They would do much better to stick to the basics of shifting merchandise and leaving the funnies to gag-writers and stand-up comics.

Creativity? Sometimes it's best to come to it cold

Some brands stand out for their creative way with language. One of them is Ben & Jerry's. I asked Kerry Thorpe, Communications Lead at Ben & Jerry's Europe, about the company's humorous tone of voice.

Why do you think Ben & Jerry's uses humour so successfully in its copy?
Ben & Jerry's was founded nearly 40 years ago by school friends Ben and Jerry. They opened their first ice cream parlour in the small town of Burlington in Vermont and wanted to use the voice of the company to take a stand on the issues that mattered to them.

When it comes to activism, the team at Ben & Jerry's found early on that to make the greatest possible impact it helps to address big issues in a way that's approachable. It's because of this that we inject humour wherever we can, from naming our climate justice campaign 'Save Our Swirled' with the tagline 'If it's melted, it's ruined' to renaming fan favourite Cookie Dough 'I Dough, I Dough' for marriage equality.

There's a lot of natural word play when it comes to ice cream too. We're known for our creative flavour names – Karamel Sutra, Phish Food – and brainstorming them is a pretty fun process to be a part of. The whole company gets involved when it's time to name a new addition, swapping ideas and puns around the office. When you know there's not an expectation to take yourself too seriously, writing new materials is something to look forward to.

What do you folk do to stimulate your creativity?
It begins when you enter our office. Our founders famously once said: 'If it's not fun, why do it?' and this motto really caught on. We have a slide in our HQ, nap pads for when we need it, we can bring our dogs to the office and each get to take home three tubs of ice cream every day.

It also comes down to the fact that at Ben & Jerry's we are encouraged to not just accept failure, but celebrate it. We know creativity involves risk, and that's OK. We have a dedicated 'Flavour Graveyard' at our HQ in Vermont, full of physical tombstones that bid a fond farewell to flavours unsuccessful in the marketplace. The graveyard reminds us that creativity – even with failed attempts in-between – will lead us to better (or tastier) results.

Does the tone of voice vary across different platforms/channels?
I wouldn't say so. Whether we're having a dialogue with one fan on social media, or addressing a big topic like climate justice, we infuse everything we talk about with a positive, approachable and fun tone. Hopefully that shines through across each platform and channel.

You're a writer, so write!

Copywriting is a lovely way to earn a living. Compared to many other walks of life, sitting at a desk in a comfortable centrally heated/air-conditioned office and tapping a keyboard for money takes some beating. But it has its duller moments. I once had a client who published dense reference books for bankers and lawyers. The copy was good, and it shifted a great many units, but candidly? Writing it wasn't particularly interesting. Too much of that sort of work can dull our appetite for the written word altogether. So my prescription is this.

Write for yourself. Every day. It doesn't really matter what you write. A journal. Character sketches of people you work with. Book reviews. Poems. Songs. Recipes. Short stories. Novels.

Just write something for yourself. There's no brief. No account director. No manager, investor or client to red-pencil your efforts. You can keep them in a drawer, or never even print them out. But they're yours.

Since I wrote the first edition of this book, I have embarked on a second career as a novelist. I write action thrillers. As of January 2019, I have published ten. Two things have happened to my creativity.

One, it has become more developed. I am able to dream up better and more exciting plots, and richer and more complex characters. And my writing itself has flourished after two decades of writing to briefs and teaching the virtues of Plain English. I write now the way I used to in my teens, unfettered by notions of what is 'best practice' or 'most responsive'.

Two, that rejuvenated sense of creative liberty had informed the copy I write for clients. I'm not saying every white paper, website and e-shot reads like a Jack Reacher book. Simply that I have unlocked a part of my brain that engages my readers' emotions and makes them desperate to read more of what I've written. Not a bad trait for someone who (still) writes what many punters dismissively refer to as junk mail for a living.

How Innocent quenches its writers' thirst

A brand that stands out for its (much-imitated) tone of voice is Innocent, a manufacturer of smoothies and fruit-based drinks. To find out how they keep their writers' imaginations well nourished, I spoke to Hayley Redman, the company's senior copywriter.

How is creativity viewed at Innocent?

Innocent is very keen to give us opportunities to flex and develop our creative skills. From creative training sessions to days off where we can work on a project of our choosing (we call them FedEx Days because we have to turn them around in 24 hours), there's a big focus on breaking out of the norm of everyday desk work to give us a chance to explore ideas that haven't necessarily been briefed in.

Is it always about writing or do you try non-writing activities?

We go on a lot of excursions together, doing creative things like trying our hands at letterpress print and creating fonts. It helps us think about our work in different ways and gives our brains a bit of extra stimulation. We go to conferences and awards shows to see inspiring work and we're all encouraged to speak about Innocent and the tone of voice at events. And, of course, there's a big focus on training that can specifically help us hone our craft.

How do Innocent writers stay in touch?

We're given a lot of space to find things that we find exciting and want to learn more about. All the writers from every European market get together for a writers' club session every six months so that we can catch up on our challenges and successes and see what incredible work has been done in different countries. It helps us maintain consistency in our tone across languages, but also gives us a lot of inspiration when we see how different markets have solved challenging copy briefs.

How to escape rigid thinking and be more creative (or not)

Being a copywriter is a lot like being a chameleon. Not the whole eye-swivelling, gross metre-long sticky tongue rocket thingy, but the ability to blend in with one's surroundings. In our case, those surroundings are twofold.

The persona of the person on whose behalf we are writing; and the mental landscape of the person to whom we are writing.

Middle-class failings

If you come from a comfortable, middle-class background and find yourself writing copy for a debt collection agency, you have a number of psychological shifts to make. For a start, what kind of person gets into the kind of money troubles (and, by the way, they will almost certainly not be thinking of them as 'financial woes') that mean their creditors will send a debt collector? What does it feel like to be owed money by someone in that situation? And what kind of person is it that runs a debt collection agency and, quite possibly, does the doorstepping?

Life would so much simpler for copywriters like you and me if all our clients were people just like us, selling to people just like us. Although, as a counter-argument, life might also be incredibly BORING. But, happily or otherwise, it isn't. Or rarely. Most of the time, we are selling to, or communicating with, all kinds of people, most of whom are very different to us. And that's where the problems can start.

Every one of us is born with in-built biases, which grow stronger as we mature into adults and our experiences confirm our biases. Some will reject authority, doing the opposite (or wanting to) of anything they are told to. Others will take risks when making decisions. Still others will seek the wisdom of crowds. Copywriters are no exception. I have met, and taught, many hundreds of copywriters. Here are some the biases, or prejudices, they have displayed, often on social media or in their own blogs.

11 prejudices of copywriters

1 'Businesspeople are rational, so there's no place for emotion in B2B copywriting.'
2 'I don't use typefaces that I find ugly.'
3 'I can't believe longer copy works better so I'm not going to test it.'
4 'Web users have short attention spans so my copy must be short.'
5 'Salesy copy is always wrong.'
6 'People don't need to be told what the benefits of this product are: they're obvious.'
7 'Humorous copywriting is naturally engaging to the customer.'
8 'Anyone who says you can't start a sentence with "And" is an idiot.'
9 'Anyone who misplaces an apostrophe is an idiot.'
10 'Anyone who changes my copy is an idiot.'
11 'People who read tabloid newspapers are idiots.'

Such rigid thinking is limiting in life generally, and damaging in our trade in particular. Our job is, or should be, to maximize profits for our client, employer or business. That's it.

We are not entertainers. We are not community outreach managers looking for 'engagement'. We are salespeople. You can test the validity of this assertion (because your in-built bias may already be screaming 'REJECT! REJECT!') by imagining a company with no sales. All the copywriters would be out of a job.

The merits of rigidity

Rigidity has its merits, of course. One of them is strength. We can take positions and guard them zealously when we think rigidly because, as highly articulate people, we have the verbal firepower to do so. It can be hard to win arguments against us when we're in this kind of mood. Which is why, I think, many clients/managers resort to the exercise of hierarchical power to win the day. Thus further reinforcing the bias that 'clients know nothing'.

Rigidity also saves time.

When we don't need to consider alternatives because we *know* we're right, we can plough ahead with copy straight away, without the need to think more deeply about the problem. It reminds me of the career arc of many contemporary politicians, who go from school to university, where they study politics, to an internship in an MP's office or a political think tank, to a position as a political adviser to a seat in the House of Commons.

This is unlikely to produce a mind capable of empathising with the plight of unemployed call-centre workers, single parents holding down two jobs to make ends meet or people who worry about the impact of immigration on their livelihoods.

Finally, rigidity allows us to carve out a persona. You are the copywriter who's hip. I am the copywriter who never works with one-person businesses. She is the copywriter who always knows more about English than anyone else.

But rigidity is an ill-mannered and lazy servant. It encourages us to prejudge situations. It prompts us to make snap decisions. It substitutes prejudice for openness.

Rigid thinking also shows up in the way many freelance copywriters conduct their affairs. It can best be summed up in the phrase 'I'm not worth any more than that', where 'that' is the fee they charge for any given piece of copywriting. In my experience, 'that' is a figure predicated on an hourly rate of somewhere between £25 and £60.

How do they know? How do they know that a client whose business they are going to kick-start wouldn't pay more? How do they know that their ability to charm money out of total strangers is worth less than a mechanic's ability to fix a car engine? Bias is how. Rigid thinking. 'That's the going rate for people like me so that's what I am going to charge.' So what is the alternative?

Aesop knew better

Linguistically, and psychologically, it's flexibility. Aesop told the tale of a mighty oak tree boasting to a reed of its strength. Then a violent wind blew up, and under its relentless power, the oak tree snapped in half while the reed bent in the wind and resumed its upward path once the storm had abated. That reed is a flexible mind, able to adjust to changing conditions. Without surrendering, but with a graceful adaptation.

How might we, as copywriters, learn or display such flexible thinking? Such *creative* thinking? I think it helps to start by compiling a list of one's own psychological biases. It's not necessarily a comfortable exercise. We might find ourselves writing lines like these:

I am an expert so I know what's right in every situation.
The familiar is better than the unfamiliar.
Arguments based on different ideas to mine should be destroyed verbally.

But this is OK because part two of the exercise it to write down ways to counter those biases.

Experts might decide to ask five questions before putting forward one opinion. Safety-cravers might change their routine. Verbal destroyers might use their linguistic dexterity to support the next argument they are presented with.

Flexible thinking also allows us to explore multiple solutions to the same problem. Instead of reaching for our 'long copy is best' baseball bat and smashing it down on the keyboard, we might think about a two-minute video script instead.

Instead of an elliptical, punning headline, we might sit down with the product and figure out how it makes the customer's life easier. Instead of resisting every revision requested by a client, we might think creatively about how to implement them and preserve the selling power of the original.

Time to let go?

This letting go of our biases is at once scary and liberating. Scary because they are often a big part of who we are, and without them we can feel naked and unprotected. Liberating because we are free to consider any and all possibilities, not just those on the approved list. I have strived to free myself from my own limiting beliefs and biases, and I see the difference it has made in my life and in my writing. Is rigid thinking holding you back?

It's time to bend like the reed.

The right and the wrong way to judge copy

02

When I, or one of the associate writers I work with, start work on a new piece of copy, there is one source of information I turn to before any other. No, not Wikipedia. The brief. If there's no brief, we don't start until there is.

It all starts with the brief

Creating a copywriting brief (whether or not it's for a copywriter) is a process often shrouded in mystery. I am still regularly asked by clients whether I have a template I can send them. Which is fine. I do, as it happens. But it's not really necessary. The template, I mean; the brief is crucial.

Here are some questions we should be asking.

Checklist: 10 things to ask before writing anything

1 What is the goal of the copy?
Is it to sell a product? Push a free trial of a service? Generate buzz about an idea?

2 Who is the reader of the copy?
Adrenaline junkies? Residents of Colorado? Car owners?

3 What are these people like?
What are their hopes and dreams, loves and hates? What are they like demographically? Psychographically? Religiously? Financially? Politically? Philosophically?

4 What are we promoting?
What are its features? How is it different or better than previous products from this company? From competing products? From total alternatives?

5 How does what we're writing about benefit the reader?
Does it improve their health? Make them (or save them) money? Make them popular?

6 What is the reader supposed to do when they have finished reading the copy?
Tap a button? Fill in a coupon? 'Favourite' something?

7 Are there any reasons why the reader might *not* do what they're supposed to?
Did the brand have terrible PR last year? Is the product 10× more expensive than its nearest rival? It is complicated to use?

8 What brand guidelines should we follow?
Is there a brand voice? Is it written down? Can we see it in action?

9 What is the timeline for the copy?
When do you need the first draft? How long for amends? When does it go live?

10 Who will be involved in the approval process?
Just the marketeer? The marketeer's line manager? The Chief Marketing Officer? The business owner? The board?

The essence of the brief boils down to this simple two-part question:

What is the product (P) and who is the reader (R)?

The job of the copy, and therefore the person writing it, is first, to figure out how P benefits R. Then, second, how to persuade R to want P enough to perform the desired action.

What to do when you have no brief/a bad brief

You've probably figured out the answer to this question without any help from me. But let's tease the question apart and consider each half separately.

The client has a responsibility to do their homework and fully understand the problem they are trying to solve, before asking the copywriter to execute against this problem.

MARK BEARD, SVP, Digital Media and Content Strategy, *The Economist*

No brief needed

Under this heading I'm going to include a situation that can feel seductively *like* a brief but lacks all the necessary information to *be* a brief. Mercifully, it has only happened to me twice in my career. But both times I came to grief. (I guess I should call it the Grief Brief.) More of that in a moment.

It's very hard to have literally no brief, since that would involve the person you're writing for (we'll call them the client) transmitting their need for copy to you telepathically. But typically, the no-brief sounds something like this:

Client:　I need you to write some website copy for our product. Here's a brochure and a couple of web links that tell you all about it.

Writer:　OK. Anything else you can tell me?

Client:　Uh, not really. It's all pretty self-explanatory.

Do *not* embark on a project specced this way. Resist, sweetly, any attempt by the client to move you into a keyboard-based activity. Instead of typing, tell them that you are almost ready to begin work, but you just need the answers to a few questions first. Don't use the word 'brief', since this may well be what put them off writing one in the first place. (Maybe they have a writing phobia. A senior executive I once coached did. He'd been beaten by monks at school for not writing 'properly'. I would have liked to have met those monks. With a bat.)

Then email the client my questions above. Explain that you want to **save them** time by writing a first draft that's ninety-five per cent of the way there. If they felt too busy to write a brief, the thought that not writing one could cost them even more is salutary.

If I were a copywriter I would reject any brief from a client if I had even the slightest whiff of doubt that the client didn't know what they wanted. As David Ogilvy said... 'Give me the freedom of a tight brief.' The client has a responsibility to do their homework and fully understand the problem they are trying to solve, before asking the copywriter to execute against this problem. A lack of clarity upfront means the work will never be judged against a clear aim, which in my opinion will always result in failure.'

MARK BEARD again

No brief? How about a big ego?

Now, how about the Grief Brief? The first time it happened to me, I was summoned to meet an inventor at the offices of his advertising agency.

'I want Andy Maslen,' he'd told their creative director. 'He's the man for me.'

He essentially repeated this to my face as we munched on smoked salmon and cream cheese bagels. He expounded at length on the features of his invention for two hours. And, basking in the righteous glow his praise produced, I completely forgot to ask him anything even vaguely relevant to the job of selling his product.

He rejected my first draft with the words, 'I wanted boiling nitric acid. This is tepid tea.'

Mortified, I went away and wrote two further ads, each completely different in concept, tone and style from the first, and from each other. I also offered to return the fee, but he demurred, saying, 'No, it's OK. I think I can use some of this.'

So when a copywriter gets it wrong, what's happened? Mark Beard of *The Economist* has this to say: 'It's usually one of two things. The client has provided an incomplete brief, which doesn't clearly spell out who the audience is and/or the message the advertising should convey to that audience (sometimes this is because the client hasn't done enough research to really understand their audience). Or the copywriter has taken some preconceived ideas they have about that brand or audience and writes what they believe is appropriate without really taking the time to read the brief and/or deep-dive into the research and data that has been provided.'

The second occasion was, I suppose, a brief of sorts. The client was a major charity. The brief ran, in its entirety: 'Stretch your creative muscles. We want something emotional we can test against our control.' Cue the sound of a copywriter rubbing his hands together. First I read the control letter, created by a specialist fundraising agency. It was performing well, I was told.

Then I wrote a letter that I thought did a pretty good job. It evoked feelings of both gratitude and guilt. It told a story, provided by a director of the charity. And it preserved the underlying anatomy of the control, which I had been told was carefully designed, based on extensive research with donors.

The response from the client was total silence. After a week of nail biting, I emailed to ask what she'd thought of the first draft. 'It made us feel uncomfortable,' she said. 'And it has the same structure as the control. We've decided not to use it.'

What I wanted to say was, 'It was SUPPOSED to make you feel uncomfortable. And you told me the structure was PROVEN to work.' What I actually said was, 'Oh. OK. You know best.' (Or words to that effect.)

In both these cases, I let my ego and my assumptions get in the way of my own tried and tested process. Please don't let this happen to you.

How to respond to a brief

Let's agree that you've avoided my mistakes and got yourself a decent written brief. Here are a few more things to think about and ask. I would begin with this deceptively simple question.

'Has everybody who's going to approve my copy approved the brief?'

You'd be surprised how often the answer is No. And this is a real problem. Because, and I'll come on to this in the final section of this chapter, if they haven't, then how will they judge your copy? On its merits as a solution to a specific business or marketing problem laid out in the brief? Or on other criteria, of which you were unaware? Their thoroughgoing dislike of stories in copy, perhaps. Or preference for a playful and much-copied tone of voice from a famous brand.

If you can, try to speak to or email all the people in what we call the approvals loop. Because otherwise you leave yourself open to a series of frustrating and wholly unnecessary rewrites as different special-interest groups get their mucky paws on your copy. And, yes, I know it's not always possible. But in that case, go back to your client (or their representative) and at least try to get some information about the way those invisible hands tend to review copy.

Next, read the brief carefully. A document that at first glance seems packed with useful information can often turn out to be ninety per cent boilerplate, listing brand values that apply to all the company's products, generic advice about SEO or some other digital best practice, and background company information that is next to useless.

Compare it to the checklist above. If there are unanswered questions, go back and get the answers. Fail to do this and you'll be sprinting towards a patch of verbal quicksand marked by a sign reading:

> Just write whatever you like – it'll be fine.

It won't.

How to 'sell' your ideas

Many people who enjoy writing copy, whether or not that is their official job title, don't enjoy selling. Which is odd. I thought it defined the job. I'm being disingenuous. I know what they mean. They mean they prefer writing to negotiating face to face with people to persuade them to buy, do or agree to something. If they didn't I guess they'd be sales executives instead.

But there comes a point when you've slaved over a first draft, writing and rewriting until you're happy. It appears to tick all the boxes on the brief. It flows well. It's in the brand tone of voice. It's clear, concise and consistent. And it's gone to the client.

Now, maybe you're special. That unicorn whose copy never gets altered. Me? Nuh-uh. OK, it happened once. But most times, your client (who could be your boss) will want changes. And that can be a frustrating moment (he says diplomatically). Try to leave aside your feelings of anger, disillusionment and homicidal rage and instead try to parse their changes into one of two kinds:

- changes that will alter the success of the copy, ie the number of orders it will generate
- changes that won't do that, but will make it different from your first draft

I know, I know. How can you possibly know which changes will reduce the copy's effectiveness? Well, as a for instance, how about a call to action that changes from

> Join today and save 33%

to

> If you join today you could save up to 33%

I'd dig my heels in on that one.

I'd advise that you let as many of the second category go as you can while salvaging a measure of self-respect (and control). And that you let as few of the first category go as you can humanly manage. But to do that, you need *reasons*. It's not enough, and probably won't work, to just say, 'My version is better.'

You're likely to receive the timeless response, 'I'm paying. Do it my way.'

The sorts of reasons that work are all versions of evidence. Can you cite tests you've run or know about that show better results obtaining from your type of copy? Are there scholarly articles backing your thinking? Or famous copywriters you can quote? Have you run a simple readability test on both versions that proves yours is easier to understand? All these things will help.

Here's my best-performing tip. When you email your copy to your client/ boss, say something like this:

Hi Jo,
Here's the first draft of the copy.
I hope you think it meets the brief.

At a stroke this achieves two things: it encourages them to *think* about your copy instead of feeling things, and it suggests that the appropriate measure is the brief, not their own subjective judgement. On which subject...

The curse of subjectivity

I've spent my entire career in marketing counting order forms. Although nowadays they tend to be virtual. And sometimes, the order forms are sales leads or downloads or sign-ups to a newsletter. Very often, I meet people – clients, copywriters, art directors and designers – who clearly have private incomes. How else to explain their blithe disregard for sales. Instead they resort to a ragbag of unsuitable measures.

The most common mistake is to treat copywriting as an art form. You can tell when this is happening, because the person judging the copy will read it, then purse their lips and exclaim, 'I don't like it.' Or, more rarely, 'I love it.' But who cares? Copy isn't there to be loved or loathed.

Nobody should be judging copy on subjective, which amounts to aesthetic, grounds. The question isn't 'Do I like it?' but 'Will it work?' Or, to be more precise, 'Will it work better than what we're using now, in a scientifically controlled test?'

Often what works better isn't pretty. And in many or all cases, most artistically inclined people will find the visual impression this sort of copy creates horrible. But the statistically significant better results are not so easy to dismiss as 'vile', as one senior in-house designer did when I suggested they test using the typeface Courier for a charity appeal.

Let's turn to the people commissioning all the copy. The people running marketing departments, in my experience, are almost always university-educated. They are sophisticated people with sophisticated tastes in everything from cars and art to restaurants and holiday destinations. Yet their customers are very often ordinary people. People who don't walk around wondering whether Banksy is a better artist than Brancusi, or whether the Paleo is more *passé* than polenta. Too often marketeers judge copy based on its appeal to *them*. Happily there are exceptions.

The editor of the *Radio Times* (a weekly British TV listings magazine) once said to me when reading some copy I'd written to sell subscriptions, 'I don't really like it. But I don't suppose it's aimed at me.' I think I may have kissed her hand in gratitude. I once asked a marketing director, who had run exhaustive testing on everything from copy length to typefaces, what she thought about Courier. 'I hate it,' she said, her face twisting, before continuing, 'and you must use it. It always does best.'

The *only* appropriate way to judge copy is to take a rigorous, intellectually-driven approach that relies on *evidence*. In other words...

Counting orders.

The impact of new channels: From mobile to social

The impact of new channels of communication on copywriting varies depending on whom you follow on Twitter.

If they are under thirty and have books out, then everything you thought you knew about copywriting is wrong, outmoded and, frankly, useless. You could be forgiven for quoting Miranda from *The Tempest*:

> O brave new world,
> That has such people in't!

Especially, since in Shakespeare's time, the word *brave*, as well as its modern meaning of courageous, connoted something bold or showy. In choosing it as the title of his dystopian novel of a future controlled by technology, Aldous Huxley took satirical aim at a naive enthusiasm for all things technological. Sound familiar?

On the other hand, if your feed is shaded towards those on the far side of forty, you might pick up a mirror image of this message. They will (deliberately mis)quote that early sage of the world of mass media Marshall McLuhan, and say, 'The medium is not the message.' Or Bill Bernbach, advertising giant of the 20th century, and his remarks about communicating with 'unchanging man' (or woman).

The truth lies where it usually does… somewhere in the middle.

> Social media is weird and evolving fast and is a mash-up of the extremely personal and the overall brand personality.
>
> NICK PARKER

What digital hasn't changed

Here's what definitely hasn't changed.

Your customers. They still want softer skin or a faster motorbike. A more secure old age or a more exciting love life. Owning a table, a smartphone and a fridge with embedded AI has not turned them into different people. Their brains still have the same working parts they had before, including the prefrontal cortex, seat of reason; the orbito-frontal cortex (OFC), seat of decision-making; and the limbic system, seat of the emotions. If they loved old movies before, they still do. If they were into playing badminton before, ditto.

Your product. If you manufacture uPVC window frames, you still do. If you were a Tier 1 law firm offering advice on real estate transactions, you still are and you still do. If you produce limited edition prints of movie posters, yes, you still do.

The reasons your customer wants your product. This is what advertising copywriter and agency founder Bill Bernbach meant by the 'unchanging man'. Human beings now are motivated by the same forces that have always driven them. Love, lust, greed, envy, redemption, guilt, piety, sympathy, compassion, ambition, fear, anxiety, addiction, obsession, disgust, curiosity, nostalgia, prurience…

The copywriter is doing the same job she always has, too. Connecting the customer to the product by concentrating on the reasons why they might want it.

… and what it has

And here's what has changed. The places where we can put our words so they are seen or heard. Back in the Dark Ages, or the early nineties as I sometimes like to call the immediate pre-digital era, if you wanted your customer to receive your message, these were your options:

- advertising
- direct mail
- door drops
- in-store

- PR
- exhibitions

And now? To the list above, add these:

Advertising

- digital display
- PPC
- social media
- in-game
- YouTube

Social posts

- Facebook
- Twitter
- LinkedIn
- Instagram
- Snapchat
- YouTube
- Google+
- etc

Content marketing

- blog posts
- ebooks
- manifestos
- white papers
- infographics
- videos
- slideshares

Writing for small screens

There's a very good chance that anything you post online whether paid-for or not will be viewed on a smartphone screen. A 2017 Pew Research study found that 85% of US adults got their news on a mobile device.* That has big implications for the way you write and format your copy (though not for what you say).

How copywriting for digital affects the humble paragraph

Let's take a single example. The paragraph. The academic definition of a paragraph is, essentially, a bunch of sentences about the same idea. New idea, new paragraph. If your reader is consuming your copy off a piece of paper, or a decent size screen, that definition might still serve. Although you'd do well to remember that nobody pays to read your copy, so breaking it up into manageable chunks will give the illusion (if not the truth) that it is going to be easy to read.

But if they're reading from a smartphone screen, everything changes. Let me show you what I mean. The two paragraphs in this grey box are set out as you might read them on a computer screen (this is my iMac).

The longest (by which I mean deepest) paragraph is four lines. Even without headings to break up the copy, it looks reasonably undaunting to read.

Now look at how they appear on my phone, in Figure 3.1A.

See the difference? The first paragraph, already fairly chunky, at five lines plus a single word, has splurged out to 11, plus the same isolated word. (Ironically, 'read'.) The second has jumped from two and a bit to five. This looks like hard work before we've even read a word.

My thinking on paragraphing has firmed up from my pre-digital days. I would have said: *A paragraph is a block of copy about a single idea, unless it goes over five lines on the page.*

Now, I say: *A paragraph is a unit of depth. Preferably three lines max.*

To show you the difference this makes to assumed readability, Figure 3.1B shows those same two paragraphs, broken up further.

Now, the same piece of copy looks invitingly easy to read. Those seven lines of white space are visual stepping-stones that the reader's brain interprets as resting places.

Figure 3.1

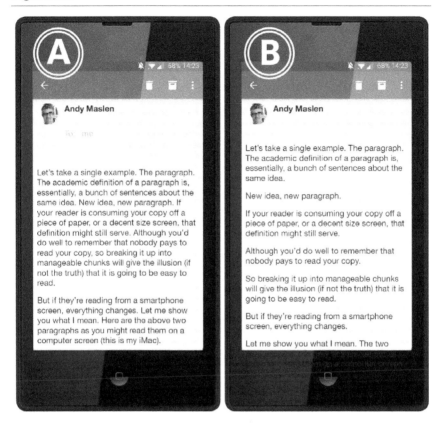

This might come as news to writers who've spent their careers to date producing technical documents, white papers and case studies, but for those of us who cut our teeth writing direct mail, the idea of the ultra-short paragraph is – how shall I put it? – old news.

As far as landing pages and eshots go, there's nothing new under the sun. They're essentially direct response copy and it follows all the same rules. But:

What we write when we write social

Social has genuinely changed the way we think about copy. Leaving aside the question of sponsored posts and tweets (at least for now), writing for social media is a far more spontaneous affair than almost anything else I can think of. If you work on a brand's social media team you're often conducting customer service conversations in public, in real time. So no pressure there, then.

In theory, you're subject to the same constraints as your digital sisters and brothers and your cousins working on ads and mailings. You have the same tone-of-voice guidelines, the same house style, the same brand, products and corporate organization. And yet there is that fluidity to social media, that dynamic quality where yesterday's sacred cows are today's horsemeat burgers. Emojis were once *verboten*. Now they're *de rigueur*. Tomorrow they may be *passé*.

I think the trick is to hire intelligent people who know how to write well, and leave them to it. You can't have someone high up monitoring your social team's output for adherence to the brand voice without stifling the spontaneity that makes social such an interesting tool.

Nick Parker is an expert on tone of voice. Anyone who's written for the scatological, scabrous and downright silly comic *Viz* , the deliberately old-fashioned *Oldie* AND major corporate brands would pretty much have to be. I asked him how he thought brand voices work on social media.

> Social media is weird and evolving fast and is a mash-up of the extremely personal (you know you're hitting up an individual in real time) and the overall 'brand personality'. It's also creating its own 'grammar' at a rate of knots: emojis and linguistic memes and all kinds of hashtag malarkey that resists 'rules' (and often makes po-faced copywriters gnash their teeth – emojis?! *Exclamation marks?!*). I think it's probably more fruitful to acknowledge that it's possible to get it without fully being able to understand, describe or 'manage' it.

Nick and I agree on one thing: writing *anything* for social media is easy. Writing something 'on brand' is tricky.

Five thoughts on what to look for when writing for new media channels

1 Always preview your copy on a range of devices, including your own smartphone.

2 Get straight to the point. You can't rely on your reader scrolling to find out what you're talking about.

3 Be as personal and as natural-sounding as you can manage. The days of corporate websites being able to get away with a stuffy sound are way, way behind us.

4 Remember that you are still writing on behalf of the brand. Be guided by the brand voice, *not* the apparent requirements of the channel.

5 Don't write anything you wouldn't want screen-captured and blasted over every smartphone on the planet within the hour.

Notes

1 www.pewresearch.org/fact-tank/2017/06/12/growth-in-mobile-news-use-driven-by-older-adults

Blood brothers or ugly sisters: How do copy and content fit together?

04

Hey! Have you heard the news? Every form of marketing before content marketing is dead. Old-fashioned. Out of date. Not tuned in to the zeitgeist. Great! You can't stand still. So let's plough ahead with our own content marketing. Yes, let's. Only let's make sure we remember to focus on the 'marketing' at least as much as the 'content'.

Who stole my cheese?

It's been said, by people with an ever-so-slight interest, that marketing in the dark ages before content marketing was like a mousetrap with a photo of the cheese. The poor punter was 'tricked' into reading and possibly buying. Content marketing, on the other hand, is a mousetrap with real cheese. The mouse is so grateful for a square meal that he or she willingly gets trapped. Here's the thing. Most content marketing is actually a huge pile of cheese with no mousetrap at all.

The problem is, by providing tons of valuable content for nothing, you are educating the very people you want as customers that what you provide is free. Always. The still-widespread perception of the internet as a free space isn't helping. Here's my point. Well, two points actually.

Don't tell physicists that gravity pulls things downwards

First of all, if you are going to follow a content marketing-driven strategy (and let's remember, there are other games in town) you need content. Duh! But it has to be good. It has to be original. It has to make people believe in you.

In my own field, copywriting, I see a lot of this type of thing:

Your web page needs a headline.

Copy needs to be relevant to your reader.

You don't need lots of exclamation marks.

Now, to be honest, this is all true. It's just not very helpful. In fact it makes you look like a rube for even writing it down.

Show me the money

Second, and far more important, before you worry about creating content, get your marketing sorted out. Without that element of your strategy, what you have is a pile of cheese with no trap.

How are you going to capture your visitors' contact details? What are you going to do with them? What are you going to say to them?

And – the literal $64,000 question – how are you going to persuade them to stop expecting stuff for nothing and get their wallets out?

Weirdly, at this point, all the content marketing gurus go silent. Because they would have to tell you that what you need is a mousetrap with a photo of a piece of cheese in it.

Measuring the value of content

Content is valuable if the *consumer* believes it to be valuable – that is the only measure that counts *as far as quality is concerned*. For content to be valuable as far as the *producer* is concerned, it must link back, preferably in a measurable way, to the bottom line. Failing that, to countable sales leads or other commercially valuable commodity.

To survive, content marketers needs to get smarter at producing content that people find both relevant and that meets a genuine need. This will consume increasing amounts of time, money and effort, so the pressure to prove a return on investment (ROI) will only increase.

Content, even digital content, is not cost-free. There is the financial cost of paying designers and deploying email campaigns, and the opportunity cost of spending potential billable time on producing the content in the first place. That means there is pressure to show a financial return *in the end*. Finance directors, who often end up running companies, do not see a great deal of value in likes, retweets, shares, linkbacks, comments or anything else they can't take to the bank. Nor do investors, accountants or bank managers.

The emperor's new clothes

I want to draw a distinction between advertising using information, and 'content marketing'. The former, which has been around for a very long time, simply means giving your potential customer useful information, relating to your product or service, that encourages them to buy from you. This is not a new idea. It has been around for centuries. Food companies publishing recipe books, tyre companies publishing restaurant guides, banks publishing investment guides: they've all been done, very successfully, and profitably. Sometimes – shock, horror! – even ads *themselves* offered useful information.

But it has always been a transaction: information for information. 'Content marketing', to me, feels a bit like the emperor's new clothes. Why do we have specialist companies popping out of the woodwork who only do content marketing? Why do we have people we've never heard of, who have never worked in commerce, trade or industry of any kind at all, advising the marketing directors of Fortune 500 and FTSE 100 companies how to connect with their customers using content marketing?

So my beef isn't with content marketing *in itself*, but with the insistence that you *have* to be doing it, that it is some sort of marketing cure-all or that it is so mysterious you can't use a regular copywriter for it but need a Content Marketing Specialist.

In the corporate sphere, where marketing managers have both an appetite for novelty and a fear of failing by missing out on a potential money-spinner, the obvious conclusion to draw is that yes, you might as well do some content marketing. Provided you are linking it to all your other sales and marketing activities.

And if it all feels a little too much like snake oil to you, this, from legendary adman Dave Trott, might reassure you:

> Don't worry if you missed jumping on this bandwagon, there'll be another bandwagon along in a minute to jump on.

Checklist

1 Don't start with your goal. Clickthroughs, signups or whatever. Instead, begin by thinking about your reader. What would they find interesting, compelling or downright unmissable?

2 Resist the temptation to turn your content into an advertisement for your product or service. The whole point of content marketing is that it creates a relationship based on trust. You are offering valuable information – for nothing – and in return your reader will think better of you.

3 Give in to the temptation to ask for something in return. The content is pure information. But the moment it's finished, have a call to action. They have committed to reading one piece of your content. Offer them more in return for their email address.

4 Do not outsource your content creation to a pennies-per-word copywriting service. Yes, you will pay £2.50 for an article. And you will get rubbish. It's called 'Pay peanuts, get monkeys'. And, contrary to what the rule says, if you have a thousand monkeys hammering away on typewriters for 100 years, what they will come up with is not the complete works of Shakespeare but 237 billion words of gibberish. Much like many blog posts you see.

5 Write in Plain English. People don't want to work at this stuff. The paradox of free information is that people like it but they don't place too much value on it. So the moment it gets hard to read they can skip off without any guilt.

6 Content doesn't have to be your own. You can curate – to use the word of the moment – a selection of interesting information you've spent time gleaning from other sources.

7 Make your content easy to share. Use social sharing widgets on every page and write a call to action encouraging your readers to use them.

8 Although the concept of keyword density has, thankfully, fallen from grace as an SEO (search engine optimization) tool, it still makes sense to think about how your reader is going to find your content. Be specific when you describe the thing you're writing about and vary the descriptions to avoid boring/irritating your reader.

9 Use hyperlinks to *a)* give your content a quasi-academic feel and *b)* push your reader deeper into your own site. Do *not* link to external sites. You are not Wikipedia.

10 Remember that the most important word in 'content marketing' is 'marketing'. Last time I checked, marketing is about meeting customer needs profitably. And guess what the most important word in *that* phrase is? If you're not making money you are wasting your time. When the bank asks for its money back – or your shareholders, private equity owners or institutional investors – telling them you have 85,000 Twitter followers will be met with the contempt it deserves.

How to write compelling content

Funnily enough, writing great content calls for the same skills as writing great advertising, or great fiction. You have to write something that your reader cares about in sufficiently clear and vivid language that once they begin, they can't stop.

Here's a short set of pointers for writing compelling content:

Create a plan for your copy

Whether it's an opinion piece or a case study, make a list of the points you want to cover. Let's say I wanted to write a blog post about headline-writing. A simple plan would go:

Introduction
- What is a headline?
- What is it for?

- What did David Ogilvy say about headlines?
- Explain what this article covers.

Three types of headline

- Benefits
- News
- Curiosity

Three styles of headline

- Questions
- Shocking statistic
- Story

Round-up

- Always appeal to reader's self-interest
- Keep them as short as possible
- Leave something for the body copy

Call to action

- Sign up for my newsletter

Start with a bang... or better still, a b—

It's free. So it has low perceived value compared to something your reader has to pay for. So grab their attention and interest from your very first word.

You're writing an ebook about sports nutrition. Forget leading with the history of nutritional science. Instead, go with this.

> *Loser!*
>
> *If you win silver that's all you are. The fastest loser.*

It's brutal but it's effective. The first word speaks directly to an athlete's insecurities. But it doesn't explain itself. So they have to read on.

Keep breaking up your copy

Just like an old-school direct mail letter, your content needs to look appealing. That means keeping paragraphs short and breaking them up with crossheads. Also graphics, sidebars, images and charts.

Return to your reader again and again

Even if you're writing a book review or a guide, keep bringing your reader into the copy by using 'you'. It's a time-honoured technique because in any piece of copy, 'you' is always the person reading. And that's the person they find most interesting.

Tell stories

I don't necessarily mean that every single piece of content you write needs to take the form of a story, But given how powerful stories are for getting and holding attention, you'd be a mug for not using some of the same techniques in your writing.

It could be something as simple as saying, 'I picked this book up at nine o'clock last night, intending to read the first chapter and then get my head down. Five hours later, I read the final sentence and was too wired for sleep.'

Use vivid language

If you're starting to feel that much of this advice about writing content applies equally to copy, you'd be right. Here, have a gold star! Just because you're providing information instead of selling, that's no reason to drop into some kind of quasi-academic writing style. Keep your reader's interest with dramatic language. Instead of telling swimmers, 'You'll *master the principles of* tumble-turns', tell them, 'You'll *crush* tumble-turns.'

Edit ruthlessly

Whether you're used to writing short- or long-form copy, it can feel like a real achievement when you've saved the final version of your 10,000-word ebook. Cutting anything feels like sacrilege. All that effort! All those hours! But now is the time to wield the scalpel (or possibly the shears). Go back over it and cut everything that doesn't add value to your content. And be bold. Start with sections, then paragraphs, then sentences, then words.

How to get your content read

Remember that for every single niche, from tattooing to accountancy, the internet is awash with content. Infographics, podcasts, videos, guides, white papers, blog posts, memes, ebooks, how-tos, maps, charts, manifestos... You could be forgiven for thinking, 'Well, it's all been done, so what's the point?'

Well, here's where it gets really interesting. Because with very few exceptions, everything has *always* been done already. It may well be that what makes your content successful is not its originality (although that definitely helps) but the skills with which you *promote* it.

In *Field of Dreams*, Kevin Costner plays a farmer who hears a voice in his cornfield telling him, 'If you build it, they will come.' The 'it' is a baseball field, but the quote sums up a lot of the talk around content marketing.

Here, I need to compare two ways that information has been used by brands to enhance their image and ultimately their profits. In the pre-internet era, brands would run an ad that offered, say, a recipe book in exchange for a completed coupon. The consumer got the recipe book and the company got their name and address, which they could use for direct mail. Now, the same company might put the recipe book on their website. But here's the crucial difference. If you buy ad space in a newspaper or magazine, you can push your recipe book into the faces of the people who might find it useful. If you simply stick it on the internet, you are building a baseball field in the middle of nowhere and hoping people will find it.

Kevin Costner had a bunch of friendly baseball players' ghosts to help him. You don't. So you're going to have to do the old-fashioned thing and publicise your content. Using guess what? Advertising. Neil Patel is a guru of online marketing. His site groans with amazing content for people who want to learn about online marketing. From the moment you arrive on Neil's site **neilpatel.com** you are served ads. Not content. Ads. Sign-up forms, pop-ups, all kinds of devices that sell his content. One way or another, Neil's going to reel you in. He gets the 'marketing' in content marketing.

Once you've created your content, whether it's a video, a podcast, an ebook or a 'gifographic', you need to pitch it to the public. And for that you need all the techniques I discuss in the rest of this book.

And the attention of search engine bots.

SEO or no?

We do need to talk about SEO. But not at length. Partly because the subject is evolving so fast that any book is out of date before it's rolled off the press.

And partly because its relevance to copywriting is not nearly so great as some people claim.

In January 2018 there were some 200 ranking factors in Google's search algorithm. Some of them refer to copy, most don't. (More at https://backlinko.com/google-ranking-factors.)

It's undeniable that Google 'likes' fresh, relevant, well-written content. So including it may give your site a leg-up in the rankings. But consider this. If everybody in your industry is pumping out content like Soviet tractor factories, they can't *all* be on the front page of Google.

PART TWO
Motivation versus reason: Tapping into your customer's deepest drives

Harnessing the 05 power of emotional copywriting to persuade your prospects

*Human behaviour flows from three main sources:
desire, emotion, and knowledge.*

PLATO

Introduction

Welcome to the wonderful world of emotion-reinforced decision-making. Or, as I like to call it, decision-making.

Copywriters promoting alcohol, tobacco, luxury watches, online poker and dating sites for married people know all too well the power of emotion in decision-making. Why else would any sane person ingest poison, spend more on a timepiece than most people spend on a car, bet against a company that makes its profits beating gamblers or risk their comfortable life for what is, at best, a fleeting pleasure?

Where it gets harder to accept is when you're selling something seemingly reason-based. Business information, training courses, supply-chain software or management consultancy services, to name a few. I have met, and trained, many copywriters and marketeers who insist that, in their business, reason is the driving force behind decision-making. They're wrong. But why are they wrong?

First of all, we have to ask them a question. Are your customers' brains wired differently to every other human's? Because unless they are, their brains are just the same as smokers', boozers', gamblers' and philanderers' brains. They all have the OFC and limbic system. And that means that motivations and emotions play a critical role in their decision-making. Whether they (or you) like it or not.

In this chapter, we're going to take a little look into that nest of electrical wiring and chemical baths and examine the emotions it produces and how we can begin to stimulate them.

*

Let's take a concrete example of how emotions reinforce decision-making in the real world. You are promoting a conference. Your producer provides a sheaf of information including a list of speakers and the agenda. You think about the headline for your promotion and, like 99 per cent of the industry, you go with the conference title, date and venue.

Now, think about the sort of person who might go to a conference. You, perhaps. You give up all this:

- Time with your family (including your new baby).
- Time with your friends (including that hot coach who just joined your tennis club).
- Time with your colleagues (including the boss you want to impress with your diligence so she promotes you not that other one).
- The comforts of home (including your own bed, your own things around you, your cool entertainment system, hobbies, car and wardrobe full of lovely clothes).
- The security of getting everywhere on foot or wheeled transport (did I mention you hate flying?).

Notice I didn't mention money. That's because money is never the reason we don't go to conferences. If the company's paying there's always budget available somewhere. If we're paying ourselves, a conference place is generally less than we spend on coffee in a year.

Engage: Motivation can pull your prospect towards you, but it can also hold them back. Use it to handle objections too.

So. Those are all the reasons *not* to go. And we're going to devote the majority of our copy to the agenda? Right. Good luck with that. Now let's figure out what might sway us into giving up all that lovely, warm, fuzzy, emotional, anchoring stuff keeping us at home.

How about:

- Time off from the family – all those rows, all that mess, all those nappies!
- Time off from friends – they're so needy!
- Time off from colleagues – including your swivel-eyed boss who thinks sleep is an optional extra.
- Time for you – in a luxury hotel, with your every need catered for by other people.
- Parties – alcohol, dancing, guilt-free fun.
- People who could hire you – and pay you double what you're making now.

How to communicate your emotions

When I was planning this book I emailed a few thousand copywriters, marketeers and entrepreneurs asking them for suggestions. One of the responses was from a copywriter asking for help when you don't feel any emotional connection with the product you're selling. She called it an emotional desert.

If only we always got to write about things that fascinated and engaged us. For me that would be music, cars, eating and drinking, psychology and gardening. Oh, and bread making, fashion and language. And machinery. And wildlife. And the countryside. Life as a copywriter would be so simple. All that emotion on tap.

So let's begin by dispelling a myth: you need to be able to communicate your emotions. No, you don't. You need to be able to evoke an emotional response from your customer.

Bad: I am delighted to announce some exciting news about the merger of Utopia Inc and AnonyCorp.

Good: You did it! Well done. You have achieved certification for your management system. We warmly welcome you as a BSI-certified client. (from a letter written by the author for BSI)

Over the years I have written copy about all kinds of products and services, some of which I felt an emotional connection with, some of which I didn't. But it didn't matter. Here's why.

You need to find an emotional connection with the *customer*, not with the product.

This, I think, is one of the most basic mistakes a writer can make. I hear it a lot when I am running training courses: 'How do I make my copy sound interesting when the product is so boring?' My answer is always the same: 'It's not boring to the customer.'

What to do about 'boring' subjects

Let me give you a concrete example. I was writing copy for an Australian company that manufactured a measuring device. What their device measured was the depth of raw sewage in a specialized storage vessel called a wet well. The device itself was very simple: a plastic cylinder with an electrical conductor suspended on a string. (I am simplifying still further but not by much.) Was I – am I – emotionally engaged with sewage measuring probes? No. So here's what I did.

I interviewed the marketing manager. He told me the story of how the company founder had started out by visiting wet wells all over Australia and climbing into them with the local county engineer to inspect them and then demonstrate how his device worked. Next I got him to tell me about the problems you'd have if you were in charge of the sewage wet wells for a county or state. Here's what I discovered.

It's really important to know the level in a wet well. If you don't know when it's full, your automatic pump doesn't stop pumping sewage into the well. So it overflows. Then you have raw sewage running down the street and into, oh, I don't know, an infant school playground. Not good. If you don't know when the well is empty, the pump keeps running – on air – and eventually burns out. Then, next time the well fills up, it keeps filling up – same result as before.

So that's one really interesting fact right there. I translated that into a line of copy that read:

> As a local utilities manager, you really don't want to make the front page of your local newspaper because you've flooded a playground with liquid sewage.

But even without that apocalyptic scenario, there were plenty of other stories we could tell. Like the dramatic drop in call-out rates, the fact that the device was ultra-reliable and that it almost never needed fixing. All headaches for the customer.

My sales copy focused on how much easier the customer's life would be with the device. The stories I told weren't necessarily going to win prizes, or engage the emotions of another copywriter, but they shifted a respectable amount of merchandise.

CASE STUDY   A sponsor letter for World Vision

This makes the communication feel personal by explaining how the letter itself came to be written.

The use of the past tense allows the reader to take in the message in a story format, further enhancing the reality of what was, after all, a true story.

World Vision is a Christian humanitarian organization dedicated to working with children, families, and their communities worldwide to reach their full potential by tackling the causes of poverty and injustice.

The brief for this letter was to explain to sponsors that, although their sponsorship of this particular child was coming to an end, World Vision hoped they would continue to sponsor another child.

I interviewed a sponsor to understand her emotions and to try to convey to the reader that we understood their own emotional response to the news:

> I loved how you seemed to intuitively grasp what we were trying to do right from the start. And your dedication to the key audience insight that went on to drive this letter – including the time you put into interviewing Sam. This was one of our boldest, most original and most personal letters in years. It's written with our target audience in mind, and it creates a connection on a much deeper level than we normally manage. The A/B test conclusively proved the value of this approach.

Mark Dibden, Marketing Manager, Product Experience, World Vision

When I sat down to write this letter to you, I wanted to find out at a personal level how you might be feeling. So I made contact with one of our other sponsors who has already gone through what she described as this 'mini-grieving process'.

Her name is Sam Turvey. Sam sponsored two girls in Zimbabwe – Prescilla and Precious – from the ages of eight and three to seventeen and twelve. I asked Sam to tell me a little about the two children whose lives had become intertwined with hers. She began immediately by saying this:

I wish you could see them. They are the most beautiful children in the world!

The very first time I met Prescilla, the girl who greeted me was not what I had been expecting. She bounded over as soon as she saw me and just screamed out 'Samantha!' and threw herself at me. She had a massive smile on her face.

They adore pink and 'girly' things, which did surprise me – they were just like every other little girl.

We talked a lot about how Sam's sponsorship had changed the lives of the children, and she told me this story about how their father had changed too.

(I should say that we never encourage sponsors to talk about even the idea of the children leaving their village. The father's comments just show the intensity of feelings many people have about their situation.)

Introducing the steady-state and target emotions

In my work as a professional copywriter, many of the clients I write for are promoting business-to-business (B2B) products and services. They recognize that, to stay ahead in the market, they need to forge emotional connections with their customers, not just bombard them with facts. Every single time I or one of my writers sits down to begin planning a new piece of copy, the very first question I want answering is this: 'How does the customer feel about the problem right now?'

This is what I call the steady-state emotion.

The second question is this: 'How do we want them to feel once they've finished reading the copy?'

This is what I call the target emotion.

Nineteen emotions and 110 words/phrases that trigger them

I want to jump right in and start to equip you with the tools you're going to need to master the art. So I'm giving you a readymade list of words and phrases you can cut and paste right into your own copy. Even if you don't feel they're exactly right, you should be able to see ways of adapting them to produce the effects you want. Some work really well as opening lines or even headlines. Like all the tips in this book, they work equally well online or offline, on big screens or small, mobile or web. The list is not exhaustive, and there are other lists you can find readily on the web. Just search 'list of emotions'. You may feel that love and hate are emotions that ought to be included. Though they might also be compound emotions made up of other, purer emotions like anger or happiness.

I understand if some (or all) of the suggested words and phrases in the table make you pause and wonder if they're really OK to use for your type of customer. If you're selling to top executives or university professors, engineers or the super-rich, maybe they do use a polysyllabic and intellectually sophisticated register for most of their day (although I doubt it). My point is that CEOs tell their partners how they feel about them using the age-old formula, 'I love you'. This is true, also, for a bricklayer. Nobody says, 'It has become apparent to me that my emotional responses for you have deepened'. *Everybody* uses emotionally engaging language. And when they do, it works. I make no apology for stating a circular argument here. In just the same way that the words, 'You're fired', 'I quit' and 'I apologise' cause themselves to come true (what linguists call a performative utterance), using emotional language engages the listener's emotions *because* it is emotionally engaging.

The one emotion that rules them all

There is one emotion missing from the following list, though it plays a part in many of them. Its 'location' within the brain is complex but it does seem to be mediated partly by the amygdala and the hippocampus, both of which are found in the limbic system. I wonder if you have already read through the list and been surprised not to find it. I wouldn't be surprised, and if you were, I'm delighted. Partly because it means my cunning plan worked and partly because it means that, as I suspected, you are smarter than the average copywriter. I'm talking about curiosity.

Table 1.1   A list of primary, secondary and tertiary (background) emotions

Primary (universal) emotions	Triggering words/phrases/ideas
Happiness	I have goods news for you. As a bride-to-be... As a mother/father-to-be... You're just the sort of person we love working with. What do you love most in all the world? When were you at your happiest? You're cool/clever/good-looking/beautiful/smart/ a good dresser/savvy/decisive/ambitious. You're going to love what I'm about to tell you. You've won! What makes you smile?

Your ring ceremony will be off to a great start with this charming pillow! This billowy soft cushion has clean white accents, with a linen sheet across the front and a flared profile for added appeal.
Americanbridal.com (USA)
www.americanbridal.com/love-pendant-ring-pillow-18842.html

Sadness	By the time you've finished reading this another [bad thing] will have happened. Have you ever felt down about something? Have you ever lost someone close to you? I'm afraid I have some bad news for you. There's no easy way to say this, but... I'm upset that I have to tell you this.

SEARCH 'sadvertising'
www.npr.org/2014/05/31/317686788/
sad-men-how-advertisers-are-selling-with-emotion

Disgust	He lies on rotting, urine-soaked bedding. The open sewer in Ahmed's street stinks of excrement. These babies are born in filthy, blood-stained wards. Imagine if your only source of water was a stagnant pond, buzzing with flies. The smell of vomit is everywhere.

Disgust in advertising article
USA Today (USA)
http://usatoday30.usatoday.com/money/advertising/story/2012-02-27/
gross-ads-fear-vs-disgust/53275918/1

(continued)

Table 1.1 *(Continued)*

Primary (universal) emotions	Triggering words/phrases/ideas
Anger	You have been lied to.
	Your values don't count.
	We don't take you seriously.
	People are killing innocent creatures.
	We're taking your rights away.
	Children are being betrayed.
	You have bad taste.
	The [X] industry's dirty little secret.

Illegal trade in otter pelts is common in India, Nepal, Bangladesh and China. Otters are mercilessly killed for their fur, which is dense and very durable, so much so that furriers consider it the 'diamond' of the fur business.
WWF (India)
www.wwfindia.org/about_wwf/priority_species/smooth_coated_otter/

Fear	Death.
	This offer must close at the end of this week.
	I have some worrying news for you.
	Did you know your house/car could be taken from you by the taxman?
	How prepared are you for a raid by customs and excise?
	Last year, 17 people doing your job were fined over £50,000 each – for a simple error.
	Are you making this common social media gaffe that could land you in court?

SEARCH 'FOMO' (fear of missing out)

Surprise	You don't need to spend thousands to look as good as this.
	Why Hollywood's A-list stars are turning away from dieting.
	This 'old wives' tale could help you pay off your mortgage 10 years early.
	If you thought your savings were secure in a building society, read on.
	How to get the [health benefit] you've always wanted – without spending a penny.

It also sticks handles to teapots.
Araldite (UK)
www.smartinsights.com/wp-content/uploads/2012/12/araldiateposter1.jpg

(continued)

Table 1.1   (*Continued*)

Secondary (social) emotions	Triggering words/phrases/ideas
Prurience	You won't believe what I've just discovered.
	Hey, wanna hear a secret?
	If sex is so natural, how come you're not allowed to do this?
	Bedroom secrets of [authority figures].
	This is just dirty!
	When I first saw this, I admit, I blushed.

The film that dares to explain what most parents can't...
Teenage Mother (USA)
http://tsutpen.blogspot.co.uk/2008/11/golden-age-of-prurience-52.html

Confidence	You deserve this.
	You owe this to yourself.
	Look at what you've achieved in your life.
	You can do this.
	I wouldn't be asking you if I didn't think you were the right person.
	We've put our heads together and agree you're the one we want.

Antiperspirant you can depend on
Sure (UK)
www.suredeodorant.co.uk/en/about/

Pride	As an expert in...
	As a distinguished...
	As a smart...
	I am not writing to everybody about this.
	You are somebody who is probably used to having folks ask your opinion.
	I'm willing to bet your are what the pundits call a savvy investor.

When it comes to stripped-down bagger style, highway comfort, modern
technology and an unruly attitude, this is the state of the art.
Harley Davidson (USA)
www.harley-davidson.com/content/h-d/en_GB/home/motorcycles/2015-
motorcycles/touring/street-glide-special.html

Embarrassment/ shame	I expected better from you.
	Would your friends/colleagues/family be proud of you if they found this out?
	Did you think how your actions would affect the rest of us?

(*continued*)

Table 1.1   *(Continued)*

Secondary (social) emotions	Triggering words/phrases/ideas
Halitosis makes you unpopular *Listerine (USA)* http://mypeanutbutterbacon.blogspot.co.uk/2013/02/20-ads-that-shook-world-james-twitchell.html	
Jealousy	There are those who'd take your rewards away from you. How would you feel if another man/woman was flirting with your wife/husband? Is somebody else getting the attention that should be yours?
My cheating spouse confirmed *Boothroyd Associates (Scotland)* www.boothroydassociates.co.uk/matrimonial-investigation	
Envy	How come some people seem to get all the luck? Do you ever feel like there's one rule for the rich and another for the rest of us? Would you like to change *your* car every year? Do your friends dress better than you? Do you know anyone who just seems to get what they want without making any effort? Your friends envy your style (but you don't have to tell them how little it cost you).
Have a figure others will envy! *Wallers (USA)* http://chawedrosin.files.wordpress.com/2009/05/envy.jpg	
Guilt	Do you ever ignore your doctor's advice? Have you ever lied and got away with it? Do you have any skeletons in your closet? Is your private life squeaky clean? I know something you'd rather keep secret. This may come as a surprise to you, but your personal emails can be seen by anyone with a 10-dollar piece of electronics.
SEARCH 'Cordaid People in Need campaign' *Cordaid (Netherlands)* www.gutewerbung.net/award-winning-cordaid-people-in-need-campaign/	

(continued)

Table 1.1 (*Continued*)

Tertiary (background) emotions	Triggering words/phrases/ideas
Scene-setters	You have been selected. Picture the scene. Imagine this. How would you feel if...?
Excitement	Front-row seats to see your favourite band. Dinner for two with [celebrity]. A romantic night with your dream date. Your wildest sexual fantasy. Training with [sports star]. An all-expenses-paid holiday in [exotic location].

You'll be able to get a ride around the track in a Ferrari, visit the pits and meet the drivers and some team members and much more besides!
Where would you like to go with the Scuderia?
Ferrari (Italy)
http://formula1.ferrari.com/join-the-team

Well-being	You have achieved much to be proud of in your life. Look around you. At your home. Your possessions. Your family. Good isn't it?

A good night's sleep in a comfy bed. Bedroom furniture with plenty of space to store your things (and easily find them again). Warm lighting to set the mood and some cosy bedding to snuggle up in. And all at a price that lets you rest easy – it is what dreams are made of.
IKEA (Sweden)
www.ikea.com/gb/en/catalog/categories/departments/bedroom/

Calm	I want you to close your eyes and take a slow breath in. Relax. No paperwork, no hassle. Stress-free. Let us do the hard work for you. You are under no obligation. You can cancel at any time.

'Sit back and relax – your miles stay with you'
Denizbank (Turkey)
www.denizbank.com/en/credit-cards/miles-more-visa-card.aspx

(continued)

Table 1.1 *(Continued)*

Tertiary (background) emotions	Triggering words/phrases/ideas
Malaise	Does it ever feel like the whole world's against you? Ever lie awake at 3.00 am wondering what it's all about? Have you ever wondered, what's the point? Do you ever just stop what you're doing and think, is this all there is?

A surprising way to cultivate contentment
Psychology Today (USA)
www.psychologytoday.com/blog/living-the-questions/201401/
surprising-way-cultivate-contentment

Tension	Bills. Insurance. Mortgage. School fees. Time's running out. What frightens you the most? How secure is your job? Do you ever worry about your kids' future? Hurry. This offer won't be open for ever.

Your Children's education is of vital importance and that's why you invest in their schooling. With your FeeSecure from Swann Insurance, you can protect your Children's education by insuring against the unexpected, those life events that
could affect your ability to pay those expensive school fees.
Swann Insurance (Australia)
www.swanninsurance.com.au/products/yourfeesecure

Cheerfulness	Spring is here. What is your favourite colour? Do you remember the smell of your Mum's home cooking? Think about your best-ever holiday.

Blast back to 1962 and cruise into psychedelic style!
Lego (Denmark)
http://shop.lego.com/en-GB/Volkswagen-T1-Camper-Van-10220

Engage: Curiosity is what makes our reader desperate to find out how what we're saying will benefit them.

Curiosity is the driving emotion that pushes us to explore our world. It is present in many animals – any dog- or cat-owner will attest to that. And how else to explain the emergence of tool-use in various non-human primates? And it is a gift to copywriters. Having a product that will make our reader's life easier is one thing. Making them sufficiently interested to read about and, we hope, buy it, quite another. Holding part of the pitch back is the simplest and the most powerful way to do this and you will see repeated instances of this trick peppered throughout this book. Recommending Wikipedia is a double-edged sword, but for an excellent article on curiosity visit http://en.wikipedia.org/wiki/Curiosity.

Much storytelling relies for its power on curiosity. Here is an excellent example from a corporate website, a species of copywriting more usually associated with narcoleptic qualities. You just have to know, why? And how?

Good: Rory Smith's life's work has already saved millions of people time, and continues to do so every day. (From the ThyssenKrupp (Germany) website) www.thyssenkrupp.com/en/produkte/formel-gegen-langes-warten.html)

Mapping the range of emotions

Of course, it is somewhat simplistic to suggest that your customer is feeling just *one* thing and that, therefore, all your copy has to do is home in on that emotion and the sale is made. Human beings are complex creatures and we may be feeling all sorts of emotions at the same time. That's why we have the line, 'I'm having mixed feelings about this'.

Later on, we'll look at building a character sketch of your typical customer. One of the things it's worth spending some time on when you're doing that is to identify the *range* of emotions driving them. They may be worried *and* excited. Happy *and* curious. Envious *and* fearful. But you will usually be able to identify the *dominant* emotion as far as it relates to your product and the problem it solves.

Having identified the emotional response you want to provoke, it's vital that you write it down as part of your copy planning process. Why? Because it's extremely difficult to do and so there's a natural temptation to avoid it, falling back on easier, simpler and faster ways of writing. With a statement near the top of your copy plan that you intend to make your reader feel anxious about missing out you can read through the first draft of your copy looking for the words, phrases or passages that do, indeed, engender that emotion. If you can't find it you have to go back and do some work until it's there.

How to communicate using emotional language

One of the techniques that you can use, which both builds the emotional connection with your reader *and* saves you time, is to concentrate on using everyday language. Our most primal urges and drives are not mediated by polysyllabic conversations and byzantine sentence structures. They rely on words whose meanings are immediately clear and structures that permit no ambiguity.

So many of our emotions, from anxiety to envy, can be triggered by these simple little phrases:

- 'I'm worried about you.'
- 'I need to see you.'
- 'Are you hungry?'
- 'Do you fancy an early night?'
- 'Let's go dancing!'
- 'I hate him.'
- 'She's so brainy.'

And here's the really important point about this style of writing. Everyone responds to it. This is not the preserve of business-to-consumer (B2C) marketeers. Until we start selling to androids, we all sell to human beings, which means we are selling to people guided if not driven by their emotions. For a long while, the prevailing wisdom in B2B marketing was that all this soft, fluffy emotional selling was all very well for ice creams, cosmetics and sports cars but it simply wouldn't wash for software, accounting services or mining equipment. Happily, that's begun to change. And there are now many B2B companies all over the world who are waking up to the fact that their customers are the exact same people who are buying the ice creams, cosmetics and sports cars.

It isn't too much of a stretch to imagine a B2B copywriter working for, say, a technology company, penning a subject line for a conference that reads: Jo, fancy a game of golf next week?

The point of the subject line is not to introduce the conference, nod to the agenda or big up the speakers. It's simply to get the reader to open the email (I could add without tricking them). And since this particular conference is set in a golf resort, it seems fair enough. I once wrote email and web copy for a finance directors' conference in San Francisco where the main draw was an Arnold Palmer-designed 18-hole golf course. Take a look:

Bad: Finance Chiefs Summit 2010

Good: A fantastic game of golf (with a not-bad finance conference attached) (from a US conference mailing for CFO Rising written by the author)

It did very well.

From theory to profit

At some point in the buying process – essentially, at the very beginning – your prospect will make a snap emotional decision to buy. Yes, they will look for information to post-rationalize their decision, but for now we aren't concerned with that part of the process. So, imagine that there were no logical reasons to buy your product. (If you are in one of the industries I mentioned earlier in this chapter, this will be a walk in the park for you.) It is still your job to write persuasive, hard-hitting sales copy that will convince your prospect to buy from you anyway.

What are the emotional benefits of buying from you? How will your prospect's life *feel* different after they buy from you? How will your prospect's spouse, children, friends, family and work colleagues feel about them when they find out? What will happen if they buy from you? What *won't* happen? By building an emotional map of the consequences of acting or not acting you can begin to understand how your prospect will view the choices you are offering them. Once you understand that, you can begin to figure out how to nudge them towards the choice you want them to make.

Which emotions from the list in this chapter would be helpful in marketing your organization and its products or services? Go back and highlight, or copy, the relevant emotions and their trigger phrases. Are you promoting products that *primarily* make bad things go away or make good things come closer?

This is one of the biggest divides in psychology and it will help you immensely to identify the specific set of emotions that come into play when your customers are thinking about products like yours. Think carefully, because the answer isn't always obvious. The latest TV may appear, superficially, to bring good things closer, such as a better experience when watching a movie. But is it really? Perhaps it is pushing away the feeling of social inadequacy that some people feel when they know they don't have the latest gadget.

Workshop

1 What's the name of the part of the brain that, if damaged, inhibits your ability to make a decision? Is it:
   a) The limbic system
   b) The pre-frontal cortex
   c) The orbito-frontal cortex

2 Which is correct:
   a) People make decisions based on information alone
   b) People make decisions based on emotion and information jointly
   c) People make decisions solely on emotion then validate their decision using information

3 What are Somatic Markers?

4 To be able to write emotionally, you have to feel strongly about what you're selling. True or false?

5 What is the name for the emotion your prospect is feeling right now?

6 Why are emotions so important to humans?

7 What are the six primary human emotions?

   H_____   S_____
   D_____   A_____
   F_____   S_____

8 Can you name a secondary (social) emotion?

9 Which of these is NOT a tertiary (background) emotion?
   well-being, calm, malaise, egotism, tension

10 Only B2C marketeers need to worry about their customers' emotions. True or false?

Putting it into action

Exercise 1: identifying your customer's steady-state and target emotions

Begin your next copy plan by answering two big questions:

- How does the customer feel about the problem right now? (steady-state emotion)
- How do we want them to feel once they've finished reading the copy? (target emotion)

Exercise 2: a conversation between two friends

Imagine your prospect feeling their steady-state emotion.

They are with a friend in a coffee shop.

The friend, noticing their facial expression, says: 'Hey, what's up with you?'

Now write your prospect's response.

If you feel it would help, continue to write a few more lines of dialogue between the pair to see where it leads you.

Exercise 3: emotional objection-handling

Download: Write down the reasons why your prospect might not do what you want them to. Then add emotion-driven reasons why they might change their mind. Use this template if it helps.

Exercise 4: Soothing your prospect's emotions

Write a list of things that worry your prospect. Circle the ones that go away when they buy your product.

Exercise 5: Basic instinct copywriting

Have a go at writing a line or two of copy for your product (or one you admire) for each of the six primary human emotions.

Exercise 6: Kicking off with emotion

Write a handful of subject lines for an email about your organization, product or service (or anything else you are promoting or selling) based around the answers from Exercise 1 (in which you identified your customer's steady-state and target emotions).

Use one or more of the trigger phrases in Table 1.1 to help you.

Tweet: How are you doing? Tweet me @Andy_Maslen

Three big ideas 06 you should use for copy before highlighting the 'benefits'

If you are nice, and keep your promise, we will be in paradise.

CAMILLE CLAUDEL

Introduction

When you're planning a piece of copy, how do you go about it? Is there a structure you use every time? Most people have come across AIDA – Attention, Interest, Desire, Action – and its close cousin, AIDCA (the C stands for conviction). This is probably the oldest sales message structure: originally developed by US salesmen way back in the 1950s, it was quickly adopted by copywriters, who realized its potential to get their arguments in the right order. But mightn't AIDCA be just a little, well, mechanistic? You know, BAM! Get their attention. Ooh! Get their interest. Aah! Make them want it. Huh! Prove it's OK to buy it. Yes! Tell them to order it. I think so – and I speak as someone who's been using AIDCA his whole career.

In this chapter, I want to show you three more powerful ways of structuring your copy. Approaches that could revolutionize the results you get from your copywriting. There you are. You *knew* it! There *is* something more powerful than a benefit. More engaging than short sentences. More magnetic than testimonials. These approaches work well for any sort of sales piece, though with some creative thinking they could work for corporate communications too. They derive their power from the emotional responses they elicit from the reader, because, in slightly differing ways, they describe the world *the way they wish it were*. Like many of the techniques in this book, they demand some hard work from you – the writer – but not much more than you would put into figuring out any other way of planning your copy.

Master these tools and you'll be writing copy that bypasses your prospect's BS detector and hits them slap-bang in the middle of their limbic system. You remember, the place where decisions are made. I also think it's more fun to write this way because the copy itself is more interesting, describing life with the product, rather than the product itself. As you read this introduction, you might notice that I haven't actually told you what the techniques are. That's deliberate. You want better results from your copywriting and I don't think you care too much what you have to do to get them.

Using promises to engage the emotions

Do you know why people buy from you? It's not because of what you provide. It's because of what you promise. Now, you may not realize you're promising them something. And if your copy is merely average, there's a very good chance your prospect will have to dig out the promise for themselves. But if you're doing it right, then you are making an explicit promise to your prospect. So what, we ask, is this promise all about?

> I promise to send you the product you ordered?
> I promise to honour the discount I offered you?

No.
Your promise goes something like this:

> I promise you that a month from now you will have lost up to seven pounds without giving up chocolate.

Or:

> I promise that the only limits on your earnings will be your own drive and determination.

Or:

> I promise that your upper body will assume godlike proportions.

Because that's what your prospect wants.

Fat people don't want to diet. Or to exercise. Nor do they want a book on dieting or exercise. Nor, deep down, do they want to lose weight. What do they want? Have a think for five seconds before reading on.

They want to be slim.

Bad: A revolutionary approach to muscle-building
Good: You too can have a body like mine (from an advertising campaign for Charles Atlas)

That's what you, marketing your revolutionary diet and fitness programme, are going to promise them. Now, you have to *prove* that your promise is going to come true. But that's later on in your pitch.

The fact that a spade has a soft-grip handle is a feature. The fact that this means you won't get blisters is a benefit. But is that *really* why our soft-handed gardener is going to fork out their hard-earned cash for it? Or is there something else? Some deeply-buried lever that we can pull? Well, yes. There is. And it's the promise.

In this case, it's the promise that they will have a garden to be proud of in half the time. 'No blisters' is a benefit but we need to process it intellectually.

'You'll have a garden to be proud of and no sore hands' is a promise and we process it emotionally.

The style and form of your promise

There are lots of promises you can make to your prospect:

- Earn your annual salary in just five minutes a day.
- Attract a mate effortlessly wherever you go.
- Dominate any social event you attend.
- Start your own business without risking a penny.
- Attain an A-lister's body.
- Safeguard your business from a tax investigation.
- Turn your sales department into an unstoppable profits machine.

- Win the war for talent.
- Turn your CV into a job magnet.
- Be the envy of all your colleagues.
- Lose your fear of public speaking.

What's interesting about these statements is that they are desirable, specific and commanding. (When you give somebody a command you are using what linguists call the imperative mood. This means your sentence is giving an order.) There's something else about these promises, too. They're incomplete. The promise is relevant to the prospect, but it doesn't explain the one crucial thing they want to know. How?

So, at a stroke, by using a promise couched in this type of language, you are engaging two emotions. First, the emotion triggered by the *content* of the promise. So, in the examples above, these are states like envy, pride, anxiety, desire, vanity, fear, insecurity, greed and self-respect. Second, and this is the kicker for any writer, the emotion triggered by the *form* of the promise: curiosity.

Engage: Make your prospect a promise and they'll lean in to hear what you have to say next.

Promises and curiosity

Curiosity is a basic human drive. In evolutionary terms it motivated us to explore our world, to discover new foodstuffs, technologies and people to mate with. When you pair curiosity in general with the desire to find out something *that will directly benefit us* you have a very powerful cocktail indeed.

Almost the first piece of copy I wrote as an independent copywriter was an advertising campaign promoting a computer magazine. At the time people were worried about buying the wrong PC – they were still pretty new in the United Kingdom and also very expensive. This magazine was aimed not at geeks or computer experts but the average middle-aged guy (or occasionally girl) in the street who just wanted to go on the internet, play around with their photos and send emails to their kids in Australia.

We made them a very powerful promise:

Bad: Over 250 PCs reviewed and rated
Good: Looking for a new PC? Pick our brains and you won't go wrong
(from an advertising campaign for *What PC?* written by
the author)

We positioned the magazine as a friendly expert who wouldn't give you bad advice. It had zillions of features, from group tests to user reviews, and many benefits, from saving money to saving time. But in a massively crowded marketplace – there were something like 20 different titles around all doing roughly the same thing – citing these would hardly have been distinctive.

All this may sound eerily similar to writing down the benefits of a product. It does overlap, it's true. But whereas a diet programme, say, might offer the benefit of losing weight, that isn't its underlying promise.

Promises carry huge emotional power. Much more than benefits. We grow up making and, occasionally, breaking promises. We know that they are important. They form part of the social contract between individuals, organizations and states. And that means we can use them to help persuade our prospect of the benefits of our product.

Try this: When you understand how your product changes your customer's life for the better you are ready to make your promise to them. Promises sound best when you phrase them as a command or a prediction. Keep it short and simple. If it helps, start your promise with the words, 'After you've bought from me...'. When you're done, just delete that introductory phrase and tweak a little if you have to.

When promises must be broken

But what if your prospect buys from you and your promise *doesn't* come true? What then? OK, this is where you might want to draw the curtains, check your mobile is switched off and make sure your Auntie Jean is in the next room watching her show on TV with the sound up nice and loud. You need a get-out clause.

What I mean is this. You are not in control of the Universe. Sorry, but you're not. And that means even if your customer does do all the things they're supposed to – follows the instructions, uses the correct ink cartridge, drives carefully, whatever – your promise might not come true. Most people will shrug their shoulders and chalk it down to experience or their own failings (because having committed to buying it, admitting it failed would be admitting *they* failed).

But I don't think that's good enough. So you need to write some copy that explains what happens if it all goes wrong. Here are a couple of ideas.

First, our old favourite, the money-back guarantee. I always phrase it as a positive that hasn't happened, rather than a negative that has. Like this:

> I think you are going to be delighted with your new smile. But if at any time and for any reason you decide you're not pleased, just write to me for a full, no-quibble refund of your fee.

Rather than like this:

> If you don't like your new smile, just write to me for a full, no-quibble refund of your fee.

Here, though, is an altogether more sophisticated way of doing the same thing:

> Will joining the Andy Maslen VIP Copy Club turn you into a copywriting god overnight? Probably not. After all, most people have neither the will nor the stamina to take charge of their own destiny.
> You could be different.

One way or another (and I would exclude terms and conditions), it's wise both commercially and ethically to allow that things may not turn out as planned – or promised. If you've done your selling properly, many prospects will simply discount the negative, preferring to concentrate on the positive: the promise.

The secret codeword that unlocks your reader's emotions

I'm going to tell you a secret but you mustn't tell anyone.

It's hard to think of a more seductive 12-word sentence in the English language. Why is this?

What is it about secrets that makes us drop whatever we're doing, look left and right and shiver with anticipation? There are two possible psychological levers being pulled here. One is the influential power of scarcity.

A secret, by definition, is not widely known. Or even known at all. So knowing it means you have something rare. Something precious. It doesn't really matter what the secret is about. The mere sniff of secrecy *itself* is enough.

Then there's the sense of being part of the in-crowd. We like to belng to groups – belongingness is one of the deep-seated human needs proposed by American psychologist Abraham Maslow. If you know the secret, you are part of an exclusive – and small – club. In fact, there may be a third lever.

The thought that we may be about to discover some juicy little titbit about someone we know is an itch just waiting to be scratched. And it's interesting that the word prurient, which means an unwholesome interest in sexual matters (the subject of many secrets), has a Latin root meaning 'to itch'.

You don't have to be a raving conspiracy theorist to believe that there are secrets locked away from the rest of us, known only to a cabal of devious, powerful individuals. Actually, maybe you do. But secrets are one of those curious cultural goods that are both good and bad. Good, because some things really shouldn't be known more widely, such as that office party indiscretion a few years back. Bad because there's a widely held belief that openness and honesty are inherently virtuous.

We all love being entrusted with a secret (some of us even keep them). And having been entrusted with it we feel more powerful than we did before. Power is one of those things most people crave, even if they don't, won't or can't admit it. Which makes it a very useful tool for influencing their behaviour.

The power of the secret

Why do secrets confer such power on the recipient or holder? For a start, once you have a secret you can decide if, when, where and to whom you release it. Power. And since people love hearing secrets (because then the power passes to them, albeit in a slightly diminished form), they will do all kinds of things to hear them. More power. Possessing secrets also confers social status: you must be on the inside track to know this stuff in the first place. Even more power. So here is an incredibly seductive word that we can use to grab our reader's attention and engage their emotions.

Engage: People love hearing secrets. That makes them a powerful word in your lexicon of persuasion.

So given that secrets have this astonishing power to gain our attention, how can we make use of them in our copy? Well, you could do a lot worse than use them in your headline.

Secrets and headlines

You can write headlines for anything using the secrets concept. It doesn't have to be some arcane meditation technique practised by monks in Tang Dynasty China (though that would certainly lend itself to this approach). How about management consultancy?

> Five leadership secrets you'll kick yourself for missing at business school.

Garden sheds?

> Top gardeners all swear by this shed. But they'll never tell you why.

Drain cleaning solvent?

> It's the secret ingredient that cuts through fat like a razor that makes Drainex the choice of professional sewage engineers.

Bad: the secret ingredient that makes white vinegar the professional's choice of window cleaner

Good: Every secret but one* is in this book. (press ad for David Ogilvy's book, *Confessions of an Advertising Man*)

If you have a product or service that has a definite advantage over the competition, you have a ready-made angle. It's called DLS and it stands for 'dirty little secrets' and it goes like this:

> The office cleaning industry's dirty little secret.

Facilities managers won't be able to resist reading on.

Or how about this:

> The secret remedy for lower back pain (and why your doctor will never tell you about it).

Or, if you can give people information to help them do their job better, or enjoy life more, you could use a line like this:

> Revealed, the secret technique for improving your memory known only to the ancient Greeks.

Maybe you could spin a little story to entice your reader:

> Could this secret brownie recipe be the real reason why MI5 arrested the editor of *Bakers and Baking*?

You don't even have to use the word 'secret' to construct a secrets-headline:

> Lawyers hate him, accountants want him dead: but this unemployed man from Birmingham doesn't care.

Key takeaway: However you choose to use secrets in your copy, from the headline down, it's a fantastically powerful device for overcoming reader resistance.

Whether you're writing envelope copy, a subject line, a blog post, a web page or even a good old-fashioned brochure, using the s-word is a tried and tested way to get more people to read more of what you've written.

Secrets and lies

A different spin on the revealing of secrets is the revealing of lies. In a way, lies are a form of secret: the liars know something you don't (the truth) and they're keeping it from you.

You would never lie to your reader. Aside from the ethical question, I'd bet that your lie would be found out, sooner rather than later, and publicized globally on social media. However, the word itself possesses immense power. It's precisely because lying is frowned upon* (to put it mildly) that it is a useful tool for writers. Here's why.

Nobody likes being lied to. If they discover they've been lied to they get angry. And we know anger is one of the six primary emotions. In fact, if you wrote down in your copy plan that you wanted your reader to feel angry, I'd say this is pretty near the top of your list of ways to achieve that goal.

Suppose you discover, in your research, that your reader has been lied to. By their government, their professional advisers, their doctors or a particular organization. Let them know!

Why stories work – and how to tell them

It is said, and I believe it, that human beings are hard-wired to love stories. It also sounds a bit like a management-speak cliché. So is it true? Refreshingly, for a bit of threadbare jargon, the answer is yes. And no prizes for guessing which part of our brain contains the wiring. The limbic system, I hear you ask? Why, yes, absolutely. In just the same way that this most primitive part of the human brain sets our rented fMRI scanner a-buzzing when we experience an emotion and make a decision, it also lights up like a firework display when we are listening to a story. Interestingly, when we are asked to explain what a story *means*, the limbic system quietens down and the pre-frontal cortex takes over. That's the basic difference between emotional and intellectual engagement.

So, long before writing was invented, cavemen, cavewomen, cave children, cave dogs and cave hamsters were sitting round smoky fires, enthralled, as

---

* In the world's major religions, the injunction against lying – bearing false witness – is one of the four fundamental rules governing social behaviour. The others prohibit killing, stealing and inappropriate sexual relations.

the tribe's storyteller created imaginary worlds, legends, myths and, occasionally, case studies of the best way to bring down a mammoth with a spear made from a stick and a lump of rock. The question is, why?

Why are we hard-wired to respond emotionally to stories? Current anthropological and psychological thinking is that stories were – and are – used to teach important lessons, both moral and practical. And that in so doing, they conferred evolutionary advantage.

An example of storytelling – from Daddy Ug

Imagine our cave children, ready to go out and play in the forest. 'Before you go to play,' says Daddy Ug, 'there is something really important I have to tell you. The red berries on the tall tree by the lake can cause severe gastro-intestinal discomfort and may in fact kill you.' Here is what the children hear: 'Blah blah blah blah PLAY, blah blah blah blah.' It's too late to give them information because they are already thinking about playing with their friends.

Now let's replay the scene, but with Daddy Ug using a different method of inculcating the lesson. 'Before you go to play,' he says, 'I just want to tell you what happened to little Og last week.' They pause, transfixed. 'He went out to play and because he was hungry he picked some of the red berries from that tall tree down by the lake. And guess what? He screamed with pain from his belly and fell down dead. Anyhoo, enjoy your playing.' Guess who's not going to eat the berries.

People who listened to stories tended to live longer so their genes got passed on to the next generation. They also told stories to their own offspring, adding behavioural impetus to the power of storytelling. It turns out storytelling works pretty well for copywriters too. Here's an example.

Storytelling for a corporate brochure

I once had to write a corporate brochure for a large US corporation. They wanted to move away from the usual overblown style that characterizes this type of document towards something on a more human level. Here's what I suggested to their marketing director.

'Why don't we tell a series of little stories?' I said. 'You can show the reader how you make their life easier through examples, rather than listing benefits.'

'Won't that come off a bit, well, flaky?' she asked.

'Not if we focus on business problems and how your products solved them.'

So off I went. The stories I wrote were focused on a series of typical working days: for a marketing manager, a mailroom manager, a finance director and an HR manager. Here's a passage from the brochure.

Bad: In 1972, we published our first report on U.K consumer markets.
Good: A marketing manager arrives at her office at 8.30 am. By 10.00 am she has received 45 emails on her Blackberry, 11 pieces of direct mail, three PDFs on her PC, two packages containing sample promotional gifts and background material for an advertising campaign, 15 pieces of internal mail, four invoices and a draft contract from her newly hired direct marketing agency. (from a corporate brochure for Pitney Bowes written by the author)

Each had the four vital ingredients of a good story:

1 A protagonist AKA the hero. This is the person we want the reader to identify with.

2 A predicament or problem. This is the problem my client could make go away.

3 A narrative – simply, what happened.

4 A resolution. How the story ended.

For one of the characters, it was getting home in time to kiss her children goodnight.

Good fiction usually involves the central character undergoing some sort of change. You could argue that the change here was becoming a customer of my client's.

CASE STUDY   A fundraising letter for The Stars Appeal

A story-based spin on the classic 'How...' headline – an irresistible opening.

The picture is of a real person – Charlie Ross – whom Jo Kelly interviewed for the letter. The caption tells the entire story in miniature.

Charlie Ross,
cancer survivor, thanks to a CT scan

CAMPAIGN

The Stars Appeal
Salisbury District Hospital
Salisbury
SP2 8BJ

01722 429005
www.starsappeal.org
Registered Charity: 1052284

Summer 2013

How a CT scan saved my life

Dear Foundation Trust Member,

A few years ago, I found a lump on my neck. My daughter insisted I get it checked out. Despite various examinations and tests no-one could tell me what it was, until my doctor referred me to a specialist at Salisbury District Hospital, who sent me for a CT scan.

Within a couple of days of my scan I had my diagnosis. My consultant told me I had Hodgkin's Lymphoma (a type of cancer), which I'd probably had for some time, and that she wanted to start treatment very soon. That scan probably saved my life.

The Stars Appeal is Salisbury District Hospital's charity. It raises money to fund extra care and equipment over and above that provided by the NHS.

This letter went out with the hospital newsletter to raise money towards a CT scanner.

Written by Sunfish Creative Director, Jo Kelly, it led with a story and generated impressive results:

Response rate: 5.6%
ROMI: 4,216.7%

We needed a compelling letter to send to the Hospital's 10,000 strong membership to encourage them to support our CT Scanner Campaign. It produced great results, helping us reach our fundraising target, enabling us to buy the Scanner sooner.

(Dave Cates, Director of Fundraising, The Stars Appeal)

Storytelling techniques for copywriters

Here are more tips for good storytelling.

Lean style

> It was agreed that steps should be taken to ensure that staff were enabled to become more engaged and motivated by our brand values going forward.

This is not what I would call lean. Technically it's a story. But it's a very boring one, written mostly in the passive voice and stuffed with management speak.

This is better:

> We took steps to engage and motivate our staff with our brand.

This is better still:

> Julie, our customer service manager, said, 'Now, I don't just *understand* our brand, I *believe* in it'.

When you're telling a story, always remember that your reader hasn't paid to read it – it's still business writing. Or, as they probably call it, junk mail, spam or marketing fluff. So it pays to keep the story rolling along at a brisk clip. Forget about long introductions, or passages of exposition. Just as with good fiction, you should aim to tell your story through action not description. Dialogue is action. Events are action. Adjectives, superlatives and clichés are not action.

Key takeaway: Every story needs a hero. Make your hero a real person and your story has infinitely more power to engage your reader.

Dialogue

Everybody knows that customer testimonials are a great way to add weight to a sales pitch (although it constantly surprises me how many organizations don't use them on their websites or publicity materials).

But it's a bit flat to have a heading that reads 'customer testimonials' followed by an unadorned list of quotes.

Why not integrate your testimonials into your copy a bit more subtly by introducing the customer as a character in your story, and treat the testimonial more as dialogue? Here's how I'd do it.

When I sat down to write to you, I knew you'd probably be sceptical. After all, a 500% increase in your inbound leads is a pretty big promise to make. So I asked our most recent client (or convert, I should probably call her) to share her experience with you.

Her name is Jean Kilbride and Jean is Managing Director of The Acme Widget Corporation. Here's what she told me when I asked how she'd found our service:

> *Oh, Andy, we were utterly gobsmacked when we prepared our first-quarter sales statement last year.*
>
> *We knew we'd had a good start to the year but 650% more inbound leads? We thought it was a fat-finger error and we'd done 65% more.*
>
> *But when we rechecked the numbers it was staring us in the face. We can't wait to move on to your Platinum Tier Service Agreement.*

Surprise

We don't want our reader nodding off because our story has become predictable. So if you can deliver a surprise – or, better still, a shock – it wakes them up. Maybe something like this:

All along, I've been telling you how enrolling in my career development masterclass is going to turn you into this year's most desirable catch for any high-paying employer. But I have some news for you.

It's probably not going to happen.

Here's why.

Most people don't have the drive, the commitment or, quite frankly, the energy to put my ideas into practice. But maybe you're different. Take this quick test to find out.

The telling detail

If marketing copy resembles any kind of fiction, it's the short story. You have to pack a huge amount of detail and emotional punch into a very small space. So long-winded descriptions are out. But given we're trying to show our prospect one particular picture – of life with our product – all we need is the one telling detail that brings it to life.

Like this:

Your new MazTech exhaust system is fitted. You're ready to drive away. From the outside, your pride and joy looks the same. You thumb the starter button and blip the throttle. Hear that? *Above* the sound of your exhaust?

You just set off all the car alarms in the car park!

That's the MazTech effect. And you control it.

Character sketches

Give your character some depth. You don't need to write a long screed describing their upbringing, career and beliefs. Just a couple of carefully chosen words that flesh them out a little. Is it their 11 cups of coffee a day that keeps them awake? Or maybe wanting to go for a run at lunchtime?

Focus on the purpose of the story. This isn't fine writing. You're still trying to sell. Make sure you show your reader how the product you're promoting solved the hero's problem.

Suspense

I don't mean some sort of Steven King-esque chiller that has the hairs on your customer's neck going haywire. Just something involving a will-they-won't-they angle. A did-it-work-or-didn't-it. A she-didn't-think-it-would-work-but-then-it-did.

Perhaps the most famous example is from an ad written by legendary US advertising copywriter John Caples. You'll know the headline even if you don't really know the ad.

Good: They laughed when I sat down at the piano. But when I started to play—

What? What happened when you started to play?

The headline has been endlessly copied and tweaked, including by Caples himself. Supposing you are promoting a new fast-drying industrial paint. Try this:

> The engineers smirked when I leaned against the fresh paint in my best suit. But when I turned around—

Present tense

Try this: For a more immediate-sounding story, write in the present tense.

'The customer hasn't bought yet, so anything I say must be written in the future tense.' This is a rookie error; it's widespread, but still an error. Compare these two sentences and rate them for selling power.

> Once you have installed MyPayRoll on your PC, it will save you hours of repetitive manual updating every month.

> At each month-end, you run MyPayRoll and smile to yourself, knowing it's saved you hours of repetitive manual updating.

In version one, the copy describes only one of two possible futures. One with the product, one without. It also makes the reader think about the effort and potential problems of installing a new piece of software. Focusing on cause and effect, it is an intellectual appeal.

In version two, the reader pictures the outcome. There is only one future and it is now. The work is bypassed. Focusing on life with the product, it is an emotional appeal.

Copywriters working in travel, especially luxury travel, use this method all the time. Like this:

> On your first evening, you dine under the stars at Treetops Lodge, the only restaurant in the Masai Mara. Something else makes it special.
>
> Your table nestles snugly on the Ironwood deck the owners have built onto the massive trunks of five, 300-year-old Baobab trees.
>
> From your secure vantage point, you look out over the plain, taking in a sight that has dazzled travellers since Livingstone.

So why is changing a verb-tense so powerful?

There are a couple of things going on.

First, it engages the reader's imagination. This is a powerful ally for any salesperson.

A reader imagining what you are describing has already bought what you are offering. How else could they be experiencing it?

Old-school types (me included) would call it an 'assumptive close'. In other words, we aren't talking about whether they will buy, merely what will happen afterwards.

The second thing going on is that we are telling a story. Weirdly, in order to tell a story set in the future and make it compelling, you write about it in the present. It's believable in the future – I understand that *if* I do this thing, *then* that thing will happen – but it still represents a possibility, not a certainty.

This simple tip allows you to make any argument more persuasive by engaging your prospect's emotion through the power of their own imagination.

CASE STUDY   Data philanthropy report for Aimia

IMAGINE living the life of a vulnerable child in a poor part of London. Your home is a cramped flat in a tower block. Your parents have split up and you care for your alcoholic mother. It's a hard way to grow up, but with support from a charity you are managing to meet the daily challenges of existence.

You go to school every day and you're making good progress in reading, writing and maths. Your caseworker is helping you, but it's the people helping your caseworker that make this story special.

As part of its corporate social responsibility programme, Aimia (the company that owns Nectar in the UK), supports charities by giving them access to its staff, expertise and technology to make better use of data.

This paper was aimed at a wide range of people, including Aimia employees, journalists and charities. I decided that to get straight past people's inbuilt resistance to reading about anything technical, I would open with a 'body swap' story that commanded the reader to engage emotionally with the material. There are seven emotionally powerful words or phrases in the first four sentences: 'vulnerable', 'poor', cramped', 'split up', 'alcoholic mother', 'hard' and 'grow up'. To preserve a professional tone of voice, and prevent a slide into mawkishness, I deliberately used the high-register language, 'the daily challenges of existence' and 'caseworker'.

Data philanthropy can be a somewhat dry subject, but behind the technical jargon are some great stories of how Aimia meets its corporate social responsibility obligations. We wanted a fresh approach that would engage people's emotions before they had a chance to prejudge the material and switch off. We felt this opening, while unorthodox, was highly effective.
                    Gabrielle de Wardener, Culture and CSR Director, Aimia

How to plan your story

Like any other style of copywriting, storytelling needs careful planning.

Here are the things I think you need to include in your plan:

1 *The hero*. Who are they? Are they a real person? If so, write down as much detail about them as you can manage. You won't be using it all, but it helps to have them fully realized in your mind.

 If they are the reader, the same applies, but you may need to use your imaginative skills as much as your research skills.

 If they are an archetype, such as a typical florist, midwife, chief operating officer or HR manager, remember to give them a couple of personal qualities as well as the characteristics of the breed.

2 *The challenge they're facing*. The specific challenge. Don't just say they needed to cut their tax bill. Say they needed to save at least 15 per cent off their annual corporation tax bill of £32 million.

 Get under the skin of the challenge and discover not just the impact on the customer but on their organization if you are promoting a business product or their friends and family if you're promoting a consumer product.

3 *The solution*. Explain how and why your product or service helped them to overcome the challenge. What particular aspects of your service made the real difference? Were they specific individuals from your organization who played a key role? Who were they and what did they do?

4 *The benefits*. How was their life changed when they bought your product? How much exactly did they save? Over what precise period? How many internet dates did they get and what happened with match number seven? These are the details that make your story believable.

Download: This download – the story mountain – may help you think about your story. Just annotate it or doodle on it to get the ingredients you want in the place you want them.

It's always hard to sell using the written word. Your reader is ever more mistrustful, stressed and busy. Storytelling allows you to bypass much of the cynicism that attaches itself to marketing messages and tap into that stone-age desire to be entertained.

 It's not just cave people who were entranced by the power of a good story either. Every major world religion has its stock of stories, from parables to fables, creation stories to origins myths. Tribal peoples too rely on stories for teaching and entertainment; and story archetypes, such as the trickster, turn up all over the world, from Anansi the spider in African folklore to Brer Rabbit from America's Deep South and Loki from Norse mythology.

When you come to write *your* story, be creative, do your research and always remember that your goal is not entertainment but sales. So make sure your story links to your call to action, either overtly or more subtly.

Stories are more likely to be read than corporate speak because we *like* to read them. Nobody ever read their children a corporate brochure before bed. (Mind you, it would probably put them to sleep quicker than *Little Red Riding Hood*.) And remember, there is no part of the human brain that is hard-wired to respond to marketing guff.

From theory to profit

Can you come up with a promise that you could make to your prospect about your product? Try this approach. Describe a scene to your prospect in which their life has changed for the better because they bought your product. Go into as much detail as possible. Are they making more money? How much more? What are they spending it on? Have they got rid of a negative emotion that was spoiling their enjoyment of life? What was it? What do they feel instead?

How about secrets? Have you conducted research that you can spin with news of a secret only you can reveal? Do your products use an old ingredient everybody else has forgotten about? Now it's a secret ingredient. Maybe you have a proprietary technology that gives you a competitive advantage. At its most basic, anything you know but your customer doesn't is a secret – or it is until you choose to reveal it. A simple headline formula that works is: Revealed: secrets of the world's best _____.

Out of all the ideas and techniques in this book, storytelling is the one I think most people buying it will have trouble with. It's not that it's difficult, quite the reverse: it's far easier than many other styles of copywriting. But it feels wrong to many marketing and business types. Too obvious. Too simplistic. Too... basic. My question to you is this: are you going to reject *the* most powerful form of communication ever invented without even testing it? Or are you going to experiment with it?

Here's what you need to do. Start with a basic story. The story of one of your customers. Find a really great customer, one who's been with you for years and is really more of a super-fan. Call them or write to them and ask them if they'd be willing to help you write a story about your organization. I'm fairly certain they'll say yes, because it's flattering (a technique we will talk about later on). With the results you get you'll be able to produce emails, ads, letters, brochures, landing pages – whole marketing campaigns.

Workshop

1 Promises should explain in detail how the thing promised will be attained. True or false?

2 You don't have to keep your promise: it's just there to hook the reader. True or false?

3 Which human emotion is triggered by the form of your promise?

4 What is the underlying force that lends promises their power?

   a) They are part of the glue that binds societies together

   b) They sound exciting

   c) They offer the recipient a 'can't lose' option in a buying decision

5 The style of writing where you give your reader an order is called:

   a) The authoritative mood

   b) The imperative command

   c) The imperative mood

   d) The commanding mood

   e) The imperious mood

5 What inherent quality makes a secret so desirable?

   a) Scarcity

   b) Potential for embarrassment

   c) Obscenity

7 What is the root of the word 'prurience'?

8 The following headline is a secrets headline. True or false?

   She made it as a six-figure copywriter. But she's never going to tell you how

9 What do the letters DLS stand for?

10 When we learn a secret, which need from Maslow's hierarchy is being met (circle all that apply)?

   a) Security

   b) Self-actualization

   c) Belonging

   d) Social status

   e) Friendship

11 Which of these is NOT a key element of a story:
events problem outcome dialogue hero

12 Which part of the brain responds when we listen to a story?

13 Which tense do you use for hypothetical stories (that haven't happened yet)?

a) The future

b) The past

c) The present

14 Can you name one useful storytelling technique?

15 What propels a story?

a) Action

b) Emotion

c) Tension

d) Exposition

e) Description

Putting it into action

Exercise 7: Features, benefits, promises

Draw up a three-column grid or use the download. Label the columns on your grid (from left to right): Features, Benefits, Promises.

Download: Now start to complete the columns in this order. First all the features. Second, their corresponding benefits. Third, the SINGLE promise you can make to your prospect that is a result of all those benefits.

Write your promise in the imperative mood. That is, start with a verb in the form of a command, as in the examples above.

Exercise 8: Promises make great headlines

You'll notice that once you have a well-written promise you can very easily build any number of powerful headlines using it as a foundation.

Take the promise you created in Exercise 7 and turn it into headlines. Aim for at least five.

Here's a little cheat-sheet for you, using one of my examples:

Promise
Safeguard your business from a tax investigation.

Headlines
How to safeguard your business from a tax investigation
The bulletproof method of safeguarding your business from a tax
    investigation
Three tips to safeguard your business from a tax investigation
How to safeguard your business from a tax investigation without hiring
    an expensive accountant
How ready are you to safeguard your business from a tax investigation?
Is your business safe from a tax investigation?

Exercise 9: Get out of jail free

We all hope our promises come true. But unfortunately we can't control enough of what happens in our customers' lives to ensure it does. So we need to give ourselves a way out.

Starting with your promise, write a few lines of copy either offering a refund if it doesn't go to plan *or* suggesting that it may not come true because the likelihood is your customer won't keep their side of the bargain, by working hard enough, for example.

Exercise 10: We spill the beans

Use the following headline formula to write a headline for your next marketing campaign.

Change 'best' to another word if it makes it easier.
Revealed: secrets of the world's best _____.

Exercise 11: Getting them to listen

Following on from that headline, write the opening to a sales email or letter where you play on the secrets theme. If it helps to get your creative juices flowing, try finishing this starting line:

> Dear <name>,
> I wasn't sure I should tell you this but my boss said to go ahead...

Exercise 12: You have been lied to

Imagine you are writing to environmental campaigners trying to persuade them to change their minds about tidal power.

Your position is that, far from being a clean, sustainable source of energy, it is actually massively damaging to the environment.

You discover that one of the leading academics whose research has been cited repeatedly by pro-tidal campaigners is being retained at a handsome fee by the world's largest manufacturer of tidal barriers, itself a subsidiary of a major oil company. This is dynamite.

I am going to give you the headline and I want you to write the first few sentences (or the whole damn email if you get enthusiastic).

> To all pro-tidal campaigners: you have been lied to

Exercise 13: Preparing your story questions

I want you to draft a set of questions that will give you the raw material you need for your story. You'll be sending them to your best customers, so focus on things like the reason they bought from you in the first place, the reason they came back, what makes you special in their eyes, and what they were looking for when they were doing their initial research.

Exercise 14: Digging up gold

Identify one of your best customers. Someone who has bought lots of stuff from you, who leaves rave reviews on your site or who writes unsolicited testimonials to your managing director.

Contact them and ask if they'd help you write a story. Email them the questions from Exercise 13 ahead of your agreed interview time.

Call them or invite them to lunch and record the interview. When it's all done and dusted, get a transcript made of the interview.

Exercise 15: Congratulations! You just wrote a story

Sit down with your transcript of the interview. Read it aloud a couple of times. Take out anything that strays from the point. Add some introductory lines like this:

> I wanted to find a way to show you what our customers really think about us. So instead of hiring an expensive advertising agency or a professional copywriter, I called one of our best customers and asked him. Here's what he said:

Tweet: How are you doing? Tweet me @Andy_Maslen

A powerful process for developing customer empathy through copy

It is insight into human nature that is the key to the communicator's skill.

WILLIAM BERNBACH

Long ago, a mentor of mine told me the difference between personal and personalized copy. He said personalized copy was easy: you just inserted data you had collected about your reader. At that point in the history of data-driven marketing, that meant Dear Mr Smith, rather than Dear Client (and I have to say, we thought mail-merging was a pretty cool idea). *Personal* copy, he explained, was much harder. Now you had to make your reader feel that you understood him and his problems, that he wasn't simply a name on a mailing list to you – he was a person.

Ironically, and all too commonly, we see examples of impersonal personalized copy. You know the sort of thing:

Bad: Dear Mr Maslen, As a professional copywriter, I am delighted to offer you a 35% introductory discount on our exciting range of printer consumables.

To call this a naked attempt to curry favour is an insult to naked people everywhere. The only message the writer manages to convey is, 'Hey! Guess what! I know what you do for a living and where you work. Aren't I clever?'

Without any further research, but with a lot more imagination, they could have written something truly personal, left out the personalization altogether and still produced something emotionally engaging. Maybe something more like this:

Good: Dear Copywriter, Has this ever happened to you? You're just about to print out the first draft of that website you've been slaving over for days when your printer bleats that it's run out of toner? Bummer!

Even if I haven't, it's close enough to my daily experience that I'll read on.

Developing insight and empathy is a hugely important exercise for any self-respecting copywriter. It's a much better use of your time than studying grammar and punctuation, for example. You can always hire a proofreader but it's really difficult to hire an empathizer. So in this chapter I want to introduce you to a simple technique you can use to strengthen your empathetic muscles. The best thing about it? It's nothing to do with being a marketeer, copywriter or entrepreneur and everything to do with being a human being. I'm going to teach you to use your imagination.

Weirdly, as I was writing these words, the phone rang and it was a new client needing help with copywriting training. He told me that despite having such rich data that he could do not just segmentation but micro-segmentation, his marketeers were unable to make much use of it, relying on generic copy that failed to engage anybody, while being personalized to everybody.

*

By now, I hope you agree with me that the most important person in any piece of writing you do is your reader. Readers come in two flavours: the single reader and the multiple reader.

If you are emailing a leading scientist to review your software, that is the first flavour. If you are writing to 20,000 scientists to invite them to buy your software, that is the second flavour.

In case you're thinking that there are two different styles of writing, depending on the flavour of reader you have, let me state something for the record...

Introducing the five Ps of effective copywriting

You write to all readers in the same way. We can sum this style up as the five Ps.

Figure 3.1 The five Ps

To repeat a point I have made before, in many places, *from their own perspective, everybody is a single reader.* (Unless they have a multiple personality disorder; although even then, only one person is reading at a time.)

No, the difference between the two flavours of reader lies in the amount you know about them.

For the single reader you can find out pretty much anything and everything you want about them. A little digging on social media sites, a pinch of search engineering, a *soupçon* of asking around and you have them, from their university to their shoe size.

Using your new-found insights wisely, you can write an email or letter of exquisitely personal tone and relevant content. One that touches your reader in exactly the way most likely to have them agree to your suggestion.

For the multiple reader, you have a much tougher challenge.

Anything you can find out about them will be, of necessity, aggregated data. It will also be infuriatingly vague.

You may be told, or discover, that your readers are aged 24–35. So, likely to be in a relationship, but a 50/50 call on whether they have children. Or a mortgage.

Or that they are 70 per cent male. Which, I feel confident in asserting, means 30 per cent of them are female. So out go all those bluff references to razor burn, football and power tools. (Or do they?) If they are in business, over 50 per cent will be director-level, leaving 50 per cent without the keys to the executive lavatories.

Try this: Picture your ideal customer as a fictional character. Give them an inner life. It's a great way to get to know them.

So what's to be done? How do we wriggle our way into their soul to discover what makes them tick? It's time for us to start thinking like novelists, or playwrights. We must invent a character. But not just any character: one that is fleshed out, believable and fully alive.

Building a customer persona

A simple way to do this is to create a persona for your prospect by writing down a list of characteristics they are likely to possess. The characteristics can be physical, material, psychological, emotional, metaphysical, social or environmental. Suppose we choose a Fortune 500 chief executive officer.

They are *likely* to have the following characteristics:

- male;
- 40+;
- wealthy;
- ambitious;
- confident;
- driven;
- works long hours;
- married with children;
- drives expensive car;
- lives in big house in nice part of town or countryside;
- likes sound of own voice;

- confident;
- aggressive;
- free-market politics;
- well-dressed;
- striver;
- anxious;
- lots of acquaintances, few close friends.

This is a stereotype. There are CEOs who don't fit this profile. Just not that many.

Even allowing for the broad brushstrokes of this approach, it gives you an insight into the character and personality of the person you are writing to. If it helps, try using this template to build a persona for your target reader.

There is another step you can take to refine your characterization. Take your list of characteristics and mark each one with a tick or a dash. Ticks mean 'shared by every example of the breed'. Dashes mean 'likely to be shared but not certain'. The ticked list represents the inner sanctum of your character, the place where whatever you write will resonate with them. I once worked with a large magazine publisher who had invested much time and energy creating target readers for each of its brands. For one particular magazine, this character was called 'Pablo' and they had even commissioned a designer to create a full-size cardboard cutout (standee) of Pablo, which stood in the centre of the open plan office. Brilliant.

If you need help creating a persona, download this 'Know your customer' worksheet and complete it.

Download: Know your customer.

Replicating the feel of a one-to-one conversation

You probably don't need me to tell you that 'you' is a very special word in the English language. Regardless of the piece of writing, whether it's printed, on-screen or spoken aloud, 'you' always refers to the same person: the reader/listener.

Try this: Use 'you' and 'I' to create a sense of dialogue in your copy. Don't worry too much about the exact number of times each word appears. Aim for a natural flow instead.

And given that most people find themselves endlessly fascinating subjects, a piece of writing that uses the word 'you' a lot must be all about them. But in the hands of inexperienced or clumsy writers, 'you' can lose a lot of its power. Here's what happens.

The writer mismatches the number of people reading and the number of people writing. Yes, there's a single reader. But there appear to be multiple writers.

Typically, this manifests itself in phrases like this:

Bad: You are the sort of person who appreciates a great deal on home furnishings. That's why we at barginacious.com have pulled an all-nighter coming up with some of this season's most unmissable bargains.

That 'we at barginacious.com' depersonalizes the message. It's just another bit of corporate garbage and may be safely disposed of. Now compare it with this, marginally tweaked, version:

Good: I think you are the sort of person who appreciates a great deal on home furnishings. That's why I was working all of last night to bring you some of this season's most unmissable bargains.

Now it feels like a conversation between two individuals.

Here's an example of some copy I wrote for a very upmarket investment house, talking to their clients about the firm's values:

> But we know there's more to life than deals. So we like to unwind from time to time. Whether it's a staff ski trip or a client dinner, we enjoy socializing and taking good care of each other.

No 'you' but based entirely on an understanding of what the firm's clients wanted from an investment adviser and how they liked to be treated.

CASE STUDY A subscriptions acquisition campaign for The Economist

We'll help you form your own view, whatever the topic

How knowing more about the world helps you in these seven situations

Dear Mr Sample

Is it possible that over the next few months you could find yourself in one or more of the following seven situations:

You might be having lunch with a new client, or dinner with friends. You may be in a meeting with potential investors, or your senior colleagues. Travelling to an unfamiliar city, or country. Or chatting to a complete stranger at a party.

For someone like you these situations are the stuff of everyday working and social life.

You have your own areas of interest and your professional specialisation. And when those subjects are being discussed I am sure you will feel more than able to contribute.

But what about when the conversation turns to a topic that lies outside your own interests? Is your knowledge of the world broad enough to be able to offer an informed opinion?

Does this sound like you?

At The Economist, we believe in the value of acquiring a broader knowledge of the world. As I am sure you do. Just to confirm my thinking (we prefer not to make assumptions at The Economist) perhaps you could think about your answers to the following three questions:

Do you read widely and have a fairly strong grasp of world affairs?

Are you thirsty for knowledge that goes beyond a shallow need to "impress the boss"?

Is knowing more about our world a worthwhile goal in itself?

For you, <u>knowing about the world informs the way you move through it</u>. But perhaps

Over, please...

The Economist magazine wanted an integrated print and digital marketing campaign that would gain profitable new subscribers. The emphasis was to be on selling the value of *The Economist*, rather than relying on offers.

The target subscriber was someone for whom knowing what was going on in the world was a deep-seated personal value, not merely a route to advancement, either personally or professionally.

As befits a marketing team who place analysis at the heart of their operations, the campaign was to be tested scientifically against their control pieces, specifically for AdWords and the direct mail pack.

The approach

Having read the extensive brief, including the customer research, I decided that for the target reader of the copy, the idea of knowledgeability was tied deeply into their sense of self. While they wouldn't necessarily be show-offs, they would value the confidence that comes from knowing they are well informed about the world. By focusing my introduction on social situations, I encouraged them to imagine how they would feel if their knowledge was found wanting. Having planted a seed of doubt in their minds, the rest of the copy showed how a subscription to *The Economist* would mean never having to say, 'I don't know'.

Despite the widely varying amounts of copy, from AdWords to a four-page sales letter, the underlying theme of the copy – the big idea – remained the same. As a bonus, the A/B test conducted by *The Economist* revealed, once again, that the longer copy (our four-page test letter) outpulled the shorter control (two pages).

'I thought I would send you a quick email to tell you that your PPC copy has outperformed the control. It is now running all across the account!'
   Matt Cocquelin
   EMEA Senior Marketing Executive, *The Economist*

Forget copywriting and try healing instead

Imagine for a moment that you suffer from arthritis. Your hands are painful. Typing makes it worse. Which of these subject lines would make you want to read the email:

> Arthritis?

> Introducing a revolutionary new hands-free keyboard

I just tried that out here in the office and fortunately for me, and the rest of this introduction, everybody I asked said the first one. 'Arthritis?' is automatically relevant, and therefore engaging, to every single arthritis sufferer. 'Introducing a revolutionary new hands-free keyboard' is only relevant to people who want a new kind of keyboard.

What I'm driving at here is the need for a shift in perspective, from what you find interesting to what your prospect finds interesting. If they coincide, you are one lucky copywriter. Let's say you work for a manufacturer of highly desirable gadgets. So desirable that even though there are superior models available from your competitors – models that work better, have more features, are cheaper and are less glitchy – people will still queue round the block for yours. Because they're *yours*. Your job as a copywriter is simple. You simply have to announce availability and use a beautiful product shot on a white background. Job done.

But supposing that your working life is a little more... nuanced. Perhaps you have a product that, once they've discovered it, people can't imagine how they ever lived without it. But they don't readily discover it. It's not fashionable, just incredibly good. There's always a temptation to trumpet the virtues of your product in the sure (and mistaken) belief that once they are apprised of same, customers will beat a path to your door. The old 'better mousetrap' fallacy. The trouble is, people don't want better mousetraps. They want dead mice. Mice that were alive in their houses and are now dead, I mean, not, like, packages of dead mice in the post. Anyway. A house without mice is what they want.

What you need to do with your better mousetrap is put it to one side, maybe against the skirting board, and put your customer in front of you instead. Remember them? You created some beautifully rich personas for them in the last chapter. Now, ask yourself this. What is their biggest problem? And the answer is...

Mice.

Empathizing with your customer

Understanding how your customer feels is crucial to establishing rapport, trust and, ultimately, the sale. In general, and this is perhaps a sad reflection upon the human condition – or maybe just upon marketing – we are not selling to contented people. No, that's not precise enough.

When contented people buy things, the part of them doing the buying is not the contented part. People buy stuff to solve problems.

Those problems could be basic: 'I am hungry.' Or they could be more, how shall I put it, middle-class: 'I need a Pilates teacher within walking distance of my beach house.'

Your first goal as a writer is to pinpoint their pain. Find what's causing their discontent and you can start building a case for a sale.

Key takeaway: Find your reader's point of pain and you've found the way in to their emotions.

(Incidentally, I'm assuming the pain we're trying to find is one your product can alleviate. If you sell rabbit hutches and your customer is suffering existential angst, you need to do more digging.)

Having identified their pain, then what? There are a number of ways you can exploit your new-found insight.

You could use it as your headline. Let's say you are marketing copper bracelets that relieve arthritic pain.

Bad: Are you ready to experience the miraculous healing properties of copper?

Good: Arthritis (from an email received by the author)

People whose hands hurt because of their arthritis are looking for something to stop them hurting. They don't care whether it's copper, aluminium, elephant hair or string.

When he was selling a treatment for hernias, US copywriter John Caples used the one-word headline... you guessed it... HERNIA.

This approach has the effect of becoming magnetically attractive to every single person seeing the ad who suffers from a hernia. It's enough to stop them in their tracks and make them want to read the next sentence. Which Joseph Sugarman, another garlanded US copywriter, claims is the single job of the headline. I endorse his view. Your headline sells the copy; your copy sells the product. But you don't have to stop at the headline. It makes a pretty good opening too.

Here are three different ways we could continue the 'arthritis' copy:

Three questions

Do you find it hard to concentrate when your hands are hurting? Have you ever had to stop doing something – a hobby perhaps – because the pain was a distraction? Are you fed up with drugs, creams and needles? Well, I have good news for you.

Startling news

Leading scientists professed themselves baffled after an 86-year-old woman in Minnesota claimed the pain she suffered in her hands from arthritis had completely disappeared... without drugs.

Shocking

'I wish I could cut them off!' That's how bad the pain in her hands was for arthritis sufferer Elaine Rich. But just two weeks after making that shocking statement, Elaine is playing her piano again.

As you get into the copy you'll want to start talking about benefits, I hope. Rather than simply listing them, you can weave them into a future story:

Imagine, within a few days of putting on your bracelet, you could be doing simple tasks without pain or discomfort: opening jars perhaps, or even just finding the right change to pay for your parking.

> Dropping off to sleep becomes so much easier without that niggling worry that the pain will flare up.

> And you can start to enjoy your hobbies again, whether it's updating your blog, emailing grandchildren or playing cards with friends.

The value of this approach lies in its universal applicability.

It doesn't matter whether you are selling copper bracelets or copper futures; lipstick or lathes; products, services or ideas.

Engage: Imagine your reader, lying awake at three in the morning. Whatever woke them matters more than whatever you're selling.

The person who's going to buy from you has a problem. That problem looms larger in their world than any product you have to sell. They have painful hands, underperforming assets, low self-esteem, unhappy customers, disgruntled workers, twitchy regulators... and you can make them go away.

So the next time you start writing a new piece of copy, try beginning with your customer's pain and work back to your product. Your view of the world and your customer's are radically different. In yours, your product occupies a central position; in theirs, it is nowhere. So to infiltrate their mind and get their attention, you need to talk about something they find interesting. Most people love to talk about their problems. So should you.

The keyboard-free method of writing great copy

I have met a number of copywriters who have told me, with not a little pride, of their ability to touch-type. I'm afraid I have always been singularly underwhelmed. Speed isn't the big deal in this line of work. Nor is accuracy. That's what proof-reading is for. But you know what? The ability to type *at all* is over-rated. Writing isn't, and never has been, about one's typing skills. Go back a ways and copywriters used to ply their trade using hand-held devices called pencils. Some (sshh, listen to this) still do. If you want, you can scan your handwritten copy, upload it to a website and have someone halfway around the world type it for you.

Or you can speak your copy into an app or digital recorder, upload the audio file to a website and have somebody... oh, you get it. (One of my favourite words is amanuensis, which means somebody who writes another's words down for them. The composer Frederick Delius famously used a young composer named Eric Fenby to help him out when syphilis-induced blindness and paralysis put a stop to his own writing.)

No, what matters is your ability to connect with your customer. So, for now, let's forget about keyboards and concentrate on gaining more insights into our customer's state of mind. I've prepared two detailed interview templates that will take you right into the heart of their world. The first one would be great to use with a real customer, but failing that you could simply conduct it in your head. Or you could get a market research agency to conduct the interviews for you (they'll have to be very good). The second set of questions are what your customer is asking you. For this one you don't need a real customer, just yourself and a massive dollop of honesty.

The process goes something like this:

1 Figure out what makes our customer tick.

2 Identify their point of pain (as it relates to the product we're selling).

3 Show them how the product makes the pain go away.

None of this involves typing.

And, in fact, you could be a perfectly good copywriter even if you couldn't type. Even if you lost your hands in a bizarre keyboard accident, you could still be a great copywriter. Here's how.

Key takeaway: Being a good persuader calls for empathy, not touch-typing.

You spend time thinking your way into your customer's world.

Twelve questions to ask about your customer

1 What are they like?

2 What drives them?

3 What do they love?

4 What do they hate?

5 What are their values?

6 How do they see themselves?

7 How do *others* see them?

8 How would they *like* others to see them?

9 If they could change one thing about themselves, what would it be?

10 Why would they change it?

11 How would they change it?

12 What does your customer want to know?

Eight questions they're asking you

Then you imagine you are face-to-face with them in a quiet space. They ask you these questions:

1 Why did you want to see me?

2 What do you want to talk about?

3 How do I know I can trust you?

4 How are you going to make my life better?

5 Can you prove it will work?

6 Who else has it worked for?

7 How do I get hold of it?

8 What if I don't like it?

To help you out, I've replicated these two sets of questions on this interview guide for you to download.

Download: Then you do this easy thing...
Using a voice recorder, you speak your answers.
Speak at length; leave no question unanswered or point unmade.
When you've finished, upload your file to an internet transcription service and get it typed.

This is your first draft. It will be packed with amazingly powerful language, couched in a natural, conversational, convincing tone of voice. Then you edit it. (OK so fingers may come in handy here.)

I came up with a headline that was almost a verbatim transcript of what I overheard one woman telling her friend in the street. It ran along the lines of:

It's what you look like on the inside that matters.

This approach has three big benefits.

First of all, by freeing you from the tyranny of the winking cursor, it allows you to focus on what you want to say, not how you want to say it.

David Ogilvy and John Caples were both fans of this approach, independently stating that the content of your copy is more important than its form.

Second, it's a lot faster, so you save time.

Third, the resulting copy sounds like a real person, not someone choking simultaneously on a dictionary and a corporate style guide.

And the net result of all of this is copy that is far more likely to achieve the goals you have set yourself.

On a course I was running, one of the participants came up to me, somewhat shyly, during a coffee break, and told me she wanted to write a cookbook in her spare time but she just couldn't think what to say and didn't have the confidence to be a writer. 'Well,' I said, 'what's the angle you're taking?' For the next 10 minutes, smiling and getting incredibly animated, she told me in a hugely engaging way, just exactly what she wanted to do with the book, how it would focus on the home-cooking of her Mum, who was from Jamaica. When she'd finished, I just said, 'Don't write your book, talk it. Then get someone else to type it up for you'. And do you know what she said? 'Oh, am I allowed to do that?'

At its heart, copywriting is about behaviour modification. Your customer wakes up in the morning with no intention of doing X. After reading your copy, they do X.

Modifying a human being's behaviour is difficult, but not impossible. But typing has very little do with it. Empathy, insight and understanding have everything to do with it.

From theory to profit

Forget about your product for the moment. It will still be there when you come back to it. Now, your customer. How much do they know about you and your product? Everything? And is their problem simply that they don't own it? Great! All you need to do is tell them it's ready for them to order (or it will be shortly – nothing like a bit of anticipation to whet the appetite). But maybe they know nothing at all about your product. Also great! Because you're not going to write about it anyway. What problem does your product solve? THAT's what you're going to write about.

When I was a wet-behind-the-ears marketing assistant, I naively assumed that marketing directors at huge global corporations would be a) excited and b) credulous when I boldly stated in my copy that this new report I was pitching would tell them 'everything' they needed to know about their industry. It didn't and they weren't. But one day I met one of our customers at a trade fair and she said, 'Oh, no, we don't base our plans on your reports, we just use your data in our presentations to the Board to show we've done our homework'. What's the reality for *your* product? What's the real problem it solves? You could do a lot worse than focus your copy on that.

Also, I don't know how good your typing skills are, and I don't care. At the time of writing I have been a copywriter professionally for 30 years and mine are, frankly, terrible. What I care about is how good you are at understanding what makes people tick. What makes your *customers* tick. Let's put it this way, when there are free apps teaching you to touch-type, the skill can't be worth very much. So, starting today, I want you to refocus your efforts as a copywriter – or as someone who writes copy for their business – away from keyboards and towards people.

Become an expert at reading people: you'll never find a free app that can teach that skill. Oh, you can? Well, get that too. Here are a few ideas: train yourself to observe the people around you, at work, at home, in the street, at the sports centre, in shops and outdoor markets, wherever you can find them. Make a conscious effort (discreetly) to listen to their conversations. Yes, note down words and phrases if you must, but concentrate on what they're saying not how they're saying it.

Workshop

1 What are the five Ps?

   a) Personal, Pleasant, Professional, Plain, Persuasive

   b) Personal, Pleasant, Pushy, Plain, Persuasive

   c) Promise, Power, Product, Pitch, PS

2 What word describes the character you have created?

   a) Profile

   b) Persona

   c) Prospect

3 You can personalize without being personal. True or false?

4 When is it OK to show your reader you are writing to more than one person?

   a) Always

   b) Never

   c) Only for lists over 50,000

5 How many times should you use the word 'you' in a sentence?

6 What was John Caples's headline for an ad promoting hernia relief?

7 What do people looking for the better mousetrap really want?

8 What does Joseph Sugarman say is the sole purpose of the headline?

9 Which one of these is *not* an approach you could use in this style of copywriting?

   a) Startling news

   b) The list of features

   c) Shocking

   d) Three questions

10 What's the time of day when your prospect is most likely to be worrying about their problems?

11 What's one question your reader is asking you?

12 What does *amanuensis* mean?

13 Name a fan of the 'what you say is more important than how you say it' school of copywriting.

14 What *must* you find out about your customer?

   a) What makes them sick

   b) What makes them click

   c) What makes them tick

15 What's the best place to discover more about horseracing enthusiasts?

Putting it into action

Exercise 16: Creating personas

For the following three 'types', create a persona as we did for the CEO earlier in this chapter. Use nothing but your imagination, empathy and knowledge of the world:

- Teacher
- Heart surgeon
- Video game designer

Exercise 17: It Lives, Igor! It Lives!

Using the same approach, create a persona for your average customer, your worst customer and your best customer.

Exercise 18: Being personal without being personalized

Using the personas you created in Exercise 17, write an email to each one announcing a new product, offer, event or promotion for your organization. Use no personal data at all but aim for a type and tone that would make each person feel it was only for them.

Exercise 19: The tale of the lost car keys

You are writing copy for a new device that tracks down people's missing car keys.

Write an ad that plays on the point of pain, not the product. Do not mention the product until the very last line.

Exercise 20: Finding their point of pain

I want you to conduct an imaginary interview with your prospect. You are a psychiatrist and they are your patient. Keep going until you are sure you understand their problem inside out and back to front. Here are the first two lines of the interview:

You: So, what seems to be the problem?

Them: Well, Doc, every morning, at exactly 3.00, I wake up with my heart pounding and a fluttering feeling in the pit of my stomach.

Exercise 21: 'I can cure your pain'

Using your new-found knowledge of your prospect's pain, write a set of three pay-per-click (PPC) ads using Google's AdWords character limits (25 for the headline, 35 each for the next two lines, plus a destination URL). REMEMBER: lead with the pain not the prescription.

Exercise 22: Interviewing your customer

Using the list of 12 questions for your customer, build a picture of their world. If you can, use them as an interview guide.

Exercise 23: Your customer interviewing you

Now using the list of eight questions, fill in your answers – truthfully – to add your side of the conversation.

Exercise 24: Look Dad! No hands!

Launch a voice recorder app or switch on your digital voice recorder and start speaking to your customer.

Explain what you know about their problem and how your product makes it go away.

Then get the recording typed up – there are cheap online services that will do this for you.

Finally, edit the resulting text until you have a natural-sounding and convincing piece of copy.

Tweet: How are you doing? Tweet me @Andy_Maslen

Copywriting hacks: Flattery will get you everywhere

08

Everyone likes flattery; and when you come to royalty you should lay it on with a trowel.

BENJAMIN DISRAELI

Introduction

How do you feel when somebody pays you a compliment? Affronted? Pleased? Happy? Suspicious? Most people pick the second and third out of those answers. It's not really surprising, is it? The reasons why we like compliments aren't that hard to figure out either. They affirm our original decision to cut our hair, pick a particular outfit, give a particular speech or raise our children a certain way. They make us feel good, or better, about ourselves. They place us at the centre of things. They reinforce all the ideas about ourselves that we hold dear. With one proviso.

Compliments must be sincere. Or, let's be honest, they must be delivered with all the sincerity the giver can muster. If we suspect, deep down, that our new 'do' makes us look like a wet spaniel, being told it's fantastic will ring hollow. But if the compliment giver protests that, no, it's not quite as lovely as the old one but the colour, at least, is fresh and different, we may allow ourselves to believe it.

So where does complimenting shade into flattery, and is that a problem? Flattery means, literally, undue or exaggerated praise. Those two adjectives need teasing out and thinking about. If the praise is undue, that means the receiver hasn't earned it or doesn't deserve it (though not necessarily that they won't welcome it). If the praise is exaggerated, it means the receiver *has* earned it and *does* deserve it, but not in the quantity or style on offer. Again, whether they will mind is debatable. William Shakespeare knew where he stood when he wrote, in Timon of Athens, 'O that men's ears should be / To counsel deaf, but not to flattery!'

My feeling is that given the remove at which we deliver the praise, and the fact that the reader cannot help but be aware that they are being sold to, a little exaggeration is no bad thing, *so long as the fundamental point is true*. This technique is definitely in the box labelled 'Authorized Personnel Only' even if it isn't in the one labelled 'Dark Arts'. It's a sharp psychological tool and, wielded correctly pays off handsomely. So go ahead, use it. I am sure you have the skills to pull it off.

*

Sometimes, when I suggest in one of my copywriting workshops that people should try flattery in their emails or sales letters, there is a murmur of protest. The objections fall into two camps.

First, it's insincere. OK, if you tell a short person that they stand as tall as a sequoia tree, or a grammar nerd that they are a linguistic free spirit, I guess you have me banged to rights. But that's crude and wouldn't serve any purpose in a piece of sales or marketing copy.

But how about substituting the word 'compliment' for 'flattery'. Now is it OK?

In his book *Influence*, Robert Cialdini (2000) observes that people are motivated to comply with people whom they like. He goes on to itemize qualities that we might possess, or actions we might take, that would cause someone else to like us. One of these is paying compliments. Robert Cialdini is not stating anything particularly startling. After all, we are bound to feel well disposed towards people who pay us compliments, however trivial.

Engage: Together with greed, ego is a massively powerful motivator for most people. Even those who claim it isn't.

I think there are plenty of compliments you can pay your reader without becoming fulsome. Wealthy folk are clearly clever with money. Petrolheads know lots about cars. Sports fans are passionately loyal to their teams. Chief executives are professionally successful. Nurses are caring. Having identified the characteristics of your customer's personality it isn't hard to parlay that knowledge into a sincerely paid compliment.

Talking about petrolheads, I had the good fortune to write a series of renewal communications for *Top Gear Magazine*. Virtually the entire series was underpinned by a single, dominating emotional appeal. I flattered the reader that they were 'one of the boys' with lines like these:

I know you love cars, so I thought you might appreciate this picture of a Bugatti Veyron.

You and I know there's beauty in cars, entertainment in cars... FUN in cars.

So what do you say? Tear off the coupon below and send it back to us and we'll even let you choose the snacks at the next services.

Nobody falls for flattery... or do they?

The other objection to flattery as a sales tool is that people won't fall for it, 'because I never do'. I am more inclined to argue with this statement. For two reasons.

First of all, I don't believe anyone who claims to know what thousands or perhaps millions of perfect strangers are going to feel, or how they're going to act. Especially not when the basis of their assertion is what *they* feel or do. It isn't scientific and it's probably not even true about themselves. I know this because I usually counter the disagreeing attendee by complimenting them on their forthright opinion – a piece of flattery they are without exception happy to accept as perspicacious and no more than their due!

Second of all, people do 'fall for it'. Alongside greed, egotism is probably the most powerful of all the factors that motivates us to action – certainly from a copywriting perspective. In our personal relationships I'm sure it's love, but in selling I'm afraid it's cupidity not Cupid that gets the victor's laurels (despite their shared Latin root *cupere* meaning to desire).

In test after test, sales copy that flatters the reader has outperformed copy driven by another appeal. The question is, why?

CASE STUDY A subscription renewal letter for CRU Group

The headline instructs the reader to engage their visual imagination. The ellipsis points indicate that they should read on to discover what to picture.

The opening story, in the present tense, evokes feelings of pride and self-esteem.

CRU Group produces global market intelligence on metals and minerals. This letter formed part of a subscriptions renewal campaign.

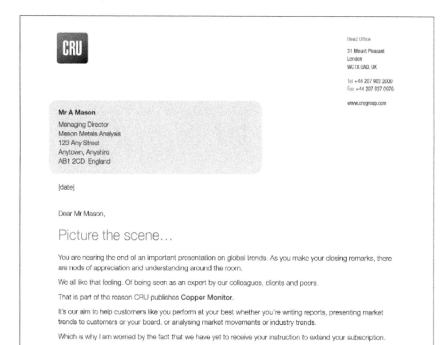

At this point in the campaign, the recipient has already received a number of communications inviting them to renew their subscription. I changed the tone to reflect CRU's anxiety at losing a customer and to instil a sense of corresponding anxiety in the reader that they themselves would soon be missing out.

> *The restructure of our renewals campaign, which used a human voice and increased the number of efforts sent, saw renewal rates rise from 76% to 85%. (Bill Brand, Marketing manager, CRU Group)*

Remember we looked at Maslow's Hierarchy of Needs right at the beginning of this book? Once your basic survival needs – air, food, water, shelter, security – are taken care of, the territory gets a lot more emotional. The three upper tiers of the hierarchy are concerned with needs of love and belongingness, esteem and self-actualization. And there – right, slap, bang in the middle of those three – is the need that is fed directly by flattery. Self-esteem *and the esteem of others.*

When you flatter your customer, be sincere. A generous compliment, honestly paid, will always be welcome.

Bad: As a valued customer...

Good: As someone who spends a lot of time in the air you are used to seeing further than most people... (from a mailing for a business magazine written by the author)

We *need* to know that others think a lot of us. All you have to do in your copy is tell your customer just how much you think of them.

When to use flattery in your copywriting

If you accept my premise, the next question you should be asking is, where is the best place to pay a compliment? The answer is, at the beginning. Flattery is one of the safest ways to begin an email, sales letter or web page. It's emotionally engaging. It speaks directly to the reader. And they won't gainsay a word of it. So you have their attention and they are willing to read on because you seem to be speaking such a lot of good sense. Here's how we might approach the beginning of an email promoting a white paper on strengths-based recruitment. It's a classic bait-and-switch opening:

Dear Judy,
As someone with a long and successful career in HR, you probably get dozens of emails offering solutions to the talent brain drain. And I'm willing to bet you discard most of them.

OK, so we have Judy's attention. That comma after 'HR' is crucial: it signals to Judy that there's more to come that will prove the truth of our compliment.

Even when she reaches the end of the second sentence, she is unwilling to stop reading. The story is unfinished. She's thinking, 'yes, and your point is?'. This is where we must start our bait-and-switch. Our next sentence reads:

But since I know strengths-based recruitment is on your radar, you'll want to hear what I have to say next.

This is actually more flattery, since we are showing her that we know what she's interested in. The second half of this sentence starts pulling away the bait and revealing the hook.

> Exclusively for senior HR managers like you, MazPeople Inc. has produced a survey of HR directors' attitudes to the war for talent. Our new white paper also gives you 10 recommendations for attracting and retaining the best of the best.

There are endless angles you can take with this approach. For every reader there are dozens of aspects of their life that you can compliment, from professional prowess to sporting success. From their skills with people to their rapport with animals. Before you start a piece of copy you should have thought and felt your way into your reader's world, so have a look around while you're there and see what would make the most compelling opening for your copy.

More subtle flattery: how to make spending money feel like a privilege

In a great many situations, people do not want things that are cheap. Expensive things are desirable often because they *are* expensive. The global luxury goods industry, which thrives whether the world economy is bubbling or bombing, knows this. I feel, though I have no evidence for it, that Ferrari salesmen and women do not complain to their bosses that the cars would sell more if only they weren't so darned expensive.

Now, if things are needlessly *costly*, that's another thing altogether. 'Costly' implies *needless* expense. Which is not so easy to sell. In such linguistic nuances are fortunes made or lost. Let's recognize that all of us like a little luxury. Luxury confers status. Luxury confers self-esteem and the esteem of others. Luxury makes us feel good about ourselves.

How can we pull off the luxury trick? If our product genuinely is a luxury then it's a walk in the park. But if we're pitching a more prosaic product – accounting services, perhaps – then it's going to be a stretch. We're going to have to be creative. A story...

Examples of flattery from hospitality and publishing

I had just returned from delivering a training course in London. I stayed at the Hilton in Docklands. Because I stay in town at least once a month I joined their 'frequent flyer' programme: Hilton Honors.

When I booked my room for this latest trip I was delighted to see that as a Hilton Honors member I was eligible for a 'Custom Upgrade'. I could choose from three different upgrades, all involving bigger rooms with better views and even balconies. But guess what?

These upgrades come with a price tag. Not huge, I admit, but a price tag nevertheless.

Hilton is doing something clever. They are upselling you just after the point of purchase, which is a pretty good time to do it. And they are packaging their selling process as a membership privilege. And it works.

Try this: Upsell at the point when your customer is buying from you. That's when they're most receptive.

A different example, from a different industry – magazine publishing – is the Automatic Membership Renewal Programme.

This really means that the publisher will continue to charge your credit card each year for another subscription period until you tell them to cancel. The technical name for this perfectly legal mechanism is continuous credit card authority – and it resembles Direct Debit.

But there's not a great deal of mileage from a sales perspective in telling your customer you're going to raid their credit card account every year. So you package it up as a 'membership programme'. Now, what do we know about human beings? That's right. They are herd animals. So they like joining things.

In fact, both the above examples do confer benefits on the customer. In the case of the room upgrade at the Hilton, you get a better room for a nominal fee – so you are effectively saving money and getting a more comfortable, relaxing stay.

In the case of the magazine publishers (or the ones smart enough to do it) they are removing admin from the customer's life and not even charging anything for this service. A line I have used many times, and freely confess to having adapted from others who went before me, was to label a continuous credit card authority deal as: Automatic Membership Continuation Plan.

So my question to you is this: Is there an aspect of your product or service offering that would make a big difference to your bottom line if more of your customers took it up? Do they have objections to doing so? Can you repackage this valuable but tricky aspect of your offer to make it seem like an additional benefit to your customers?

OK, that was three questions. But they're worth asking. And answering. Oh, and by the way, the answer is purely copywriting. You don't need to re-engineer the product offering – it's all already there. This is purely about words.

In business, as in life generally, it's never a good idea to leave money lying on the table. If you are facing customer resistance to an idea that could make you more money and help them out in the process, all you need to do is sell it a bit better.

People love upgrades, membership privileges and the rest. So put your thinking cap on and get writing.

Key takeaway: Don't be afraid to sell your customer something else – but focus on selling one thing at a time.

From theory to profit

If you're going to use this technique successfully, there are a few hoops you have to jump through. First, can you square its use with your own ethics? I ask only because it seems to cause some people problems. It shouldn't be a problem because of what comes next. How are you going to determine the things you can compliment in your customers? You're going to need to think about them. Again. What are their skills, their qualities, their characters? Where does their self-esteem reside? Are they secure in their place in the world or do they rely on the opinions of others for emotional stability? Answering these questions will help you identify the sorts of compliments you can pay that will get them nodding as they read, and receptive to whatever you decide to say next.

When it comes to flattering people by offering them upgrades, it doesn't matter whether you are in the luxury goods sector or not. What matters is whether you can borrow some of its clothing – and language – to position either your product or an additional service as a privilege, upgrade, 'Diamond Service' or premium. Remember that people love to belong to groups and clubs of all kinds, so one of the simplest approaches you can take is to create a subscriber club. Get a membership pack together, write a welcome letter and send it to every new customer. And here's where it gets interesting. Figure out a way to encourage either repeat purchase or a bigger purchase. Only you don't call it that; you call it an upgrade.

Workshop

1   Which human need does flattery meet?

2   Where's the ideal place to use flattery in your copy?

3   Flattery only works if it's appropriate to the reader. True or false?

4   Benjamin Disraeli said that when it came to royalty you should apply flattery with a:

   a)   Trowel

   b)   Towel

   c)   Shovel

5   Talking about 'liking', Robert Cialdini asserts that we are more likely to comply with people who:

   a)   Make us laugh

   b)   Pay us compliments

   c)   Are physically attractive

   Tick all that apply.

6   What's the emotional reaction that makes people like being offered upgrades?

7   Which of these would NOT work as a title for your luxury scheme?

   a)   Goldcard

   b)   Executive Plus

   c)   Privilege Club

   d)   Frequent Buyers' Club

   e)   Inner Circle

8   What's the difference between expensive things and costly things?

9   If your customer is moaning about price, what haven't you shown them?

10   Which of these is the best product to work into a luxury deal?

   a)   Something that costs you a lot to produce and has a high price tag

   b)   Something that costs you virtually nothing to produce and has a low price tag

   c)   Something that costs you a bit to produce and has a high price tag

Putting it into action

Exercise 25: Honestly, it suits you

Think of one of your close friends. Or a colleague perhaps. Make a list (I suggest you do this somewhere you can be sure they won't stumble upon it) of their positive qualities. For each of these qualities, write a couple of lines of sincere praise in as natural and conversational style as you can manage.

Exercise 26: Honestly? You stank!

Think of a public figure. Make a list of all their negative qualities. (I imagine this won't be too hard. Vanity, at the very least, will surely make the cut.) For each of *these* qualities, write a couple of lines praising them for the exact opposite, again, in as natural and conversational style as you can manage.

Exercise 27: Flattery will get you everywhere

Write a sales email that opens with a strong appeal to your customer's ego. Make your praise both sincere and assertive. Try starting with 'As a...' if you need help getting going. Remember to switch from the bait to the hook quickly and make the desired action consonant with the aspect of their character you are praising.

Exercise 28: Finding the money left on the table

I want you to identify something that already exists within your organization's product range that would be very profitable if every customer bought it along with their main purchase.

Exercise 29: Joining the privileged few

Come up with half a dozen ideas for the name of your add-on sales programme. Use words such as 'club' or 'society' to denote the idea of exclusive membership.

Exercise 30: Are you ready to join our elite customers?

Write some add-on sales copy for your newly defined luxury product or service. Try using it next time somebody places an order. Major on the benefits of membership rather than the benefits of the product itself.

Tweet: How are you doing? Tweet me @Andy_Maslen

The Ancient Greek secret of emotionally engaging copy

09

All human actions have one or more of these seven causes: chance, nature, compulsions, habit, reason, passion, desire.

ARISTOTLE

Introduction

Among the first people to start thinking systematically about the power of language to move people to action were the Ancient Greeks. Rhetoricians developed many of the techniques we still use today to create compelling arguments, from repetition to contrast, irony to metaphor. English has its own direct steal, 'rhetorical question', meaning a question asked to prompt thought rather than a direct answer.

You may think it's a stretch to get from some bearded guy in the market square in 480 BCE Athens, sounding off about foreign policy, to you trying to write a Facebook ad, but it's really not. How easy do you think it must have been to move a populace to war just by talking? Or to overthrow a government? On a scale of 1–100, where 1 is 'Ooh, I think I left the gas on' and 100 is 'Quick, pass me that spear'? Yet that's what happened. Not every day, but often enough for us to look at what was going on with language and try to see if we can learn something.

The main thing we're going to look at in this chapter is the way we can build an argument. If you think that means another formula, you're right. If you think it means another acronym, you're right. If you think it means another mechanistic this-goes-here-and-that-goes-there approach, you're wrong. This approach is conceptual, rather than structural.

Like many of the other techniques in this book, it's worth putting in the effort to understand it thoroughly and practise using it because it will distinguish your copy from the run-of-the-mill hackery bombarding your customers on all sides. And, at heart, it's incredibly powerful because it includes a strong emotional component. It's also more fun to write. (Not that having fun should be our primary concern, but, hey, who said work should be boring?)

*

Picture the scene. You're in Athens for a training course. Your course leader is one Aristotle. His CV is impressive, and one of his clients is none other than Alexander The Great. He's already written a treatise, On Rhetoric, which you've been trying to order on Amazon, but the river is flowing sluggishly and is also several thousand miles away and nobody outside of South America has heard of it. And nobody has heard of South America either. You are there because you've heard Aristotle has formulated what modern business school theorists would no doubt call a three-point strategy for effective oral communications. To be a compelling speaker, he advises the use of three components: ethos, pathos and logos.

Here is what Aristotle himself has to say about his idea:

> Persuasion is clearly a sort of demonstration, since we are most fully persuaded when we consider a thing to have been demonstrated. Of the modes of persuasion furnished by the spoken word there are three kinds. Persuasion is achieved by the speaker's personal character when the speech is so spoken as to make us think him credible. Secondly, persuasion may come through the hearers, when the speech stirs their emotions. Thirdly, persuasion is effected through the speech itself when we have proved a truth or an apparent truth by means of the persuasive arguments suitable to the case in question.

Or, my translation: Ethos, pathos and logos:

Ethos refers to the speaker's character. In other words, why we should trust them (and their words).

Pathos is the emotional appeal of the argument. Getting people's feelings engaged with their arguments.

Logos is the intellectual component. The reasons why the listener (or reader) should believe them.

Key takeaway: Character, emotion, argument: the three Ancient Greek components of a successful sales pitch.

That's precisely the approach we should be taking in our copywriting. When you're trying to sell something – or modify your reader's behaviour, feelings or opinions in any way – you can do a lot worse than to follow Aristotle's three-point plan.

You can use this approach in all sorts of subtle ways, and its impact is, I think, immediately visible. I often find myself writing copy for a money-back guarantee of some kind. And I tend to phrase it like this:

> I am sure you will be 100% satisfied with product X and its triple-tested internal widget. But to give you complete peace of mind, I want to offer you my PERSONAL guarantee.

'Triple-tested' and '100%' are logos.

'Peace of mind' is pathos.

'I am sure', 'satisfied' and 'personal' are ethos.

Download: Using this template, jot down the aspects of your sales pitch that fit into the EPL model of persuasion.

CASE STUDY   A video script for Petrochemical Alert

Platts delivers
real-time information

Polymers
aromatics
olefins
solvents
crude oil
naphtha
LPG
styrenes
plastics
methanol
and other feedstocks

The on-screen captions reinforced key sales points but the actor's words were aligned with natural speech patterns.

Platts is a division of McGraw Hill Financial (NYSE: MHFI), a leader in credit ratings, benchmarks and analytics for the global capital and commodity markets.

For this project, Platts wanted a script to be hosted on their website alongside copy and graphics.

Writing scripts calls for an ear attuned to the rhythms of everyday speech. The viewer has to believe that the actor they're watching really is a trader. In this script I made sure I included all three of Aristotle's argument-winners: Ethos – the speaker's character; Pathos – his appeal to the viewer's emotions; and Logos – the intellectual force of his argument.

Table 5.1   Transcript

Narrator	Supers
When you do a job like mine – trading in tough and complex markets – you need access to the absolute latest information, or you're out of the game.	Platts delivers real-time information
As the market changes – hour by hour, minute by minute – Platts Petrochemical Alert gives me everything I need to decide on my response, from news to prices.	Minute-by-minute updates
It tells me what's happening in global petrochemical markets *as it happens* and gives me real-time prices on the commodities I'm trading. If it's heard in the market, I get to hear about it, too.	Polymers, aromatics, olefins, solvents, crude oil, naphtha, LPG, styrenes, plastics, methanol, and other feedstocks
Platts Petrochemical Alert gives me news flashes... long-range analysis... forward curve assessments... basically I get what I need to stay on top in volatile markets.	From plant closures to industry and market performance
For me, it's gold-dust. Completely indispensable if you're making crucial trading decisions. Which for me means pretty much all the time, every day.	Information that supports timely decision-making
Basically, I choose from hundreds of price assessments to create my own customized dashboards. I can even build in bespoke pricing charts that help me visualize price assessments and figure out what's affecting my trades and positions.	Real-time news flashes, long range analysis, pricing charts – on your own bespoke dashboards

(continued)

Table 5.1   (*Continued*)

Narrator	Supers
If I want, I can sit back and simply track global petro-chemical prices – it's that easy.	Spot prices bids and offers
Plus, I've got deal reporting and end-of-day price assessments. They help me home in on the factors moving the market today: so I'm better placed to make critical trading decisions tomorrow.	Integrated, Transparent, Global
Platts Petrochemical Alert in a nutshell? For me it all boils down to three factors. Efficiency. Timeliness. And access. I get the data I want. In the format I want. When I want it. So as a trader, what do I do...? I use Platts Petrochemical Alert.	Register now for a free demo... ... contact your local sales representative

If your reader trusts you, they are more likely to accept your arguments as truthful. If you engage them emotionally in your position, they are more likely to want to go along with you.

And if you give them concrete reasons why what you're saying is true, they can accept their emotional response intellectually and also believe more strongly in your character.

Bad: Joaquin Dorada is one of Spain's leading dental surgeons.

Good: Hello, I'm Teresa. I have been a Nutritionist for over 20 years. I provide consultancy services and nutritional training for professional chefs. (from a sales letter for Menuanalyser)

Three approaches, using ethos, pathos and logos

Let's have a go with three versions of a paragraph of web copy for the fictitious S Todd Knife Makers.

Ethos: Hello, my name is Sweeney Todd. I have spent the last 30 years of my life perfecting the art of blade making.

For the first 10 of those years I studied under Japanese blademaster Riuchi Yakamoto. And shortly after establishing my own cook and hunting knife business, I was inducted into the World Council of Master Bladesmiths.

When you invest in an S Todd Cook's Knife, or one of our Hunter's Choice range, you are placing your trust in a knife whose creation reflects a tradition stretching back over a thousand years.

Pathos: Picture it. You're cooking that fancy new sushi dish you promised your wife. Ruby red tuna belly and translucent eel are laid out on your board. This is no time to start using a sub-par knife. You want to get those fish just so – and keep all your fingers.

With an S Todd Sushi Knife you're in safe hands... and so is your sushi. More important, your wife has that smile she wore on your wedding day.

Logos: It's a fact. Most modern cook's knives just aren't up to the job. In tests, over 90 per cent of blades on the market were found to use an inferior tempering process known as hot-roll-and-press. It's a mass production technique used to manufacture the cheap knives you see in department stores.

At S Todd we use a method of knife making perfected by the Japanese in 987 AD. It's called cold-carbon tempering and it takes 14 hours and over 30 separate processes to create a single blade.

Ideally we want a version that combines all three approaches. We'll call it EPL. The best copywriting must simultaneously convince the reader to trust the writer, want whatever they're selling and, crucially, believe that there are sound reasons for buying. Using Aristotle's EPL, we have a ready-made triple-whammy that guides us to this goal.

Engage: If you only have space for a small amount of copy, go for a pathos-led approach. Remember, emotions drive decision-making.

From theory to profit

I suspect that you are already pretty strong on the logos part of your sales pitch. Most people are. We tend to be schooled in the idea that logic will prevail and that facts and figures sway minds. I hope, by now, you have become more sceptical of that view. At any rate, the citing of features is perhaps the most obvious use of logos to make the sale and I don't think you need much help there. But what about the other two components? What are you going to do about *ethos* and *pathos*?

Try starting with *ethos*. It should feel fairly comfortable for you to discuss with colleagues the idea of your organization having character. In modern management speak, we are firmly in values territory. But wait! Do not run off and start worrying about writing a vision statement. For a start it will take months and for a finish it will end up mangled by the combined but disunited efforts of your Board, your General Counsel and your Compliance Department. Instead, how about describing your organization as if it were a person?

For *pathos*, keep going with the techniques we've been exploring so far in the section. Remember, also, that your customer is pre-wired to respond emotionally, so they don't have to decode that style of argument. It already feels natural to them.

Workshop

1 What does *logos* refer to?

   a) Your brand identity

   b) Your argument

   c) Your sentence structure

2 Which famous warrior-king was advised by Aristotle?

3 'I have something I simply have to share with you' is an appeal based on:

   a) Character

   b) Emotion

   c) Logic

4 Advancing a logical argument enhances your character in the eyes of your reader. True or false?

5 If benefits are *pathos*, what are features?

Putting it into action

Exercise 31: It's character-building

Pick one of your current or forthcoming campaigns and write it using an *ethos*-dominated style.

Exercise 32: Getting all emotional

Now rewrite it using a *pathos*-dominated style.

Exercise 33: Let's have an argument

Finally, write it in a *logos*-dominated style.

Tweet: How are you doing? Tweet me @Andy_Maslen

Copywriting and connecting on social media 10

We take our bearings, daily, from others. To be sane is, to a great extent, to be sociable.

JOHN UPDIKE

Introduction

Much of the debate about copywriting for the web rests on the false assumption that people's behaviour has been changed by the channel, most notably in the oft-repeated assertion that people have shorter attention spans. But social media *is* different. Before social media it simply wasn't possible to communicate so quickly, so richly and so prolifically (and we could probably add so weirdly, so idiosyncratically and so self-aggrandisingly), with so many different people, all at the same time. At the time of writing, the main reason most people take photographs has shifted completely, from printing out and adding to bound albums (or, more commonly, storing in a box in the attic) to sharing on social media.

Facebook spawned Facebook ads, Twitter followed with sponsored tweets, and that's not counting the trillions of self-promoting posts on the hundreds of sites on the web grouped under the social media umbrella. All of which has raised anxiety levels about the 'right' way to behave and write on social media.

In this chapter I want to share my personal experience – and view – on how to write for social media. I'm talking about writing for business here; when you post on your own account it's none of my business what you say or how you say it. I'm slowly coming round to the idea of social media as a reasonably effective way to promote, influence and sell. In fact, a delegate on one of my open courses who booked because of this tweet chided me (gently) for lacking faith.

Figure 10.1   Tweet

Andy Maslen

Less than 8 hours left of my early-bird offer for bit.ly/1g3XgGh Digital Copywriting Essentials course.

I want to offer you some things to think about, grouped into three main clusters: what to talk about, how to talk about it and how to protect your reputation. If you send somebody a badly written direct mail letter there's a chance they will scan it, edit it, resize it and then post it on Twitter. If you do the same with a blog post or Facebook update it's much more likely you'll find yourself being lampooned, or worse, within minutes.

*

Are you on Facebook? How about Twitter? LinkedIn? Instagram? Google +? I'm guessing there's at least one 'yes' coming from you.

And *why* are you on social media? Do you distinguish between 'work' and 'personal' sites? Do you tweet on behalf of a company or brand or as yourself? These things matter because you need to set yourself a few rules before getting into it too heavily. For one thing, you can end up spending every waking hour checking your notifications, likes, followers and all the rest. For another, this is a commercial activity, at least in part, so you should have at least a smidgen of commercial thinking behind your social media activity.

This part of the book is concerned with emotions and motivations, so let's stop, just for a moment, to consider why people love social media so much. Well, why do they? I think the clue is in the title. It's a social space. And human beings are social animals. I don't think pandas would have much time for Twitter, whereas meerkats would probably be on it all the time.

But there's more to it than simply that sense of clubbiness. After all, for some sites, like Facebook, we already belong to the club of our friends and family. So if our contacts are spread out, maybe it's a way of staying connected or of feeling that we are connected. But then, wouldn't it be *more* connected to pick up the phone and talk to them person-to-person?

Eight aspects of social media

To me there are eight aspects of social media that make it interesting from a psychological point of view:

1 It's conducted in **public**. If you tell a joke to one person, one person laughs. If you tell it to a crowd, the crowd laughs. That feedback is like a one-hour full-body massage for your ego.

2 It's conducted with **strangers**. Yes, many of your followers will be friends or colleagues, but many will be social media contacts only. Yet we share the same information with everyone.

3 It's conducted in **real time**. Ping! A new update. Ping! A new notification. Ping! A new follower! You can talk to all those people throughout the day. Who needs work?

4 It's **fast**. No need to plan what to say. No waiting for someone to pick up the phone. Just say what you want to say and you're done.

5 It doesn't need much **effort**. Most social media posts are super-short (and we'll pick up on this aspect later on). Which means you can just bang out posts as they occur to you.

6 It offers **fast rewards**. Did that last post hit the sweet spot? You'll know in seconds. Reply to a follower's tweet and get a reply back instantly.

7 It's **free**. It's on the company, your data package, your home broadband subscription.

8 It's **pleasurable**. Chatting is so much more fun than working. Watching cat videos or reading blog posts is easier than doing chores. Getting 'liked' or 'followed' makes us feel good.

Social media posting and responding is tied up with ideas of self-worth, social status, belongingness, admiration, adoration, being liked and being influential. It is also compulsive, addictive even. And guess where the whole process of addiction kicks off? Our old friend, the limbic system. So it's pretty powerful stuff. Being social is a big part of what being human is all about. Which means it's a natural arena for communicators. That's you and me.

Now, I don't want to argue about whether social media is 'worth it'. That's a discussion for a different kind of book. Instead, we'll assume that it is. So what are you going to write? And how are you going to write it? I've been tweeting away merrily for a few years (admittedly with a year's break). I have a LinkedIn profile and even my own group.

Key takeaway: Do social media because you want to, not because you feel you 'ought' to. If your heart isn't in it everyone will be able to tell.

Ten rules for social media

So here are 10 observations for connecting on social media. I hope some of them work for you.

1. Be careful

An old one this, but only say things you'd be comfortable with your gran reading; your vicar, priest, imam or rabbi; your boss, boyfriend or BFF.

Don't shop on eBay when you're drunk, and don't engage in slanging matches on Twitter when similarly inebriated.

The golden rule is an old one: if you wouldn't feel comfortable seeing it on a poster outside your office, don't say it at all.

2. Be original

Sometimes, unfollowing is the only option when you read gems like these:

> 'Benefits are more important than features.'
> 'Today's word of the day, 'arcane.' – hidden or obscure.'
> 'INFOGRAPHIC: 10 types of Twitter user.'

Incidentally, if you *are* tempted to create an infographic, bear in mind these two things: one, it's just a fancy word for 'diagram'. Two, if the copy would make sense on its own, then what exactly are the pictures for?

I'd rather have my thinking challenged by tweets/posts on:

> 'Why features are more important than benefits.'
> 'The moron's approach to headline writing – and why it's better than yours.'
> 'INFOGRAPHIC: neuroscience, copywriting and EBITDA.'

3. Be fresh

If everyone else is posting photos of their products, post one of your dog. If the market is saturated with cool infographics, create an ad in the style of an 18th-century engraving.

If the people you follow all blog about their business lives, start blogging about your holidays, home-yacht-building project and cooking disasters (pictures please).

Key takeaway: You'll never succeed on social media if you only view it as a 'channel'. It's much richer and more complex than that.

4. Be cheeky

Social media mores are different to website, email and print mores. You have licence to be a little less buttoned-up.

I happen to think the odd bit of mild swearing is perfectly OK – even moderate invective can work but I tend to asterisk a couple of letters.

Flirting, bickering, mickey-taking: they're all OK, provided you follow the golden rule – see rule 1 above – and think before you post.

5. Be opinionated

Hedging is boring. We all do it. We cover our backs when expressing a strong opinion in case we're wrong or liable to get into an argument.

Hey! Get into it. What's the worst that can happen? (See rule 1 above.)

I think there are at least two types of opinion you can express on social media and get a good reputation in the process. Firstly, a sincerely held opinion: 'Whale hunting is a national disgrace,' you might write. 'Please RT this if you agree.' Secondly, a completely made-up opinion that you do for the hell of it: 'Am I the only person here who thinks Princess Kate looks a little like Tony the Tiger?'

In my experience, the latter gets more likes and retweets.

6. Be authentic

This may sound as if it's contradicting my point about expressing made-up opinions, but I do think you need to be yourself. In the singular.

Nothing is worse than those dreary corporate posts. I saw this on Twitter recently, from a top-four accountancy firm:

'A personal blog can add credibility and transparency to your profile.'

No sh*t!

What I mean is, make sure your social media writing comes from the real you – sense of humour, pugnaciousness, Flirty-Gertie-From-Number-Thirty and all.

7. Be truthful

Social media is a bit like advertising. So stay honest. Only make claims you can back up.

Your tone of voice can be as off the wall as you want – or your director of brand communications will allow – just so long as the content of your posts is truthful.

Actually, I think honest is a better word than truthful. Tell jokes, fantasize, make stuff up – but don't be a heel, a fake or a charlatan.

8. Use pictures

You're a writer, but think about when you could include pictures in your posts to make them more interesting to your reader.

Remember that people love pics on social media, especially Facebook, so they're an excellent way to hook attention.

I guess that's partly where all those INFOGRAPHICS come from.

9. Be social

I think if you see social media as just another 'channel' or 'route to market' you're going to have a hard time making it pay – or even enjoyable.

If people reply to your posts/tweets, get into a conversation with them.

Look at what other people are posting and reply, in turn, to them.

Necessarily, Twitter demands economy, but don't let that dictate your tone, which should always be respectful. Thx is OK for thanks, pls for please, but people get really twitchy if they detect arrogance (believe me, I know!).

10. *Remember to sell*

You don't have to be cheesy, but why not at least try to sell on social media?

I know, I know, it's about brand building, establishing a voice, customer communications, community... but it's costing you money so you might as well have a little think about ROI.

There are so many measures of success to choose from on social media: the most common being quantity. Number of likes, follows, retweets, fans etc.

But try running those past your finance director/accountant and see what they say.

At some point, you are going to have to make your investment in social media pay. Everything else has to show a return, so why not this?

Whenever you take to the sugar-rush world of social media, remember this. The people you want to connect with haven't changed. The things you want to talk about haven't changed. *You* haven't changed. It's just the medium that's changed.

Where social media and content marketing meet

Though this chapter is mostly about social media, it is an appropriate place to discuss the relationship between social media (the ultimate short-form channel) and content marketing (a more nuanced space, where short- and long-form copywriting, not to mention audio video, graphics and animation, happily coexist.

It is undeniably true that Facebook, Twitter, LinkedIn and the rest are ideal places to develop relationships with customers; the limitations of the form mean that we often need somewhere else to deepen those relationships and make money out of them.

That is where content marketing comes in. Content marketing bridges the gap between the evanescence of social media and the long-term impact of transactional copywriting. Blogging, briefings, presentations, videos, webinars: there are many ways to demonstrate your knowledge and expertise and now you have the luxury of long-form copywriting. If you want it.

Many of the rules that apply to great copywriting also apply to content. It should be engaging. It should build trust. It should be clear and concise (no wasted words, please). And it should be written in a friendly, accessible and even – if you feel like it – chatty style. Just make sure you avoid the temptation to sell outright and concentrate instead on delivering information that your reader will find interesting and relevant in its own right.

Having created your content, using social media is one of the most effective channels to promote or publicize it. At which point we are back to the main subject of this chapter.

CASE STUDY A presentation for Collinson Latitude

The personas were dramatized using storytelling techniques, writing in the present tense as if each was a character in a story.

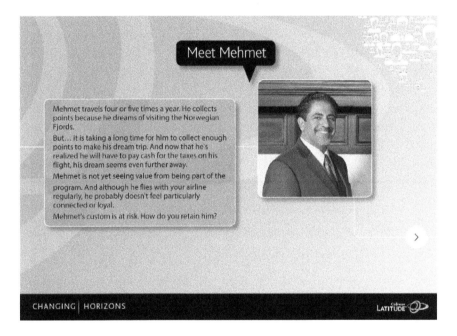

Collinson Latitude is part of Collinson Group, which helps companies shape and influence customer behaviour through loyalty, lifestyle benefits, insurance and assistance.

Our brief was to create content to explain to clients how the company's products could help them grow sales and increase loyalty. This particular piece is a presentation looking at ways to deepen customer relationships. Using customer personas, we created mini-stories that dramatized how the company's various marketing programmes could help its clients increase their sales.

Writing for mobile and social: the art of UBC

We've looked at how to *be* social. Now I want to look at how to *write* social. I am thinking principally about short-form copy here, since writing a 1,500-word blog post really isn't that different from writing a 1,500-word magazine article. Or not if it's done properly. I'm talking about Facebook updates, LinkedIn posts, tweets, profiles, texts – stuff like that. As mobile commerce booms, we are all going to have to become Zen masters of succinct yet attention-grabbing copy. But before we get carried away by the zeitgeist and fling our fountain pens down in despair, what about classified ads? What about slogans? What about envelopes? What about billboards and posters, bus-sides and shelf-wobblers? I've written them all, both before and since the advent of smartphones, and I have to say, I didn't have many three-figure word counts. So, yes, brevity is key. But hasn't it always been?

Although *what* you say doesn't need to change for the web, or mobile, the *way* you say it might. Because, like it or not, when they're using the web – on any kind of screen but especially a smaller screen – your customers may prefer to get their information in smaller chunks. Or you may be forced to deliver it that way – subject lines, tweets, AdWords and banners all call for a style of writing I call Ultra-Brief Copy (UBC).

Bad: Surround yourself with those who appreciate your expertise.

Good: You guys, can we agree to stop using '2.0' now? #itsOver #moveOn (tweet from @spydergrrl)

How much you write *in total* is up to you, but there are times and places now where the amount you can write *in one go* has changed. And for social media there is licence, if not outright demand, for a less formal style. This is especially true for corporations, who regularly trip themselves up with either lame attempts to be social savvy or pompous attempts to turn social media into a clone of their corporate brochures.

In a sense, publishing guidance on writing for social media and mobile in book form seems counter-intuitive. It's changing so fast there's a real risk that by the time you read this it won't apply. Hey, what're you gonna do? <shrugs>

How to write scannable subject lines

Let's start with subject lines. Depending on whose research you read, the ideal length for a subject line is somewhere between 29 and 39 characters (why not 40 I have no idea). But there appears to be another spike in open-rates at over 100 characters. Go figure.

At any rate, it seems clear that the beginning of your subject line is the most important. Unlike when reading print, people scanning their inboxes tend to run down the first few words of each subject line, rather than scanning religiously left to right. Visualize a giant capital F overlaid onto an email inbox. This is the so-called heatmap showing where people's eyes come to rest most frequently.

We need to cram as much of our message into the first few words as we can. This is no place for teasing lines that only reveal the killer point at the end.

If you were promoting a new fitness centre, you could run with a line like this:

If you look in the mirror and think you could stand to lose some belly fat, come to MB Fitness this month.

But what your reader will see is:

If you look in the mirror and think you could stand...

And what they'll process is more like this:

If you look in...

Not so good.

So you need a subject line more like this:

Lose belly fat at MB Fitness this month

Or these:

> Lose your belly at MB Fitness
> Lose your gut at MB Fitness
> Flat tum month at MB Fitness

The trick is to keep slicing away at the fat until you have the bare minimum of 'valueless' words such as *and*, *it*, *if* and *by*. That way your prospect gets a message rich in meaning that requires the minimum of space on screen and processing power in their brain.

Bad: Why do I need a photocopier?

Good: The nurse said 'do this or die' (from a spam email received, and opened, by the author)

Experiment with word order too, until you get the biggest concentration of meaningful words all jostling for pole position. Tell yourself your reader is only going to read the first four words, or the first three, two or one. It focuses the mind.

If your list includes first names, test including them at the start of the subject line. Over time, I have run dozens of first-name tests, and including first names gets higher open and clickthrough rates.

What to do about tiny screens

Back in the olden days – the mid-nineties – when people used the internet they did so exclusively on desktop screens or, rarely, on laptop screens, all of which were… BIG. (I'm writing the bulk of this book on my iMac, which has a 37″ screen.) That meant paragraphs looked different. Take this one. It has 90 words – so a short paragraph, by any standard. At a line-width (measure) of 114 mm, standard for a book like this, it occupies about 7 lines. It looks relatively easy to take in.

Now let's set it for the line width of a smartphone. I'm using my current Samsung as a guide. It looks like this:

> Back in the olden
> days – the mid-nineties –
> when people used the
> internet they did so

exclusively on desktop screens or, rarely, on laptop screens, all of which were... BIG. (I'm writing the bulk of this book on my iMac, which has a 37' screen.) That meant paragraphs looked different. Take this one. It has 90 words – so a short paragraph, by any standard. At a line-width (measure) of 90 mm, standard for a book like this, it occupies about 10 lines. It looks relatively easy to take in.

Oops! Not so good. Even at a smaller point size, it's still going to spill over the screen and need to be scrolled.

Which might not matter if what your customer is reading is the book they just paid for and downloaded. But if what they're reading is a *promotion* for the book, well, I think your copy now looks daunting and boring, *simply because of the depth of the paragraph.*

So you have to make adjustments. The simple truth is that the paragraph is no longer a unit of meaning with some sort of grammatical or intellectual coherence. It is purely a unit of length. And, yes, I know, this overturns the actual definition of paragraph. But grammarians weren't dealing with people reading on eeny-weeny screens.

Let's adjust our paragraph to make it more readable on a small screen.
Back in the mid-nineties people used the internet on desktop or laptop screens.
All of which were... BIG.
(I'm writing the bulk of this book on my iMac. It has a 37' screen.)
That meant paragraphs looked different. Take this one.
It has 89 words – so a short paragraph, by any standard.
A 90 mm line-width is standard for a book like this.
At this measure, it occupies about 10 lines. It looks relatively easy to take in.

What it lacks in grace, it more than makes up for in readability, and scannability.

The art of social – writing tweet-friendly copy

Here's a conundrum. How do you write commercial copy in a medium that's *named* for its non-commercial ambience? Social media is supposed to be just that. Social. Last time I looked that meant 'relating to society and the relations between human beings'. Now, I guess you could heat that up and hammer it around on your verbal anvil for a while until business relationships became included, but it would be a very brittle weapon you'd fashioned.

But write for social media we must. It's a channel. And it can work. *I've* made it work.

Here are a few aspects of writing for social media we need to consider. It's social (duh!).

This is all about belonging. It's no accident that the language of social media is all about followers, friends, groups and connections.

This means that some of the recommendations in this book – and others – won't work. Humour, for example, can be an effective way to build rapport in social spaces. Although I still cleave to my basic point that a laughing customer is rarely reaching for their credit card.

I have worked with a global media brand on social media campaigns, and one of the findings from their testing and research was that their followers (and they have millions) didn't want the same old offer that was being punted out elsewhere. They regarded themselves as members of a club with special privileges. We wrote about a special offer to foster the feeling that this was something especially for them.

It's informal...

If you want to play here you have to follow the rules. That means eschewing the more hardnosed aspects of copywriting in favour of a softer, more informal style. Over-strict brand guidelines are unlikely to be your friend here, since the linguistic prescriptions they tend to favour result in copy too stilted for the dynamic, chatty world of Twitter, Facebook, and the rest.

Try this: Remember: the key word in social media is 'social'.
If you're going to write socially you can't be a corporate stiff
so try writing in a more relaxed way than you normally do.
... and short.

You don't usually have much space with social media. Of course there are exceptions, but the more your copy tends towards traditional long-form styles, the less you need this chapter anyway.

What this means for our writing is we need to be more like Hemingway than Henry James. Short, terse, muscular phrases, not rambling, beautifully crafted eight-and-a-half-page paragraphs. We're back to some basic advice: prefer shorter words to longer synonyms. Choose full stops over commas and colons. Economy not prolixity.

Viral headlines

This book isn't the place for a full-scale discussion of the rights and wrongs of headline writing. If you want one I can recommend *The Copywriting Sourcebook*, one of my other books on copywriting.

But in terms of getting people to click, we can learn much from some of the content-aggregator sites currently garnering zillions of eyeballs for videos of kittens playing the banjo, babies conducting the Boston Symphony Orchestra and minor celebrities falling down manholes.

The key emotional play here is curiosity, 'I just have to know what happens'. There's a secondary emotional play, 'Maybe I can share this with my friends and get kudos'. These headlines enjoy the lovely name 'clickbait'.

Typically, these lines run something like these:

This old lady thought she was just buying cat food. What happens next will make you cry with laughter.

---

37 of the most shocking photos on the internet. I couldn't look at number 19.

When you see what he collects, you'll see why this man really needs to get a social life.

---

21 WTF moments from the new series of 'Copywriters'.

> These celebrity wardrobe malfunctions caused more than blushes.

Peel away the bleeding-edge attitude and what you reveal are some old-timey headline-writing approaches. The story. The appeal to prurience. Self-interest.

But, a word of caution. These are not product ads. The content is free to the consumer. Free in cash terms, anyway. They pay with their time, of course. This means we can see what pulls people in to watch the video or look at the pictures. But we can't tell whether these techniques would be any good at persuading people to spend money. Plus, as we know, clicks do not equal conversions.

Try this: If you want to be viral, work the curiosity angle for all you're worth. And make sure the content lives up to the promise.

From theory to profit

I think it helps when considering what you're going to do about, or with, social media, if you have a goal. In other words, why are you there? And what do you want to achieve? There are hard, measurable goals, such as selling stuff; there are medium-hard, measurable goals, such as getting likes and retweets and followers; there are softer goals, such as building relationships with your customers, which are harder to measure but which instinctively feel right. My feeling is, the goals are key. This is a business activity, a *commercial* activity: if you don't know what you're trying to achieve you won't know how well you're doing. And social media isn't free. It isn't even very cheap, if you factor in the opportunity costs of all that activity.

Make sure you have some way of parlaying all those followers into an inbound marketing strategy you can eventually make money out of. Getting to grips with social media means getting to grips with a new set of rules, new levels of openness and genuine dialogue with customers. Figure out an authentic voice you can write in and you'll find it much easier to build long-term and, hopefully, profitable relationships.

I'm assuming you are involved in social media and possibly mobile for business, so let's try to formulate a strategy for writing well. Somewhat counter-intuitively in this most instantaneous of communications spaces, you need to plan. And plan well. If you mess up five lines in a 16-page brochure it's really not a problem. If you even *have* five lines for most UBC projects that's a luxury you can't afford to waste. Yet planning can be the enemy of spontaneity, which is often where this here-one-moment-gone-the-next writing really comes alive.

Will you shoot me if I suggest writing corporate tweets in a word processing package then cutting and pasting them into Twitter? You have a moment's pause between finishing and posting when you can reflect on a few things: is it spelled OK? Is the punctuation OK? Do I come across like a dork or a moron? How about trying your UBC out on yourself and your colleagues? Read your copy on your phone or tablet and have a look at it from a purely visual perspective. Is it attractively laid out on the smaller screen? Is it inviting? These things matter more than normal because your reader is making a read/trash decision in a microsecond.

Workshop

1 Why do people love social media so much?

2 What's the golden rule of posting on social media sites?

3 When is it OK to post things that aren't strictly true?

   a) Never

   b) It doesn't matter

   c) If your followers can tell you're joking

4 How closely should you follow your organization's brand guidelines?

   a) To the letter

   b) They don't apply – it's social media

   c) As closely as they say you should

5 Because it's social media, the old rules of commerce don't apply. True or false?

6 What's the ideal character limit to observe for email subject lines?

   a) 29–35

   b) 29–39

   c) 46–104

7 In A/B subject line tests, how does including first names affect the result?

8 What is the driving emotion behind clickbait headlines?

a) Happiness

b) Envy

c) Curiosity

9 What is the best punctuation mark to use in UBC?

10 Which of these subject lines looks most likely to outpull the others?

a) Introducing a new way to get relief from your lower back pain

b) Now: a new way to get back pain relief

c) Back pain? Try this 'ridiculous' cure

Putting it into action

Exercise 34: Who are you again?

Write your ideal social media profile. Make it truthful, authentic, personal and do *not* make it boring. Write a profile that would make YOU want to befriend or follow that person.

Exercise 35: A dozen different voices

Write a tweet about the same development at your organization in each of the following styles:

- boring;
- crazy;
- professorial;
- cheesy;
- shouty;
- childish;
- cheeky;
- aggressive;
- confident;
- funny;
- sad;
- mysterious.

Exercise 36: Goals? Really?

Write a short document (say, no more than 300 words) setting out your goals for each of the social media platforms you either use or plan to use.

Exercise 37: Going social

Write copy for a social media campaign for your product including the following:

- three tweets;
- two subject lines;
- one viral headline.

Exercise 38: Alternatives to images

Review all the images on your website (or, if there are too many and you think you'll go mad, your email campaigns). Do they all have Alt tags? If not, write them. Remember that these are ideal places for a little stealth selling. Imagine an email loading on your customer's smartphone with 'Download' images switched off. What will they read? Not see; read. Nothing or your sales message in outline?

Tweet: How are you doing? Tweet me @Andy_Maslen

Creating calls to action: Top Tips to bring home the bacon

I ask you to pass through life at my side – to be my second self, and best earthly companion.

CHARLOTTE BRONTË, *JANE EYRE*

Introduction

I wrote this book to help you perform better as a copywriter. That means getting better results from your writing. And that means we need to spend some time thinking about money. Specifically, how to ask for it. I have said this before, but it bears repeating: if you can't ask for the order, you are going to starve. Perhaps there is a cultural aspect to our attitudes towards money. There is certainly a cultural aspect to our ability to talk about it. Broadly speaking, I have noticed that British people are noticeably more reluctant to talk about money than their cousins in the United States. This extends from how much we earn to our ability to state the price of whatever it is we're selling. (One notable exception is the price we paid for our house and its market value today. That holds such fascination that it occasionally seems as if there is only one topic of conversation fit for the dining table.)

Somehow it seems much more natural, much more *appropriate*, to open a sale with all the emotional stuff – the storytelling, empathizing and psychology. We get our prospect all juiced up at the thought of how wonderful their life is going to be just as soon as they sign on the dotted line, then we have to ruin it by getting them to fill out an order form. I mean, 'order now' is hardly the most emotional of commands is it?

But ask for the order we must. The question is, how can we get our prospect to confirm their purchase without breaking the spell we have spent so much time and effort weaving? The answer, I think, lies, as it always does, in looking at the world from our prospect's perspective. Perhaps because many marketeers and copywriters see order forms as mundane pieces of boiler-plate, they fail to maintain focus when it comes to writing the call to action. As a result, what gets bashed out is a variant on that lamest of all lame headlines – Order Form – followed by something equally uninspiring. Yet your prospect has just made an emotionally driven decision to buy from you because they *feel* it's the right thing to do. All you have to do is prolong the mood.

*

All this emotion is all very well when you're setting the scene. But what about the sharp end: asking for the order? How do you make that engaging? Here's a clue: don't start thinking about the money. That's what you want, not what your reader wants.

Instead, keep thinking about fulfilling your promise to your reader. If they are going to get a flat stomach, F1 driving skills or a fully functioning fighter plane (1:18 scale) talk about that. Above all, don't let your prospect see that droplet of sweat beading on your forehead as their finger hovers over the 'Confirm Purchase' button. Be cool.

Engage: Keep your call to action emotionally engaging by staying focused on the promise, not the purchase.

You'll find this tip in at least one of my other books on copywriting, but it's so important I will take the liberty of offering it to you again here:

Never. Write. 'If'.

As in:

If you would like to order.

'If' says, you might not.
   'If' says, even I'm not convinced and I wrote this.
   'If' says, you don't have to.

Bad: Write back if we can do anything for you.

Good: Here is the link to today's issue. Just click the button like yesterday and it's all yours. (from a sales email for Platts written by the author)

OK, now that's out of my system, what are we going to do instead? Let's start with the words you use.

Twenty-six calls to action

Here is a list of 26 words related to the call to action. I'd like you to re-arrange them into two lists: one labelled intellectual; the other, emotional. Ready?

book	meet
buy	order
charge	pay
choose	pledge
congratulations	quick
deliver	reward
despatch	rush
enrol	save
help	select
hurry	send
invest	sponsor
invoice	subscribe
join	support

How did you do? Any you weren't sure about? Here's how I split them:

Intellectual	*Emotional*
book	choose
buy	congratulations
charge	help
deliver	hurry
despatch	invest
enrol	join
invoice	meet
order	pledge

pay	quick
select	reward
send	rush
sponsor	save
subscribe	support

And here's how they might look in calls to action:

Intellectual calls to action

Book your place on our course today.

Buy this 100% cashmere dress now.

Charge my credit card £298.

Deliver my brake pads to

Despatch my protein shakes to

Enrol in our distance-learning programme today.

Invoice me now.

Order form.

Pay in four quarterly instalments.

Select the option that best meets your needs from the list below.

Send me my EasySushi Kit.

Sponsor a child today.

Subscribe before 31 January and save £7.98.

Emotional calls to action

Choose life. Choose MazCo Omega-3 Oil.

Congratulations! You're about to make the smartest decision of your life.

Help us save lives in Moldoravia.

Hurry! I need my NiteSite™ laserscope right away!

Invest in your future wellbeing.

Join your peers at the forefront of biotechnology.

Meet other petrolheads at the Festival Of Power.

Pledge your help now.

Quick! Get me my NuKlear Carp Bait today.

Reward yourself with a pure silk dressing gown. You earned it.

Rush me my free stockpicking guide. I'm in a hurry to get rich!

Save a month's rent: sign up with EZRental today.

Support your local priest.

Too often, what we see are order forms, e-commerce pages and sign-up forms that sound as if they had been written by the finance department, the legal team or the HR department.

I suspect this is because they are often the last thing to be written on a website, brochure, sales campaign or landing page.

So here's a tip.

Try this: Write your call to action first. (First after you plan, I mean.)

Now, imbue your call to action with all the emotional power you can muster. How did you say you wanted your reader to feel? That you're a fun company to do business with? Confident they've made a sensible decision? Nostalgic for a simpler, friendlier time? This is your first (and last) chance to evoke that emotional response.

Three ways to ask for the order

Just taking those three emotions, in order, here are possible approaches for a call to action:

NOW! You heard me, I want them NOW! Rush me my hand-stitched angora keyboard wipes or take the consequences.

I'm ready to invest in my children's future while taking no risk today. Please send me my free, no-obligation guide to saving for school fees.

Yes! I remember when we had more time to sit and stare. Please sign me up for the introductory landscape painting for beginners' class.

CASE STUDY   Subscriptions leaflet for *Motor Sport* magazine

'Join' is an emotional word and much more powerful than 'subscribe'.

The money-back guarantee serves to overcome the unstated object, 'what if I change my mind?'

The quote from Sir Stirling Moss acts as a reinforcement from an authority figure.

Motor Sport has been published since 1924. As you can see from the testimonial above, it has many famous racing drivers among its subscribers. The inside spread of this subscriptions acquisitions leaflet is really just one big call to action.

We gave the reader reminders of the content they would miss if they didn't subscribe. We included a testimonial/endorsement from Sir Stirling Moss – a universally respected figure and former champion. We created a subscription guarantee 'certificate' promising their money back if the subscriber wasn't happy with the magazine. And we ran a call to action headline across the top of the spread, pointing to the form, which restated the call to action.

Do you notice something about those three lines? They are all written from the perspective of the customer, not the company. This style allows the reader to step right into the call to action and take control. This is all about them. There's no grubby money or form filling involved – this is all about the promise.

You could also add a photograph of a trusted or trustworthy figure right by the tickbox. Maybe your brand spokesperson, an existing customer or your managing director. Give the photo a caption, enclose it in speech marks and focus on something really important, such as customer satisfaction, company reputation or your MD's personal feelings about doing business.

Try this: Reinforce the safety features of your promise, such as a money-back guarantee, customer testimonials or a trial period.

Ultimately, there are limits to how far you can take emotional engagement with what is, essentially, a commercial transaction. But think about how a really good car salesperson deals with it.

You're about to commit to five years of crippling monthly finance payments. But you don't care (not really) because out there, on the forecourt, is... the car. Your new best friend that you've already chosen a name for. (Oh, that's just me? Never mind.)

Somehow, the salesperson has to get your signature on the contract without your refocusing from car to commitment. There isn't another legal word for a

Join us at *Motor Sport* for 12 issues and get 3 more FREE ▶

H ow do you follow your favourite sport away from the track?

With coverage of F1, rallying, sports cars, historic racing, motorcycles and more, there is only one answer for the knowledgeable motor racing fan …

"*Motor Sport* magazine".

Nigel Roebuck

Y

"A fighter with a **lion's heart"**

O

Opinions and interviews – Including *Lunch with…* drivers, team owners and technical innovators

DAVID COULTHARD

F1 – the cars, the drivers, plus Nigel Roebuck, one of the most respected voices in motor racing

Racing history – *Motor Sport* is the best place to find reminiscences of the sport's pioneers

Putting it on the line… Again.

T

Every type of motor racing covered, from sports cars to historics, F1 to motorcycles

The experiment that struck Gold

contract: that's what it is. But that doesn't faze our friend. They hold the door open for you and usher you towards their desk with the immortal line: 'Now, we'll just take care of the paperwork and you can be on your way' <big smile>.

Paperwork. It's not emotionally engaging, but it's not supposed to be. It's supposed to be neutral. A little bit of boring admin before you put your pedal to the metal, the rubber hits the road and you leave the showroom in a squealing spurt of clichés. So you go. And you sign.

From theory to profit

It's hard to make a sincere and believable call to action if you aren't convinced by the value of what you're selling. So, as this section of the book draws to a close, it's the perfect time to stand back and take a good look at your product or service. What is its real value to the customer? How does it make their life easier, better or simpler? How do they feel once they've bought it? What do they say about it on social media?

Once you can see – and internalize – the value your customers place on your product, you are in the right place to start asking other people to buy it from you. More for British readers than anyone else, this next point, but do not be embarrassed about its price. Nor about asking for it. Next, why not run an audit of your organization's calls to action? Yes, all of them. Stick them all in a spreadsheet or a presentation and then rate them for emotional power versus administrative efficiency. This product is life changing; who wouldn't feel proud about asking somebody to buy it?

Workshop

1 Why shouldn't you use the word 'if' in a call to action?
2 Is it OK to use emotion in a call to action?
3 When is the best time to write your call to action?
4 The best way to write a call to action is from the perspective of the customer. True or false?
5 Which of these words is not an emotional word:

   a) Join

   b) Pledge

c) Buy

d) Rush

e) Congratulations

Putting it into action

Exercise 39: I need *you* to buy this

Taking your product as a model, write half a dozen calls to action using only the words from your emotion list in this chapter.

Exercise 40: A short play about selling

Write a short scene between a salesperson and a customer engaged in selling/ buying your product. Keep the dialogue natural and imagine how each person is feeling.

Exercise 41: A web of orders

Work through your website, identifying every single call to action, and rewriting those that lack an emotional appeal alongside the administrative one.

Tweet: How are you doing? Tweet me @Andy_Maslen

PART THREE
The pleasure principle:
Making your writing more enjoyable and compelling

Balancing pleasure and profit: five techniques to write fantastic copy

12

The noblest pleasure is the joy of understanding.

LEONARDO DA VINCI

Introduction

About once a month I get an email from a budding copywriter. They, variously, want a job, advice on how to get one, feedback on their writing or an opinion on whether they could cut it as a copywriter. One that sticks in my mind pursued, from its opening to its closing, a convoluted metaphor involving cake and floorcoverings. This writer was talented, or at least, talented as a writer. I can imagine people paying to read her stuff and quite possibly laughing once they had done so. Sadly for her, and for me and for you, nobody does pay to read our stuff. In fact, quite a few people would probably pay not to read our stuff. Her mistake, I think, was seeing pleasure as the ultimate goal of copywriting, rather than as a means to an end. Like a lot of aspiring copywriters, she had projected her own love of wordplay onto a general positive emotional reaction to puns, rhymes and arcane humour in copywriting.

Now, she may well have been right: maybe people do love all that. But there is a huge and unmistakable difference between an emotional reaction and a commercial response. I want people to respond emotionally to my copy not because I am some sort of therapist, but because I believe that if they feel good about buying, they probably will buy. Am I a cynic? No. I am a copywriter. And my clients hire my agency to help them solve commercial problems, the most common of which is, 'we need to sell more stuff'. However...

I believe that no harm can come from writing copy that, while it has an explicit commercial purpose, is pleasurable to read. I just don't believe in raising the feeling of pleasure to the status of ultimate goal. Nor, for that matter, do I believe in striving for pleasure, or in showing off. I never forget that the copywriting should be invisible. So how can you be simultaneously invisible and pleasurable? The answer, I think, lies in creating an environment in which your selling message is more readily absorbed because it is written in language that doesn't jar or upset the reader. A bit like swimming in the Mediterranean in summer: the water is pleasant to be in, even if you are not aware of its being in contact with your skin.

*

There comes a point in every copywriter's development when you start asking, 'Well, now what?' You know how to tell a feature from a benefit. Writing for your reader is second nature. And you never ask a question where your reader could answer, 'no'. What then?

Well, one thing you can do is think about how to make your writing more pleasurable to read. Now, this might seem like a strange approach to take for a copywriter. Isn't copy supposed to be invisible?

Aren't we supposed to be painting a picture so enticing to our prospect that the real world fades away and all that's left is a glorious future of 'life with the product'? Well, yes. Let's assume that's all happening.

Then the next step is to make reading itself pleasurable. Even for a reader of the most modest educational attainment, reading can, and should, be enjoyable. As the writer's writer, Samuel Johnson, remarked, 'What is written without effort is in general read without pleasure.'

But what does that mean in practice? And how can we do it?

Bad: ... it came as no surprise that when ReQualtic, a neutral and unbiased researcher of financial services, looked at the Over 50s Life Insurance sector recently we received their recognition in the format of a maximum scoring of 5 Star Rating for our Over 50s Life Insurance.

Good: Here we are again at the end of another week! How was it for you? Successful? Stressful? We had a super week (thanks for asking) and we still managed to spy some cool online scribblings to share with you. (from a newsletter written by Jo Ciriani)

How to make your copy pleasurable to read

Here are five aspects of your writing that affect the reading experience:

1 rhythm;

2 pace;

3 musicality;

4 imagery;

5 surprise.

And here's how to use them in your copy.

Rhythmic copywriting

We are all of us adept at spotting, and responding to, patterns around us. Linguistic patterns are beguiling because they combine this natural desire to find patterns with the communication of ideas.

One aspect of rhythm that you will be aware of if you've ever read or written a poem is metre. What is metre?

It's the tum-ti-tum-ti-tiddlyness of language.

It's why, 'truth, justice and the American way' is more pleasurable to read than, 'the American way, truth and justice'.

And why, 'As a delegate, you'll meet your peers, share your thoughts and learn from those at the top of their game' is easier on the ear (and eye) than, 'As a delegate, you'll meet your fellow copywriters, share thoughts and learn from top writers.'

Pacing your copy (and your reader)

One of those Copywriting 101 moments is when your tutor, mentor or annoying boss leans over your keyboard as you're typing and intones, sonorously, 'You do know you should keep your sentences short, don't you?' And they have a point. Providing they add the words, 'on average'.

If you write your copy entirely using short sentences, something odd happens.

Your sentences collapse.

They become short. Too short.

Each one a missile. Lobbed at your reader. From a barricade.

They have impact. Sure.

Like a half-brick does.
But they never let up. One after the other.
Bricks flying. Bottles smashing.
Stressful. Exhausting.

And, ultimately, like a riot of words, sentences and paragraphs clamouring to be heard, something to be escaped from, ignored, rejected out of hand as, simply, too much.

Try this: Read your copy out loud and you hear rhythm, pace and tone. If you can hear them, you can judge them. And fix them if you have to.

Pacing means giving your reader a break, allowing them a few graceful dips and turns among the skipping quick steps of the dance.

Good: The best fruits and vegetables? Perfection? Top quality?
All natural products with no compromise on taste? Absolutely! (from Hortex website (Poland))

Feeling the music in your copywriting

Remember we were talking about patterns a moment ago?

Musicality is all about patterns. Not about rhythm or beats this time, but sounds. Alliteration is a simple type of musical pattern in your writing. Handled well, it never fails.

You might write, 'If there's a softer seat on the market we'd be surprised'. Not so obvious as 'sing a song of sixpence' but it's there and it feels pleasant to read it.

Good: The new First Class seat is your private and exclusive sanctuary in the sky. (From the Singapore Airlines website)

Can rhyme work in copywriting? It's trickier, certainly. The problem with a 'straight' rhyme – 'I'm so much in love, like a hand in a glove' – is that it can call too much attention to itself. The pattern obscures, rather than complements, the meaning.

But if you rhyme internal vowels in words – the technique called assonance – you can create something memorable, sticky, if you like. It's very effective when you're writing slogans and straplines rather than body copy.

Like these:

Beanz Meanz Heinz.

Gillette: the best a man can get

Born to perform (Jaguar)

CASE STUDY   Homepage for Addcent Consulting

The headline talks directly to the reader, using 'your' but even though it uses part of a famous speech, it leaves it unfinished, encouraging the reader to proceed to the body copy.

Beyond the headline we concentrated on old-fashioned selling copy, where every line was suffused with benefits copy.

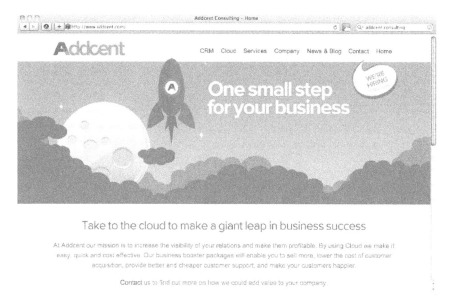

Addcent is a Swedish customer relationship management (CRM) consultancy that uses Cloud-based computing. The client wanted a catchy strapline and intro to its website based around a 'space' theme.

Resonance is the technique of borrowing emotional impact from a well-known story, phrase or name. Here, we referenced Neil Armstrong's famous lines as he stepped onto the surface of the moon.

Verbal imagery in copy

One of the best ways to engage your reader's emotions, and therefore bring them closer to a sale, is to use the power of language to create visual, or other sensory, imagery.

Compare these two lines of travel brochure copy:

Bad: For centuries, the limpid waters of the Ionian sea have brought succour and a sense of peace to the weary traveller.
Now it's your turn to experience the surprising qualities that have made Taormina Sicily's most popular resort since the time of Juvenal.

Verdict: High-register. Sterile. Intellectual appeal.

Good: Dip your toes into the water lapping gently at your feet.
Be prepared for a surprise. Number one: it's warm. Number two: it's so clear you feel you could reach out and touch the sea urchins clamped to the rocks 10 feet down. Welcome to Sicily. Welcome to Taormina.

Verdict: Low-register. Visually rich. Emotional appeal.

You needn't limit yourself to visual language, either. Your customer has other senses and you can appeal to as many of them as you can manage. And you can do it in one of two ways.

The direct approach: if your product stimulates the senses, then describe how. A new rollercoaster at a theme park might make you feel as if you'd left your stomach in the next county. Put that! A new restaurant might make its own bread every morning, creating that nostalgic just-baked bread smell for everyone eating lunch. Put that! Or your new industrial coating might be as smooth as a baby's bottom. Don't put that, it's a cliché!

The indirect approach: there is a hypothesis, popular in neurolinguistic programming (NLP) circles, that each of us has a preferred 'sensory modality' for communications. Proponents claim X per cent of us are primarily visual, Y per cent are auditory and Z per cent are kinaesthetic (the sense of physical movement or activity). Following this hypothesis, you might structure your copy in such a way that you use visual language at the start – 'can you see what I mean?' – then move to auditory language – 'if this sounds too good to be true, read on' – before introducing physical words – 'grab this opportunity before its too late'. I was doing this long before I had even heard of NLP, but it's nice to know that there might be some science behind it.

Key takeaway: Remember, your prospect knows she's reading advertising. Or junk mail. Or marketing speak. She is suspicious. She is sceptical. She is very possibly getting bored.

Surprise your prospect and keep them reading

Part of the process of emotional copywriting is managing your prospect's attention levels. In a longer document (which, historically, has been shown to have a better chance of leading to an order) there is a greater risk that your prospect will lose interest and start to skim over your carefully wrought arguments. Quick! You need to say something to grab her attention. Something surprising. One high-risk tactic is to use bad language. The upside is that you will definitely regain your prospect's attention. The downside is that you may well alienate the very person whose money you want. It probably works better in a very personal communication like a blog post. Or when you are writing for a super-savvy, street-smart reader. Which probably means nobody over 25. Sorry.

Or you could employ a shocking image or phrase. There's a lovely headline by veteran direct response copywriter Eugene Schwartz that always tickles me.

> The Sex Food So Potent, Priests Were Forbidden To Eat It

Or maybe you could go straight to the limbic system with an image so powerful they're helpless in your grasp:

> Our goal is to make your event stick in the memory like your first kiss.

(I wrote that one.)

Repetition reinforces your point

This simple technique hammers your point home without sounding off-putting to your reader. In rapid succession, you are going to say the same thing, or virtually the same thing. That creates a pattern, and we know that the human brain is wired to search out patterns. Patterns are more memorable because they suggest order. Order suggests significance. And significance suggests benefits. Maybe you'll get something good to eat. Maybe you won't be something nice for something else to eat. Maybe you'll find a mate. (I mean, not right now – in evolutionary terms.) Here are a couple of examples:

> Ask not what your country can do for you. Ask what you can do for your country. (John F Kennedy, Inaugural Speech, January 1961)

> Many people in this country have paid the price before me and many will pay the price after me. (Copyright © 2010 by Nelson R. Mandela and The Nelson Mandela Foundation)

And a couple of rather more everyday examples:

> Are you a copywriter?
> A copywriter who's going places?
> A copywriter with drive, guts and ambition?
> Yes? Then you're going to love what I have for you.

> Calling all engineers.
> We think engineers are brilliant.
> We want to hire more engineers.

For some reason, repetition works really well in groups of three. What rhetoricians would call a triad. If you want to add icing to your cake, make the last instance a turnaround – where some or all of the syntax is reversed, giving your reader a payoff for continuing reading. Like this:

> Strategy isn't just lots of tactics strung together.
> Strategy isn't just a fancy word for planning.
> Strategy is a rule for making decisions.

Good: Make good cars that are the safest, most environment-friendly and most energy-saving, make users happy with Geely cars, make Geely distributors happy in marketing. (from Geely website (China))

When a fancier variety of word comes back for an encore, the reader is distracted and, therefore, not paying attention to you at all. Like this:

> This is a strategic opportunity to capture market share in Asia-Pacific. Our strategic goals have always included seizing opportunities and it would be strategically difficult to move forward without this one.

If they keep reading at all, it is only to search out, point and laugh at, and possibly tweet about, further instances of poor writing. You have lost a reader and gained a proofreader. On which subject...

Seven copywriting traps and how to avoid them

Sometimes the best writers make the worst copywriters. Their very facility with the language becomes a problem. Why? Because they fall, all too easily, in love with the fun they can have with words. There isn't a sentence that can't be improved by adding a playful metaphor, a headline that won't work as well unless it contains a pun, a call to action that won't pull harder without a cutesy little wink to the reader's sense of humour. My question is always the same: how will this make it more likely that you win their business?

Having said that, bad writers aren't much good as copywriters either. Lacking the skill to play with the language, they settle for a kick about in a muddy field instead. Cliché, jargon and the well-worn phrase are their stock-in-trade. Every corporate development, however mundane, is exciting. Every offer, no matter how pedestrian, is fantastic. Every new product, no matter how average, is revolutionary.

Both of these get the boot in the world of advanced copywriting. Because they don't even attempt to connect emotionally with their customer. The good writer is too busy pleasing themselves to think about the customer; the bad writer doesn't really give a stuff one way or the other. You though are different. So I want to give you a map that will help you avoid the worst traps lying in wait for the over- and under-skilled copywriter. (And I am sure that you are neither.) We'll look at what goes wrong when we forget the basic rules of great copywriting: put the reader at the heart of your writing; what it does is more important than what it is; you are here to sell; what you say is more important than the way you say it. And we'll have a quick reality check with some basic diagnostic tests to ensure our writing breaks none of them.

I think it's time to repeat an old copywriting mantra. 'It's not about what you want to say, it's about what your reader wants to hear.' Which makes our lives very easy. Because our reader doesn't want to hear much beyond, 'I have a solution to your problem'. Is this reductive? Probably. But we are not novelists, poets or journalists (though we might borrow some of their approaches). So our readers are not looking for entertainment or news.

Key takeaway: Think of your writing as a window. You want your reader seeing the view. Not the glass.

Your reader is also impatient and naturally inclined to be dismissive of shoddy phrasemaking, basic mistakes and self-regarding writing. With that in mind, and to ensure they are looking at the view through the window not the smudges on the glass, here are some of the traps we must all avoid.

Trap 1 Concentrating on what it does instead of why that matters

Product copy all too often focuses on how it works, what it does or who put it together.

We must forget all that and concentrate on why it matters to the reader.

For example, if an expensive music system is as small as a hardback book, why does that matter to people who live in large houses with spacious sitting rooms? If you think this is me telling you (again) that benefits matter more than features, you're right.

Always test what you believe to be benefits copy by using the 'So what?' test. Put simply, if you hear your prospect saying 'So what?', you haven't written a benefit. What would you say is the benefit of the book-sized hi-fi system?

Trap 2 Being lazy

When we're short of time, we are all too easily tempted to use bad ideas just because they're quick.

You often see this with headlines, where a cheap pun is slapped down because it echoes the picture. If you don't have the time to do something fresh, either find more time or do something else until you do. It's comforting to send your copy off to the client, developer, designer or mailing house: one more thing off your to-do list. But unless that in itself is your ultimate goal, it's better to wait.

Trap 3 Confusing your reader

It really doesn't matter whom you're writing to, there's no excuse for needlessly complex language.

Remember, as long as you're writing copy, ie advertising, your reader will make little or no effort to decode it. Confuse them and you lose them. So your readers are chief executives, engineers or university lecturers? Big deal! They all understand Plain English don't they? Even though they may use complex language, their aim might not be the same as yours. *They* may be seeking social, intellectual or political advantage. *You* are try to sell something to a stranger.

I am not advocating the use of purely monosyllabic copy. If the product involves simplified derivatives trading you'd better come straight out and say so. But if it's a good night's sleep, I'd say that any day before calling it a scientifically demonstrated sleep solution.

Trap 4 Trying to be an entertainer

I'm calling time on feeble attempts at humour of all kinds. Puns, wordplay, lame 'jokes'.

Partly because humour doesn't travel and partly because even if it does, we don't want our reader laughing, we want them reaching for their credit card. Is there an exception? For social media and blogging it's a fairly safe bet. But you are splashing around in the shallow end of the influence pool. You could amass thousands of followers with your cracked sense of humour, but if that's the reason they follow you they may take less kindly to following you on a journey that ends with them paying for something.

Key takeaway: Distract your reader and risk losing the sale. Remember, you're trying to close a deal not provide entertainment.

Trap 5 Not checking for mistakes

It's late. The copywriter just wants to go home. They give the draft a cursory glance on-screen and send it to their boss/client for approval. Or, worse still, they send it out. To customers. With mistakes in it. Ah. That.

This is linked strongly to number 2. Checking your work is not an additional job. It is an integral part of the writing process. Your emotionally engaging story, laden with telling details, dialogue and subtle ploys to persuade, is brought to its knees by a mispunctuated its. You will also find that your once-busy customer has suddenly discovered they have enough time not only to check the rest of your copy for mistakes, but to post them all on Twitter.

Trap 6 Showing off

Despite claiming to be busy, copywriters will often spend ages researching their subject. But, regurgitating stuff from Wikipedia will not shift merchandise. Nor will combining it with your imagined grasp of fine writing. 'As Doctor Johnson, that renowned Eighteenth Century belle lettriste, might have said, were he browsing our site today...'

Picture this familiar scene. Tatiana, a copywriter, is writing a corporate brochure, or a website, or a press release, and shimmering into view on the horizon she sees a delicious figure of speech. It's a metaphor, no, it's a simile, or is it a saying? Maybe it's an epigram. In truth, she has no idea, but she is definitely going to use it in her next sentence.

She writes, 'The prospect of a comfortable retirement is the proverbial carrot dangling in front of us'.

She has made a common mistake – assuming that any figure of speech is a 'proverbial' one. In fact, only things derived from proverbs are proverbial. So you might, just, be forgiven for saying, 'It's like shutting the proverbial stable door after the horse has bolted'. This is still clumsy, but now, at least, accurate.

Our copywriter should have written, 'The prospect of a comfortable retirement is the *metaphorical* carrot dangling in front of us'. But given that her readers know it's a metaphor (unless they are particularly dim), it would be better as, 'The prospect of a comfortable retirement is a carrot dangling in front of us'.

For the same reason, we should avoid using 'literally'. Partly because it is often misused as a synonym for its direct opposite – 'figuratively' – as in, 'I was literally sweating blood'. Or because it's redundant, 'The Acme Widget is literally unique'.

Another example of this writerly anxiety to be noticed is when 'interesting' words or phrases are enclosed in speech marks. For example...

> *On Your Hind Legs* is the speechwriter's 'Bible'. [Subtext: *On Your Hind Legs* is not the speechwriter's Bible. We just wish it was.]
>
> *On Your Hind Legs* is the speechwriter's Bible. [Subtext: *On Your Hind Legs* is as important to speechwriters as the Bible is to Christians.]

Drawing your reader's attention to the fact you're using a figure of speech is never a good idea. Either it's a strong enough image to stand on its own two feet or you knock it down and come up with something better.

Trap 7 Writing for the wrong reader

To be fair this can sometimes be unavoidable. There are three wrong readers you can write for. Your boss, yourself or a colleague. When your boss (or client) won't sign off a piece of copy until it reads the way they think it should, you will almost always end up aiming to please them. To do otherwise requires a strong stomach and, possibly, a well-padded bank account.

If you write for yourself, including words or phrases that you enjoy using or reading, that's almost always the wrong thing to do. What would your reader think or feel in response to these words? Would they be more likely to buy? That's what matters.

You may have a colleague whose opinion matters in the organization. They, in turn, may have influence over the copy irrespective of whether it meets the brief. Dig your heels in. Write for the customer.

From theory to profit

This chapter, like all the others in the book, has universal applicability. It is just as relevant if you work in a heavy engineering firm as if you work for a funky fashion brand. Every reader is capable of finding the process of reading pleasurable, and as long as you follow my advice and don't see pleasure as the reason you're writing, you will be fine.

At the very least, you can make sure that your copy is always relaxing to read. In practical terms I am talking about our old friend sentence length. Sticking to between 10 and 16 words for your average sentence will mean nobody feels confused by what you're saying. For technical specs, product documentation and legal matters, that may be all the pleasure you need or want to inject into your writing. But for anything that you might call customer facing, and certainly anything pre-purchase, try to give your copy a little character as well as content. Remember that these techniques – and all the others in the book – are just as applicable to non-sales communications.

Finally, how would you rate your writing in terms of the seven traps? Maybe you should take a couple of recent pieces home with you and read them in the peace and quiet, away from the office. (If you wrote them at home, maybe you should take them to work and read them in the hurly-burly, away from your sanctuary.) It's only natural that as a good writer, or even a brilliant writer, you are occasionally going to indulge yourself with a bit of levity or linguistic gymnastics (linguastics?). If you were pushed for time when you wrote them, maybe you'll see a few passages that make you cringe. Don't worry! We've all done it. I once had to admit, shamefacedly, in one of my own workshops, that copy I had drafted would have made me cross, were I the intended reader. Don't worry, I revised it thoroughly. The point is, now you know what to look out for, you can be vigilant.

Workshop

1 What is metre?

a) Average words per sentence

b) Overall length of your copy

c) Rhythm of your copy

2 What is alliteration?

a) Words starting with the same letter

b) Using a metaphor or simile

c) Using a literary reference, eg to Shakespeare

3 You should limit all your sentences to between five and eight words. True or false?

4 Metaphors and similes are both forms of visual language. True or false?

5 What three-letter word will waken most readers from a doze?

a) And

b) You

c) Sex

6 Why is accidental repetition a bad thing?

7 What's the ideal number for a group of repetitions?

8 Repetition only works with complete phrases. True or false?

9 What does your reader discern when you deliberately repeat yourself?

   a) That you've run out of ideas

   b) A pattern

   c) A musical quality to your writing

10 Who were the first people to consciously use repetition in argument?

   a) The Ancient Geeks

   b) The Ancient Pekes

   c) The Ancient Greeks

11 What's wrong with putting speech marks around a figure of speech, like a 'double-edged sword'?

12 What is the phrase for the act of deleting passages of writing that make *us* happy?

   a) Murder your darlings

   b) Kidnap your babies

   c) Beat up your besties

13 When is it OK to use humour in copywriting?

   a) When you don't need to sell

   b) Whenever you feel like it

   c) When you want to make your reader laugh

14 Who is the only person you should be writing for?

15 It's OK to say 'We're putting the cart before the proverbial horse'. True or false?

Putting it into action

Exercise 42: Taking pleasure from headlines

Choose one of the five pleasure-inducing techniques described in this chapter and use it in a headline, subject line or other piece of short-form copy.

Exercise 43: I sense you are interested

Try writing a short passage of copy describing, in the present tense, what it's like to use or experience your product. Use at least two different forms of sensory language, eg visual and kinaesthetic.

Exercise 44: Perfect tens

Take a recent piece of copy you wrote and analyse it for all five of this chapter's pleasure techniques: rhythm, pace, musicality, imagery, surprise. Give it a score out of 10 for each of them. Rewrite it as needed if any aspect scores less than a seven.

Exercise 45: Repeat after me

Write repetitions – in sets of three – using the following words:

- customers;
- happy;
- innovation.

Try to vary the style of sentence for each one, as I did above.

Exercise 46: Repeat on opening

Write the beginning of an ad for your best-selling product using repetition. Focus on a benefit as the substance of your repeated point.

Exercise 47: Rinse and repeat

Write a headline for your ad also using repetition. It doesn't have to be a triad, or the repetition of a whole word. Play around with sounds and initial letters too.

Exercise 48: Do you swear to tell the whole truth?

Rewrite the following passage of copy, for a fictional firm of solicitors, removing all the bad writing and replacing it with something better.

Maslen and Kelly: we go the extra mile

At Maslen and Kelly, we firmly believe that running a law firm is a bit like running a marathon. There's no point stopping at 25 miles. So we make sure we go the full 26. We have a team of seven partners, five associate partners and five paralegals. Between us we have over 68 years' combined experience in every type of legal service, from family law to litigation, conveyancing to probate. Unlike Jarndyce and Jarndyce, the fictional (thank goodness!) firm of lawyers in Charles Dickens's famous 1853 novel Bleak House, we do not seek to prolong cases unnecessarily merely to inflate our fees. Our aim is always to secure an optimum legal outcome for our customers. This methodology, *ipso facto*, is in the best interests of you, our clients. Some of you may wonder whether going to law is going to be expensive and stressful. Well, come and talk to us for an informal, no obligation conversation and then you be the judge!

Exercise 49: And the scores are...

Take a recent piece of your copywriting and score it out of 10 for each of our seven traps. If you avoided the trap altogether give yourself a zero. If you took a run-up and jumped in head first, give yourself a 10. Add your scores together for all seven traps. If you scored 21 or less, that's pretty good: you just need to work a little harder at rooting out those lapses. 22–42, sort of OK, but you either need to spend more time editing or more time on your first draft. 43 or above, hmm, I applaud your honesty, now apply some of that candour to an improvement plan. Start with the lessons in this book and I am sure you'll be down below 14 in no time.

Exercise 50: Give. Me. FUNNY!

I want you to write something funny. Genuinely funny. Why? Well, first because at this point in the book I think you deserve to have a little fun. And second, because it is, actually, a very desirable skill. You may never have more than a couple of chances to use it in your career but when you do, Oh boy! How will you know if you've succeeded. Either send it to me and I'll tell you if I <smiled>, LOLed or ROFLed. Or get a friend to read it and see what they say.

Tweet: How are you doing? Tweet me @Andy_Maslen

How to engage your imagination and free your creativity 13

I saw the angel in the marble and carved until I set him free.

MICHELANGELO

Introduction

As copywriters, you and I are expected to come up with creative concepts and the words that express them a) when needed and b) without leaving our desks. So let me ask you a few questions. When was the last time you had a really brilliant idea? Not just for copywriting, for anything. Now, where did you have it? Was it sitting at your desk? And when did you have it? Was it within working hours? No, I didn't think so. There is something about the routine of everyday life that militates against creative thinking. Maybe it's, oh, I don't know, because it's routine. This chapter is my attempt to explain my creative process and help you discover what works best for you.

If we are honest with ourselves, much copywriting can be completed successfully – and profitably – without expending vast amounts of energy sweating blood over a keyboard. Projects that repeat themselves with just a name change, or a new feature, do not require gargantuan levels of creativity. You just take what worked last time and run with that.

But there are also those writing projects that call for the wow-factor – a phrase that a senior executive at a large media company used when briefing me on some letters she wanted writing.

These are the jobs where you have to come up with the goods. And in my experience, the goods are not to be found in the drawer labelled, 'Things that work around here', the box with a label reading, 'Templates' or the shelf under your desk with, 'Everyday ideas' stuck along the edge.

So, where do we find them? The answer is, I think, in our subconscious. I don't mean this in some mystical, freaky-deaky, recovered memory syndrome kind of way. Just that any idea we have must come from inside our heads. If we can't access it immediately, from our conscious mind, it must lie a little beneath the surface: *sub*conscious. Of course, that begs another question, which is, how do the really good ideas get there in the first place?

*

First question: how do the ideas get 'in there' in the first place?

Whenever I read those 'What I read' features in glossy magazines and the interviewee claims only to read biographies and non-fiction, because 'novels aren't real' my heart sinks. They are cutting themselves off from the world's richest source of ideas.

Novelists play around in the same sandbox copywriters do: human behaviour. Specifically, human emotion. So whether or not our celebrity interviewee wants to read fact or fiction is irrelevant. *We* should.

Part of the process of having great ideas is accumulating them in the first place. For as long as I can remember, I have been mad about books. In fact, not just books: magazines, newspapers, comics, advertising posters, cartoons, food packaging, public signs – anything with words on it. I devoured them. But gluttony without exercise only leads to obesity. To have your own ideas, you need to burn calories, not just ingest them.

I think that your best ideas come from making connections between existing ideas. Maybe you put two literary references together and come up with something new. Or, better still, maybe you put a literary reference together with a pop-culture reference and really blow the lid off it.

All my life I have been fond of making puns. In our family, and, I suspect, many others, this particular form of humour is known as 'Dad jokes'. They have an appallingly low strike rate: perhaps as few as one in a thousand. But, boy, be around for the zinger that gets the family laughing.

That willingness (or desperate drive) to get a laugh means I am constantly experimenting and playing with language to see what I can get it to do. I am not shy, I am not afraid, I am not embarrassed (though, perhaps, I should be). I just do it.

One important component of this process is that I don't judge the idea until I have said it out loud. Well, I do judge it, as I rehearse it internally in my head, but I still say it, because, you never know, your audience might like it better than you do.

Second question: how do we get the ideas 'out of there'?

How to have great ideas is the subject of an entire stream of scientific and sociological endeavour, and I don't propose to lay it out in detail here (partly because I don't have the intellectual chops to do it). But from my own experience, here are three things that help:

1. Changing place

I rarely have my best ideas sitting at my desk. I am fortunate to live in a very beautiful part of England, with mile after mile of rolling countryside. I also have a very lovely dog, a whippet, called Merlin.

Every day, he and I go for a walk. There is one particular spot we both enjoy visiting – a river running through a meadow with a little stone bridge and a grassy spot on the bank to sit on. I have had some *epic* ideas there.

This is where I come to think. Where could you go to free *your* creativity?

2. Changing time

My normal working hours are 9 am to 5 pm plus or minus an hour each end, like a lot of people. But occasionally I wake up at 5 or 6 am and can't get back to sleep. So I get up and go to work. I can hear birdsong from my office, which is next to the house, but other than that, it's silent. My head is unusually clear, too, and I find I can come up with new ways of saying things, funnier ways of saying things, *better* ways of saying things, than I can in the middle of the day.

3. Changing materials

I write most of my copy using a keyboard–screen combination of some kind. But now and then, particularly when I am writing a direct mail letter or long-form email/web page, I switch to the implement I used to use back in the day. I use a fountain pen. (For any digital natives reading, a fountain pen

Figure 13.1   Every writer needs a thinking place

The author's whippet, Merlin, pondering the best way to start a web page.

is a slim, handheld, wireless printer that uses liquid toner and reproduces your thoughts on paper without needing a keyboard.)

Would it be boring of me to say, also, that you need to work at it? Maybe, but there it is. No doubt there are some free spirits out there blessed with so much natural creative talent that ideas come to them like bluebirds alighting on Snow White's outstretched finger; but for me, I find working at it helps.

What do I mean by 'working at it'? Well, you may be relieved to hear it doesn't mean I just sit there, staring with agonized desperation at a blank screen or piece of paper. It means I prepare. Here are some things I do to tilt the odds in my favour (because, who knows, maybe Snow White had breadcrumbs and bird lime up her sleeve).

The playground test

I make sure I understand the thing I am selling thoroughly. So thoroughly that I could stand in the playground at my children's school and explain it to anyone who happens to be standing there *so that they understand*. If I can't I don't start writing. I go back to the client and ask them a series of increasingly pointed questions (some would say dumb, but I don't care) until I do.

The user test

Then I try to get hold of the product and experience it for myself. This isn't always possible, especially if you are promoting military hardware, luxury watches or million-pound software installations, but it's worth having a shot.

The 'do I know what I am trying to say?' test

We all want to come up with that killer line. But first it can pay to know you can state your commercial objectives clearly and simply. I try to sum up my pitch in a couple of sentences. A good friend of mine used to command a regiment in the British Army. I asked him what his job was and he said this: 'We blow up the enemy's stuff, and try to stop them blowing up ours.'

I don't think you can improve on that.

The planning test

OK, this isn't so much of a test, but I'm locked into the 'test' motif now. Let's call it the 'do I have a plan?' test. In my first book, *Write to Sell*, I explained my planning process in detail, and I don't propose to take up your time with it here. But here are the bare bones.

I have a **written plan**. I don't believe I am clever enough to hold a plan in my head *and* write copy at the same time.

I write my plans **longhand**. Computer-generated type is too perfect for what should be a free, fluid process.

I start with my **commercial goal**. Nothing is more important than achieving what the client wants – not smiles from the reader, awards, nothing.

Download: I always use my own planning mnemonic – **KFC**.
What do I want my reader to Know, Feel and Commit?
Download a KFC planning template.

I always set aside **enough time for planning**. Which I define as roughly a quarter of the total amount of time I have allotted to the project.

One of the best-performing bits of copy I ever wrote was a subject line. It was for a conference. I have written about it before but it fits so well in this section that I'll go over the process that led to its creation again.

CASE STUDY   Email campaign for Euromoney

At 44 characters, this subject line just exceeds the 40-character limit widely believed to be the sweet spot. But the company name and evocative phrase 'Billion Dollar Baby' are well within the scannable portion of the line.

The conference was called Airfinance. It was to be held in New York. And it was in its 21st year.

In conversation with the marketing manager and the editor of AirFinance magazine I unearthed the fascinating fact that over the course of the 20 years the conference had been running in New York, around a billion dollars' worth of deals had been concluded.

At this point I could have written something workmanlike:

> Now in its 21st year, the conference that spawned a billion dollars' worth of airfinance deals

And it might have done OK.

But this was the year that Hilary Swank won the Best Actress Oscar for her role in the film *Billion Dollar Baby*.

Somewhere, a light bulb went on in my brain and out popped:

> Euromoney's Billion Dollar Baby Comes of Age

Here is what Jason Coles, the marketing manager, said in an email:

What a wake-up call. Our tried (or should that read 'tired') and tested headlines were blown away by your 'Billion Dollar Baby' subject line. Our open and click-through rates went through the roof, and delegate registrations spiked dramatically within hours of broadcast. Great job – here's to the next campaign.

Result!

A practical tool for generating ideas

Are there shortcuts to great ideas? Yes! There, that was easy, wasn't it?

Here's one I find works for me. Word association.

Try this: Playing isn't just for children. Play with language until you find something new and appealing. Just make sure it's relevant.

Here's what might have happened with the Billion Dollar Baby idea above.

21 > key of the door, never been 21 before > coming of age

Billion dollars > billion dollar baby > baby grows up > comes of age

So, you start with a few words taken directly from the brief – the product name, perhaps, or one of its features, or who it's aimed at.

Then you free-associate, without consciously trying to come up with 'copy' or even a workable idea.

Keep going until you dry up.

Then see what you have and play around with it.

If we were working on a relaxation product for new mums, maybe it would go like this:

mums > tums > bums > thumbs > sucking thumbs > sucking thumbs is dumb > for dummies > babies' dummies > relaxation for dummies

relax > lie down > breathe > yoga > calm > oasis > palm trees > mirage > imaginary > imaginary friend > your best friend

At any rate, you're just trying to open the floodgates, so try to avoid feeling self-conscious. I find it helps to be away from my screen. For a start, a hastily scribbled idea looks less 'professional' than one in perfect 11-point Helvetica on a screen and therefore less embarrassing if it later turns out to be no good.

Key takeaway: If you're searching for new ideas, don't bother looking in the same old places. Genius isn't top of mind or tip of tongue. Dig deeper.

Another technique – word games

Given that we are using the written word, it can also work to play word games.

Take your keyword and come up with the following:

- a list of rhymes;
- a list of synonyms;
- a list of antonyms;
- a list of alliterations.

Rank each list in order of word length.

Say them all out loud, listening for the beat.

And another – resonance

Why not try jotting down as many cultural references as you can think of that refer to or contain your keyword?

This is known as resonance. It means we are borrowing the significance of an existing idea to lend weight to our own. If, say, you were writing a futuristic thriller about a man trying to save the human race from being exterminated by killer cyborgs, and you needed a name for your hero, you could call him John Drake. Cool-sounding, macho, unaffected. Zero resonance.

Or, you could call him John Connor. Cool-sounding, macho, unaffected. Oh, and the same initials as the founder of Christianity. Resonance. (Kudos to Stephen King (2001) for alerting me to this point. Buy his book, *On Writing*. You'll be the better writer for it.)

One more – linguistic precision

In some ways, this chapter is a polemic against adjectives and adverbs. You know, describing words. That's how our teachers sold them to us, at any rate. And, so long as you use them correctly, it's true. They do describe things. You don't just want people to save the Siberian Tiger. You want them to save the *endangered* Siberian Tiger. But beware the empty vessel that sounds so freighted with meaning yet contains nothing. Ready? Save the *magnificent* Siberian Tiger. Why? What's magnificent about it? Well, you say, it is being *cruelly* hunted. Oh dear, as opposed to *kindly* hunted, you mean? Or do you mean that poachers armed with Kalashnikovs trap and kill mothers and their cubs before hacking off their heads using chainsaws? In that last sentence there were precisely no adjectives or adverbs. Still worked though, I feel.

What we should be aiming for is a way of writing that derives its power from the exhaustive search for precisely the right nouns and verbs to a) convey our exact meaning and b) evoke the exact emotional response we're looking for in our reader. If we need adjectives and adverbs, fine, let's go ahead and use them. But let's remember to use them to add information (*endangered*), not emphasis (*magnificent*).

Writing like a journalist

Another example. I was driving back to the office from a client meeting when the news programme I was listening to featured a live interview with a reporter walking around a compound in Iraq where prisoners had been held. In halting, gasping speech she described what she could see:

> There is another body in front of me. A man. He is dead. Kneeling with his head twisted sideways on the ground and his hands tied behind his back with wire. There is a fist-sized hole in the back of his head. A lot of blood. The smell is bad – everywhere. These were assassinations. Murders.

I almost had to pull off the road, it was so intense. Her voice itself was unemotional. Dispassionate, even. Her words rendered the injection of emotion unnecessary. And they themselves were devoid of emotion. Just not of detail.

This section is about finding ways to discover that ability in you. To report what you see, not what you know. To convey to a complete stranger the impressions you have of your product in language at once emotionally rich and linguistically simple.

Finding the hard-won phrase

What do poets share with war reporters? Naturalists with painters? Doctors with detectives? They are all expert observers. They are attuned to detail. They record what they see (and hear, smell, taste and touch).

They do not reach for readymade phrases or generic language to describe things; they painstakingly describe the scene in front of them. From this precision, this attention to detail, comes truth. And the truth they describe can be heartbreaking, uplifting, shocking, exciting, infuriating, convincing, amazing, provocative, depressing, joyous or inspiring.

As writers, as persuasive writers, we must learn to do the same. We must learn to spend time understanding what it is we are writing about, what we are *truly* writing about.

I once ran a writing workshop for a major nature charity. In one of their promotional leaflets I came across this phrase: 'the unmistakable flight of the heron'.

Bad: the unmistakable flight of the heron

Good: ...horse riding with the owners on a ranch in the Pampas of Argentina... night-time safaris in Brazil's Pantanal wetlands area where you could come face-to-face with a jaguar, 2.5 metres from nose to tail ... (from a website written by the author)

Try an experiment with me. Lean back, close your eyes and imagine you have never seen a heron in flight before. (This may be true, in which case you will excel in this experiment.) Using the adjective 'unmistakable' to guide you, try to visualize the heron in flight. Is it helping?

Now go onto your favourite search engine and search 'heron flying'. Watch a few films, then come up with a description of what you see that would convey the distinctive images in front of you to a heron-deprived reader. Test it on someone you are fairly sure has never seen a heron in flight and ask them what they 'see'. To save you a little time, here's one I found: **www.youtube.com/watch?v=eqhcajrS4PQ**

When I ran that little exercise with communications executives from the charity in question, they said that it was hard. Of course it's hard, I said. That's the point. But so is persuading complete strangers to commit to a regular monthly payment to save creatures they've never seen just by writing to them.

They did, in the end, manage to come up with some fine descriptions, and the conversations between them as they began digging down into the real details of what happens to wings, feet, necks and body posture were a pleasure to listen to.

Show don't tell

But hang on. Doesn't all this description fly in the face of all those books on copywriting that tell you to sell don't tell? And to concentrate on benefits not features? How can describing something accurately turn a sceptic into a customer? Well, it can't. Not really. Let's take that phrase 'sell, don't tell'. In creative writing classes it morphs into 'show, don't tell'. Anton Chekhov, the Russian writer of plays and short fiction, said, 'Don't tell me it was night; show me the moon reflected in a shard of glass.'

Key takeaway: The more time you spend thinking about your product, the less time you need to spend describing it.

Suppose you are trying to persuade somebody to buy a product from you. Your product saves them money. It does this because it has a widget inside it that uses less electricity than its competitors.

The widget is the feature. The using less electricity is the advantage. The saving money is the benefit. So far, so ho-hum.

Write:

> Thanks to its revolutionary electricity-saving widget, Product X saves you money.

and you are telling.

Write:

> Imagine what you could do with the money you save when you switch to product X.

and you are selling.

Write:

> Imagine switching on Product X and seeing the counter on your electricity meter actually slowing down. I just tried it and I couldn't believe my eyes. My smart meter told me I was already saving money within seconds of plugging in Product X. That was a week ago. According to my smart meter, I have already saved £4.76. By my calculations that means I will save £247.52 every year. You could too.

and you are showing.

To show, you need to observe. You need to play around with Product X, use it like a customer would. Subject it to scrutiny until there's no aspect of it that you don't understand.

In my time I have written a lot of sales copy for business books, especially heavyweight statistical compilations, fact books and directories. Whenever I talk to a marketing executive whose job it is to promote these books, they always say the same thing: 'Obviously there's no point reading it – it's just a load of statistics – so I'll just send you last year's brochure.'

I then have to plead with them to send me a copy of the book. When I receive it, I spend a day or so going through it, getting a feel for the type of information it contains and trying to figure out (if there's no research to tell me) how a customer would use it. Then I can write about it. From a customer's perspective.

I understand that, to a marketing executive working for a business book publisher, a book full of statistics on the global automotive industry may not light their fire. But it isn't aimed at them. It's aimed at analysts working in banks, consultancies and component manufacturers who are fascinated by this stuff.

Try this: Really get to know the thing you're selling. Use it, play with it, observe it. Do not rely on other writers' copy as your sole guide.

Charts aren't 'at-a-glance', they are 'full-colour bar, pie and scatter charts'.

Manufacturer profiles aren't 'in-depth', they contain '28 separate performance measures including productivity per employee, return on capital employed (ROCE), product recall ratios and inside leg measurement of all board members'.

A few years back there was a rather good advertising campaign for BMW. The advertising agency sent its creative team to Germany to visit BMW's factory and spend time with its designers and engineers.

The process was later described by the agency as 'interrogating the product'. Out of these far-reaching discussions into the processes involved in the manufacture of a BMW came a memorable campaign focusing on individual components, such as pistons that were forged in one piece then broken and glued back together around the crank shaft to ensure a fit at the molecular level. Does this all sound like features not benefits?

You're right. It is. But the deep-seated emotional benefit that the copy conveyed was that 'you are behind the wheel of the ultimate driving machine: we do not compromise and neither do you'. Pretty powerful stuff to people who care about their car's performance and handling.

From theory to profit

When I am running a writing workshop, there inevitably comes the point when one of the participants puts their hand up and asks a variant on this question: 'How do you get your best ideas?' And I give them a variant on this answer: 'I go somewhere quiet and think.' But it seems to me that thinking is an increasingly undervalued activity in marketing departments. Oh, sure, I know marketeers are supposed to be *constantly* thinking. But they are never given the resources to do it properly. Most I've met work in large, featureless open-plan offices where the main sounds are calls from their colleagues in sales who occupy the next 50 cubicles or, failing that, the sound of a million keystrokes. So my question to you is this. Thinking back to your answer to my initial questions – 'Where and when do you have your best ideas?' – how are you going to incorporate that into your work?

How much do you know about your products? Do you own or use one? Have you experienced your own service? Or do you just rely on marketing brochures and web pages to get the information you need? The essential first step to bringing your product to life is bringing it into your own. An example: I wouldn't be without a subscription to *The Economist*, and when I was hired to write copy for a subscriptions campaign, I felt I had a deep understanding of what the magazine was all about. The publisher was incredibly helpful in giving me insights into the *readers*, but the product I had down.

David Ogilvy, legendary 20th-century adman and copywriter, declared that it was common courtesy to use your client's products. Jo Kelly, our creative director, tells the story of a former colleague smoking the 'wrong' brand of cigarette in a meeting with a tobacco client. Leaning across the table and proffering one of his own, the marketing director smiled as he said, 'Try one of these – I think you'll find they taste of bread and butter'. So, it's polite and it's also the best way to see your product for what it really is.

Workshop

1 What's one test you can use to prepare for some creative thinking?

2 Give an example of a technique you can use to generate new ideas.

3 What must you never do to an idea until you have written it down?

   a) Judge it

   b) Smudge it

   c) Fudge it

4 Name one thing you can change to stimulate new ideas.

5 Why might using pencil and paper be an effective way of thinking more creatively?

6 Complete this simple mnemonic for visual copywriting: _____ don't tell.

7 Adjectives are there to add _____
not _____. *Fill in the blanks.*

8 Anton Chekhov said, 'Don't tell me it was night; show me the moon reflected in a _____'.

a) Puddle

b) Mirror

c) Shard of glass

9 You need to be emotional to convey emotion. True or false?

10 The only copywriters who can benefit from trying their own product are in B2C. True or false?

Putting it into action

Exercise 51: Creative pitch

For your own product, write a brilliant, unexpected line to pitch it. Use all the ideas, tests, questions and tips in this section.

Exercise 52: Get yourself into a different state

For the next piece of copy you have to write, make a determined effort to change state. Go somewhere different. Or use different materials. Or sit with different people.

Exercise 53: That looks fun

Start a swipe file of things that strike you as creative, original, unexpected or exciting. They can be images, pieces of writing, logos, graphics, typefaces, toys... anything at all. (So it might be a big file.) Every now and then have a rootle through it and pull stuff out. Don't try to consciously ape anything you come across, just let yourself be immersed in their difference. THEN write.

Exercise 54: The 20:80 description

Go and find an object from your office or home, wherever you are reading this book.

Place it in front of you. Now, look at it for two minutes, put it behind you, then spend eight minutes writing a description.

Exercise 55: The 80:20 description

Place the object in front of you again. This time, look at it for eight minutes, then put it behind you and spend two minutes writing a second description.

Exercise 56: The power of observation

Compare your two versions. (You saved them, right?) What are the differences between them? Which one do you prefer? Show them to a friend or colleague. Ask them for their reactions.

If you did it right, the second piece, even though you had a quarter of the time to type it, should be better than the first. More vivid, more engaging, more true to life.

In two minutes we can discern the shape of a thing and perhaps the colour and a few primary features. In eight, we can relax and look at its texture, the subtleties of light and shadow, the greys in the white, the unevenness of the planes. All these details bring an object to life and help your reader see what you saw. This is the beginning of emotional writing.

The uses of this approach don't stop at describing objects. You can use it to describe less tangible things, such as movements, colours or sounds.

Tweet: How are you doing? Tweet me @Andy_Maslen

Tone and technique in copy: Finding your voice (and that of others)

14

We often refuse to accept an idea merely because the tone of voice in which it has been expressed is unsympathetic to us.

FRIEDRICH NIETZSCHE

Introduction

When I was just starting out as a copywriter I remember one of my contacts coming up to me at a conference and saying, 'Andy, I saw a mailshot the other day and I just knew you'd written it. I recognized your style'. At the time I was pleased. Looking back, I should have been horrified. I had committed the cardinal copywriting sin of becoming more visible than the product. Since then I have worked hard to erase all traces of my style from my copywriting. Maybe it's a sign that I have been successful that nobody has ever told me they recognized my style from a website or email since that original incident.

As a freelance or agency copywriter, you might be writing about professional indemnity insurance one day and self-loading rifles the next; skateboard gear the day after and a wedding planning service before you go home for the weekend. As an in-house copywriter you might have lucked out and landed a berth at a company whose brand image exactly mirrors your personal one. But it's unlikely. In both cases, your style – your voice – should vary with the client or campaign. But there is one field when you have licence to write how you want to write.

Content marketing is where you have the opportunity to engage your reader not just with your content but with your style as well. I've been publishing a monthly newsletter about copywriting since October 2000. Right from the outset I decided to write it the way I wanted to, and not to worry overmuch about what people thought about it. I figured if they liked it they'd be great clients and if they didn't, well, that might save us both some time finding out we were incompatible. I also blog, tweet and create standalone bits of content including books and postcards. In every case, they're mine. Nobody has the final say apart from me.

For another take on the power of your voice to create and sustain interest in you and your brand, take a look at the work of Doug Kessler, joint founder of content marketing agency Velocity Partners. Doug has this to say about how to write content: 'How you say it is just as important as what you say. Having a voice will help your message stand out from all the me-too, same crap flying around.' Doug is brilliant at setting out his ideas in a distinctive voice and you can find his presentations online at **www.slideshare.net/dougkessler**.

So, let's have a look at developing yours.

*

In the world of creative writing, fledgling writers are desperate to find their 'voice'. What does this mean? Put simply, to find a style of writing that a) they feel comfortable with; b) reflects their view of the world; c) expresses their thoughts about language; and d) makes them recognizable to their readers. To read Hemingway then Austen is to read two very different voices.

Do we, as commercial writers, need to find our voice, too? Well, as they say, it depends.

Our reputation is unlikely to be contingent on our writing style. As long as it's clear, concise and persuasive we should thrive. Our readers are unlikely to be buying what we write, so it's equally unlikely that our voice will be seen as adding value to the transaction.

If we are writing speeches, they should manifestly not be in our voice. If we are writing marketing or advertising copy then we will be writing in the voice of the brand or its spokesperson. Over the years, I have written in the voices of TV presenters, magazine editors, company directors, senior doctors, professors of nursing, engineers and many others.

But. (Oh, good, there's a but. That means we do need a voice after all.)

What about blog posts, e-books, white papers, social media updates, articles, personal emails and letters? Here, I think, there is definitely scope to develop your voice as a writer. Shall we de-frill it and just call it 'the way I write'? There. Now we can start to figure out what we might do to develop it.

Key takeaway: The best way to develop a strong and identifiable voice is to write. Lots. Write *what* you want to, in the *way* that you want to.

Twenty factors that affect your voice

Here is a non-exhaustive list of qualities of your writing that a) are under your control (well, they are all, aren't they?) and b) have an impact on your voice:

1 **Sentence length.** The longer your average sentence, the more sophisticated, formal and educated you sound. The shorter the average sentence, the more conversational, everyday and down-to-earth the voice.

2 **Foreign words.** I am talking here of words that are recognizably foreign, such as *je ne sais quoi* or *mi casa es su casa*, rather than so-called loan words such as bungalow or verandah. Their effect on your voice is complex. Longer words, such as *weltanschauung* (German for world-view), give you an academic, high-toned sound, whereas shorter words, such as *mamma mia!*, sound playful.

3 **Long words** (three or more syllables). Again, longer words move your language into a higher register, one that suggests higher social class and education.

4 **Quasi-religious language.** Even readers who are not religious usually pick up on the cadences and vocabulary of religious writing. In the Judaeo-Christian tradition, for example, *smite* is a powerful word and might work well in a speech to a sales department describing how you intend to obliterate your competition.

5 **Question tags,** eg Every writer needs to find a voice, or do they? Great for creating rapport with the unseen reader, informal in style.

6 **Personal pronouns.** Without them, your writing will sound dry and academic or corporate. (This may be precisely the effect you are striving to create.)

7 **Old-fashioned terms.** This can sound arch, or knowing, or just old-fashioned. Often it works best when you mix high-tech and low-tech in the same passage or even sentence. 'This cloud-based storage is just too darned complex for an old-timer like me.'

8 **Slang.** General slang, gang slang or activity-slang, eg skater-speak: they can work, but avoid 'trendy vicar' syndrome at all costs. Nobody will ever believe you are down with the kids. Unless you are one of them.

9 **Jargon.** A bit like slang, it will give your writing a certain sound. And it can help build connections and credibility with an interest group. But

beware of using jargon when writing for lay readers. Your voice will sound standoffish and boring to them.

10 **Punctuation,** eg subordinate clauses, complex lists. Simple punctuation is best if your sole concern is comprehension. It will also render your writing a little like an instruction booklet aimed at small children. Used correctly, punctuation should always clarify meaning, so more involved sentences are OK and will vary the pace of your writing.

11 **Asides to reader** (you know, in brackets). This suggests a degree of complicity between writer and reader – the sharing of a joke or emotional rapport. Also as though you are leaning in to whisper to them.

12 **Mixing of register,** eg Senator Wilson has a 'blokeish persona' (a phrase I read in an edition of *The Economist*, surely a paragon of good writing). This effect is exciting to the reader, who must recalibrate their perception each time you switch from high to low or low to high. Good for maintaining attention.

13 **Literary references,** eg Like Uriah Heep, I am 'ever so 'umble'. If your reader gets the reference you have added to the rapport you are building between you and your reader. But it can sound pretentious and showy as if you are drawing attention to your education (which you might well be doing).

14 **Wit/humour,** eg You could try searching for a better deal. Here, we've packed you some sandwiches for the trip. This 'cute' approach to writing is much beloved by advertising agency copywriters and others working on brand campaigns. Do it well and your reader is smiling and receptive. Fluff it and their BS detector goes crazy.

CASE STUDY Quad – app promotional video

http://vimeo.com/72978470

'Once upon a time, on a campus not too far away…' is how this funny video for an organizational app kicks off. Referencing aeons of storytelling and Star Wars, it proceeds to tell the tale of a badly-run zombie nation on a school campus.

Tens of thousands of downloads later, it just goes to show that, maybe, with the deepest respect for Claude Hopkins, who said spending money was a serious business, and people didn't buy from clowns, humour does belong in copywriting.

The copywriter behind this undead fun is Natalie Mueller, of Chicago:

> *We took the client's inkling for something zombie-related in a completely unexpected direction for a fresh and engaging story complete with plot twists, subtle humor and some quality rhyming. (Natalie C Mueller, Freelance Copywriter and Creative Director, Chicago)*

But beware, rookies, this lady is a comedienne as well as a copywriter, so she knows funny.

15　**Deliberately poor grammar,** eg In the end, it ain't going to work. End of. There are two groups of people who use bad grammar: people who don't know any better and do it randomly and very well educated people using it for stylistic effect. If you're going to join the latter group, make sure your reader will be left in no doubt of your intentions. The alternative is that they assume you're a member of the first group.

16　**Childlike phrasing,** eg I saw the new feasibility study and you know what? Me not like. This kind of quirky writing will certainly get your reader's attention. In the example I've just given, it's paired with a sentence containing the decidedly non-childlike word 'feasibility'. That, I think, is the clue. All childlike is merely childish.

17　**Reticence in place of boldness,** eg Might you be interested in a free trial? Do let me know and I shall set you up with a user name and password. This is a great way to send a message that you are super-confident without coming across as arrogant. The implication is that you would love it if they did what you ask, but, you know what – it doesn't actually matter because you're doing just fine anyway.

18　**Boldness in place of reticence,** eg I don't *think* you're going to come to my course. I KNOW you are. Why? Because you are the kind of engineer who knows that in nanotechnology you are either moving forward or moving backwards.

19　**Attitude,** eg You *could* visit another art gallery. I mean, there are tons in this city to choose from. But hey, there are tons of vacant lots too and I don't suppose you'll be visiting too many of them. So unless you have some kind of problem seeing the artist who won this year's Venice Biennale, I guess I will be handing you a glass of champagne next Thursday evening at 7 pm. Sharp.

20 **Surreality**, eg, Last night, as I was planning this email, my goldfish started talking to me from its tank. This happens on a fairly frequent basis so I wasn't surprised. (It's not as if the angel fish was talking. That would be weird. He's so shy he never speaks.)

I say these tools are under your control, but many people will do these things entirely randomly. Everything *you* write must be purposeful. By all means write a 35-word sentence stuffed with as many '*Weltanschauung*'s and '*quid pro quo*'s as you can manage, but do it on purpose.

Key takeaway: When you're developing and using your voice, save it for those projects where you want to be identified as the writer. That means something that has your name at the bottom.

How to modify your tone of voice

If the last section of this chapter was about finding your voice, then this one is about varying it. That doesn't immediately sound straightforward, I admit, so let me try to tease out the separate aspects of your writing. When your reader reacts to your voice, they are reacting, possibly emotionally, to how they feel about your writing. When your reader reacts to your tone of voice, they are reacting, entirely emotionally, to how they feel about your message. This means that tone of voice is a more useful tool for sales communications, where we want the reader to feel that going along with our suggestion is a good idea. This is a fairly subtle distinction, but I hope, as you work through this chapter, it becomes clearer.

Debunking the 7 per cent rule

One of the biggest challenges we must meet as copywriters is the lack of face-to-face contact with our customer. At a stroke, our chosen medium of communication renders invisible such determinants of meaning as non-verbal vocal cues and body language.

But let's pause for a moment, before we throw our pencils and pads out of the window and retrain as accountants. There are a great many communications 'consultants' eager to sell you the idea that only 7 per cent of what we say is communicated through the words we choose. But this, my friend, is rubbish. The originator of the statistic is Albert Mehrabian, currently Professor Emeritus of Psychology, UCLA, whose original research was investigating how much people *liked* the person doing the communicating.

Explaining the genesis of what has popularly come to be known as 'Mehrabian's Rule', Professor Mehrabian says:

> Total Liking = 7% Verbal Liking + 38% Vocal Liking + 55% Facial Liking. Please note that this and other equations regarding relative importance of verbal and nonverbal messages were derived from experiments dealing with communications of feelings and attitudes (ie, like–dislike). Unless a communicator is talking about their feelings or attitudes, these equations are not applicable.

This means that you can communicate information very effectively in writing (in fact, given that it's less likely your emotions are clouding the picture, probably more effectively than face-to-face). However, when you are trying to communicate on an emotional level in writing, clearly there is a problem. How, then, are we going to reproduce the effect of non-verbal communication with only a screen or a sheet of paper between our reader and us?

CASE STUDY   A direct mail pack for CareSuper

CareSuper is the largest Australian industry fund that specializes in superannuation for people in professional, managerial, administrative and service occupations.

The aim of this campaign was to increase the number of active members in the fund by encouraging lapsed members to nominate CareSuper as their fund of choice.

> *To overcome the apathy of recipients, it was important that these mailers be different from the usual communications to super fund members.*
>
> *We wrote the mailers with the aim of being empathic and subtly humorous. With its simplicity and notably 'casual' tone, including the use of colloquial language, the copy in these mailers was distinctly unlike the dense, formal copy used in most communications from super funds and other financial institutions.*
>
> (Dr Ryan Wallman, Head of Copy, WellmarkPty Ltd (Australia))

This is a classic headline formula, in this case playing to the reader's emotional reaction to dealing with anything pension-related

5 ways to avoid dealing with your super

The curiosity-evoking outer envelope message fulfils exactly the same role as an email subject line

Ignoring this will not make it go away.

The inside pages explain the '5 ways', with copy and design working in harmony to maintain the witty tone

1
Assume you win inherit the fortune of a mystery benefactor.

2
Reject that planning ahead is just not how you roll.

3
Decide that there are better places to keep your money.

4
Figure that if you do it needs to worry about Super because it's actual to turn out that face away.

5
Take the mature approach - put your fingers in your ears and say la la la.

This campaign prompted an unprecedented response from lapsed members, and won an Association of Superannuation Funds of Australia (ASFA) 'Excellence in member communication' award.

The sound of business writing

Most of the time, we tend to write in a generic business language, using a narrow range of tones of voice, depending on the job of our writing. These tones often look like this:

- marketing copy: excitable, portentous, matey;
- business documents: lofty, pretentious, cool;
- internal communications: aloof, dictatorial, bossy;
- social media: hip, flippant, informal.

That's not to say there aren't plenty of counter examples. But *they* don't need to change.

The main thing to note about tone of voice is you have to decide what tone you're going to adopt *before you start writing*. Do not let it develop by chance. Do not fall back on established patterns of writing. Do not, definitely do not, let it be dictated by emotion.

Bad: This high profile corporate lunch provides an afternoon of superb entertainment, fine dining and plenty of laughter, whilst also raising vital funds for charity.

Good: Whatever kind of a week you're having, a quick flick through our pages can cheer up your day and lift your spirits. (from a sales letter for *Reader's Digest* written by the author)

Now, that last injunction might seem to you to sit a little awkwardly with the whole premise of this book. But hear me out.

Without wishing to suggest that you counterfeit emotions you don't feel, you must remember that all business writing is basically trying to do the same thing: modify the reader's behaviour. So, yes, you want to arouse emotions in your reader, but you don't necessarily want to display your own. Evoke, don't emote, in other words.

Typically, the heat starts to build when we receive an email from a customer or colleague that rubs us up the wrong way. Without pausing for breath we fire back an intemperate email in a tone that exactly mirrors our inner emotional turmoil. But here's the thing. Are they more or less likely to see your point if you send them an angry, sarcastic or rude email rather than a polite, wounded or apologetic one?

We're back to planning.

Planning tone of voice

Try this: Tone of voice doesn't happen by accident. Decide in advance how you want to come across. Write it down in your copy plan.

Before you write anything, you need to have a plan. At its simplest, your plan will say what you want to happen next. Let's say a major client has emailed you with a long list of minor criticisms of your work on a project. They are clearly pissed off and have made no attempt to hide their feelings.

First of all, how are you feeling now? Happy? Respected? Content? No, I didn't think so.

So. Take a deep breath. And write your plan. Start it like this:

What I want to happen next is: _____

And you write down the action you want your client to take after they read your email.

Now you're ready to start your first draft. You are calm (hopefully) and you have a plan, so the only emotions that will be manifest on the page or screen are those you want to be there.

Engage: Remember, tone of voice is judged by the reader, not the writer.

Five simple tools for getting tone of voice pitch-perfect

But how do you actually create or vary a tone of voice? How do you sound friendly, or cross, or professional or enthusiastic? Here are a few thoughts that might help you:

1 **Get into the mood.** If you want to sound excited, go and do some vigorous exercise. Get your heart pumping, smile while you're doing it (this releases endorphins – 'happy hormones' – in your brain). If you want to sound worried, think about something that makes you anxious.

2 **Dress the part.** Do you want to sound professional and authoritative? You might find it easier if you are suited and booted, not slopping round your office in jeans or joggers.

3 **Keep a swipe file.** Every time you read a piece of writing (copy or otherwise) that seems to have a distinctive tone of voice, save it. See if you can spot the words, phrases or other linguistic tricks the writer has used to create the tone.

4 **Do not worry about going over the top.** Write freely and only think about editing it afterwards. This is a pretty good tip for writing generally, but it's especially helpful if you are striving for a particular tone of voice.

5 **For positive, friendly tones, use lots of personal, everyday words and simple syntax.** Saying please and thank you helps enormously. For more serious tones, use more complex sentence structures and avoid colloquialisms and too much down-to-earth vocabulary.

From theory to profit

Remember, your voice as a writer is a discrete entity. It's not the literal voice you speak in – it's a writing style that people might recognize and enjoy. What you are looking for is, above all, clarity. And consistency. As communication skills – particularly written communication skills – assume ever-greater prominence in organizational and business life, having a distinctive voice can be a competitive advantage for you personally.

Here are three places where you can use a recognizable voice. Any sales messages that you sign personally. Any or all content you create for your own organization with your name at the bottom. Anything you publish as the named author, such as books, articles and speeches. When the world is awash with dreary corporate voices and me-too attempts to ape the latest darling of the advertising world, creating a recognizable voice is one way to stand out from the crowd. Have a look at your corporate communications or, if you are a freelance, those you write for clients. Divide them between those that come from the company and those that come from you. For the latter, why not experiment and have some fun. What's the worst that can happen? Who knows, people might start following you just because of the way you write. Now wouldn't that be something.

And now, consider how you want to come across to your customers. Before you answer that, maybe you need to map out the varying types of interaction you have with them. Because tone of voice is absolutely not a one-size-fits-all technique. There's the depth of relationship you have with them. And the duration (though these aren't the same thing). And the nature of the issue you are writing about. Even with a very good client, telling them they owe you money is going to need a different tone of voice to telling them they've won a prize in your annual sweepstakes. This is all about feelings. You may want them to like you but it's more likely you want them to feel something more than that. Like guilty, if they owe you money, or reassured if you're suggesting they buy an untested product. So figure it out, plan it in and use these techniques to make it happen.

Workshop

1 Name three different aspects of a writer's voice.

2 Trademark stylistic techniques are fine provided they:

    a) Are recognizably yours

    b) Are used in moderation

    c) Get a laugh

3 When should you avoid having a distinctive voice?

4 Name one technique from those listed in this chapter that will make you sound educated.

5 Name one technique that will sound playful.

6 What is the easiest way to judge the tone of voice of a piece of writing?

7 For every type of communication, only 7 per cent of your meaning is carried by the words you use. True or false?

8 Truthful is a tone of voice. True or false?

9 Can you think of a technique that would make your tone of voice sound friendly?

10 Which is better, emoting or evoking?

Putting it into action

Exercise 57: Listen to my voice

Unless you are a very experienced and talented writer, writing is going to feel harder than talking. So forget about the keyboard. Use a voice recorder instead.

Switch it on and say what you want to say. Keep going, relax into it, don't stop if you make a mistake or fluff your 'lines'. If it helps, jot down some notes first to keep yourself on track.

Now, get your recording transcribed and read it back to yourself. First aloud, then in your head.

This is your voice. Your authentic 'you-ness' typed up when you can take a look at it.

Exercise 58: Switch on the voice analyser

Now analyse your transcript. Refer to the list of qualities above and see how many of them apply to your voice. What are you doing? Where are you doing it? *Why* are you doing it? What effect does it have on the message? On the reader? On their mood?

Exercise 59: Introducing... your voice

Are there tics in the way you speak that you want to change? Maybe you use certain words a lot, or begin lots of sentences the same way.

Edit your writing and read it out again. *Now* how does it sound? Once you have a piece of writing you like, pin it up somewhere where you can see it. This is your voice.

Exercise 60: Name that tone

Write a list of as many descriptive words for tone of voice as you can think of. Give yourself five minutes. Here are five to get you started:

- anxious;
- flirtatious;
- obnoxious;
- self-important;
- wistful.

Exercise 61: Diff'rent strokes for diff'rent folks

Now write a list of all the types of written customer interactions you deal with in your organization. From your list of tones of voice, choose the one that you feel will create the impact you want to have on your customer for each of your interactions. This list of pairs is your tone of voice checklist. Refer to it whenever you are writing to customers.

Exercise 62: Varying tone but not content

Let's have a go at writing the same basic passage in a number of different tones of voice. I want you to write a call to action using any five of your list of tones of voice from Exercise 60. Here's an example, using my five:

Anxious – Are you going to order? Oh *please* say you are. I can't bear the thought of you going a day longer without our Wonder Widget.

Flirtatious – So, why don't you just pop your details down here and I might just come round personally to deliver your Wonder Widget.

Obnoxious – Apparently, you haven't ordered yet. Which makes me wonder whether you're as smart as I thought you were or just some idiot who got onto a mailing list by mistake. Which is it?

Self-important – I am convinced the Wonder Widget represents not only value for money but also extremely high quality. No doubt you agree with me, which is why I am looking forward to receiving your order.

Wistful – Do you remember when widget shopping was quick and easy? I know I do. If only we could get back to that simplicity. Shall we start a trend? Why not send me your order now. By post.

Tweet: How are you doing? Tweet me @Andy_Maslen

The definitive guide to when grammar matters in copywriting

15

Writing has laws of perspective, of light and shade just as painting does, or music. If you are born knowing them, fine. If not, learn them. Then rearrange the rules to suit yourself.

TRUMAN CAPOTE

Introduction

Do you know what links pedants and pendants? They both look good hanging from a chain. There! That should upset the grammar police. Does it matter if a car company tells us to Live Bold instead of Live Boldly? If a software firm suggests we Think Clever instead of Think Cleverly? If a toy manufacturer exhorts us to Play Happy instead of Play Happily? I don't think so. I have bigger fish to fry. But what if a bank writes to its customers telling them, 'As a valued customer, I am delighted to offer you an introductory discount, you can apply online now'? Or a utilities company says in a press release, 'The new pipeline, which was made possible by funds from the UK Government, the EU and investors are going to be fully operational at the start of next year'?

I believe most people are smart enough to know when language is deliberately being used playfully and the rules are being flouted for effect and when the writer is an ignoramus who should be tied up, beaten and flogged to within an inch of... Oh, sorry. Got carried away there for a moment. Where was I? Oh, yes. Grammar.

Over the years, I have become progressively less interested in the 'rules' of English grammar. Possibly this is because, as a native English speaker,

I was raised on them. Possibly it's because there are so few that really matter. Possibly it's because there are other things that matter more. I once had an argument with a client about whether you could use 'they' as a singular personal pronoun, rather than 'he/she'. This must have been at the very height of my clever-dickery because I actually faxed some pages from the *Oxford Guide to English Usage* to him. Sorry, Lou. I should tell you that I have also had some fairly heated arguments with me in the other corner, arguing that what matters is results (*are* results?) while my interlocutor tries to brain me with a dictionary.

But grammar does have rules; as does a prison. However, the rules of grammar are there to help you fly. Not to tether you to the ground. You need to know the rules of grammar because, in governing sentence construction, they also make meaning, and shades of meaning, possible. Without them, all would be chaos. The problem many of us have in the world of copywriting isn't sticking to the rules, it's dealing with the ill-informed, the prejudiced and the just plain ignorant. Most of the commandments the know-alls claim we sin against aren't really rules at all. They're 19th-century attempts to force the rough-hewn peasant that is the English language into a fake classical costume more befitting a romance language like French or Italian.

So what's to be done? Abandon the rules and embrace anarchy? Or don our pince-nez and join the tut-tut-a-split-infinitive brigade? Read on.

*

Does grammar matter? Well, it might. It all depends on what you think of as 'grammar'. If, for example, you mean the rules that govern the relationships between words and clauses, then clearly, yes, grammar does matter.

Key takeaway: The only grammatical errors worth worrying about are those that distract your customer.

Without grammar, a sentence would be what anyone decided it was; and meaning – the ultimate purpose of grammar, and of language itself – would gradually become submerged under the silt of ignorance.

If, on the other hand, you mean a set of needlessly prescriptive 'rules' used to bully people who don't follow them (that's you and me, by the way), then, no, it doesn't matter.

Two views on the importance of grammar

What do we mean by 'does grammar matter'? Does it matter if you write:

> Me and John went to the conference.
> John and I goed to the conference.
> That's the conference John and I went to.

How about:

> John went to the conference and me.

Or:

> Conference went to John I and.

Yes, grammar matters

English isn't Latin: word order matters. At its simplest, grammar regulates word order. So, yes, grammar matters. An argument against the *teaching* of grammar has been made on and off since at least the 1960s (when, incidentally, my father was a teacher). It runs, in its full, idiotic glory, as follows: Teaching grammar stifles children's creativity.

Now, if by creativity, you mean the ability to have ideas, then we are very, very deep into philosophical territory involving the ability of ideas and language to exist independently of one another. And you can see that when it comes to painting, or music or drawing, a child doesn't need to know about grammar to be creative. Nor, for that matter, do they need grammar to have an idea for a story.

No, grammar doesn't matter

But if you want children to *write their ideas down*, and allow others to decode it *without their being present*, then grammar is going to be essential. This, I think, is the crux of the debate. The creativity brigade muddy the water by talking about ideas. The grammar brigade stir them up further by, essentially, frothing at the mouth every time a greengrocer misuses an apostrophe (like it matters).

Does grammar matter in advertising copy

Figure 11.1 Does grammar matter in advertising copy

Write clever

Give your ad a head start with an ePen. It's the pen
your hand would choose.

ePens Inc.

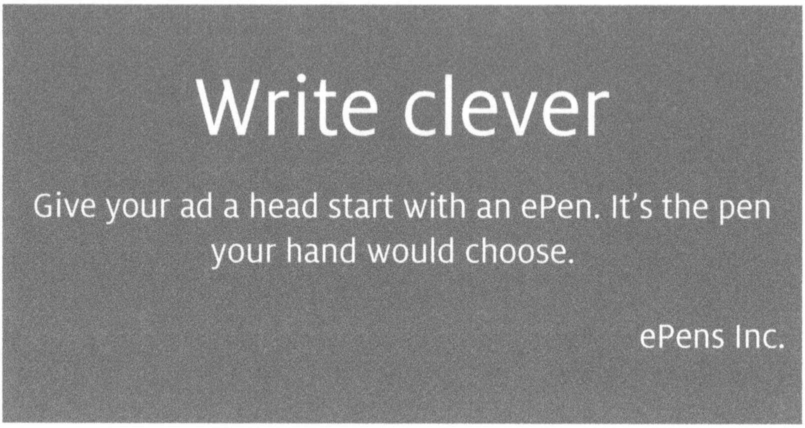

Copywriters as a breed tend to become super-uptight whenever they spot an
advertising slogan containing 'bad grammar'. Regardless of the fact that it
has been created (almost certainly) by another copywriter.

A particular sin is the adjective pressed into service as an adverb, as in the
(fictitious) ad for a pen company above. Publish an ad like this and you can
be sure social media will light up roughly three nanoseconds later.

'It should be "Write cleverly"', the grammar nerds exclaim. Well, maybe;
if your agency was run by English teachers. I would suggest that this sort of
'error' is a knowing misuse of grammar designed to add to the stickiness of
the slogan – it is more memorable precisely because it doesn't use 'correct'
grammar.

Or how about the following real example – a mailer for Inspire, a US
marketing agency.

A deliberate spelling error in the call to action – 'meat' for 'meet' is playful, entirely within the spirit of the mailer and 100 per cent unlikely to upset
or confuse the intended reader.

CASE STUDY Grill Mailers for Inspire Marketing Services

Inspire Marketing Services is a Chicago-area, promotional marketing firm.

These mailers aimed to entertain and spark interest among potential clients. Each postcard came with a grilling-related gift for the recipient: a bottle of branded barbecue sauce, a grilling recipe book and, lastly, a refrigerated box of premium-cut steaks.

> *Even a postcard with the cleverest of headlines is often going straight to the recycle bin. Some companies forget that even if their target is a business, their reader is a human being. We opted to appeal to the gatekeeper directly, with a series of surprises and supporting notes to brighten their day and pique their interest.*

It was important that the gifts not overshadow the nuts and bolts of who Inspire is and what they can do for clients. We decided to go big or go home with Grade A dad puns to not only amuse, but clearly convey Inspire's offering and connect that offering to the gifts at hand.

(Natalie C Mueller, Freelance Copywriter and Creative Director, Chicago)

Why grammar is like brain surgery

Let's use an analogy.

You wake up one morning with a blinding headache, visual hallucinations and a strange sense of having left your body.

On being admitted to A&E you are scanned and pronounced to have a small, benign brain tumour.

You need surgery.

When you are introduced to your consultant neurosurgeon, Mr Hegarty, he pats you reassuringly on the arm and tells you not to worry, 'I'm sure it will be fine'.

'Just out of curiosity,' you say, 'how much training in brain surgery have you had?'

'Training?' he laughs. 'Oh, no, I didn't train. Learning all those rules just stifles my creativity. I just dive in and cut out what looks icky.'

Every trade, from bricklaying to copywriting, is founded on a set of rules that govern the way things are done.

A brain surgeon avoids slicing into arteries to prevent your bleeding to death. A bricklayer (a good one, anyway) lays bricks in overlapping patterns that stop your house falling down.

A copywriter (any writer) makes verbs agree with subjects so people can figure out what she is trying to say.

Why grammar matters (really)

The problem is that 'good grammar' is a cultural shibboleth. To possess it is to be smart, classy, educated, socially superior; to lack it is to be stupid and low-status.

But many if not most of the people who work themselves into a froth about grammar fall into the latter group. And, funnily enough, many if not most of the advocates of a rule-free existence fall into the former.

The pedants confuse prejudice with rules. All the old favourites are trotted out, from sentences beginning with 'And' (I am still regularly told this is wrong) to sentences ending in prepositions. 'Apostrophe fails' (which, by the way, are errors of punctuation, not of grammar) are held up as a harbinger of societal breakdown. Nouns pressed into service as verbs are decried as being on a par with hate crimes. (Many so-called rules are actually matters of style not of grammar, as a cursory reading of *Fowler's Modern Usage* will confirm.) The hippie-linguists (don't tie me down with rules, maan) pretend to an anarchy they eschew in their own writing.

So where do we go from here? What is the right approach? No rules, all ideas? Or hang the ideas, let's just get our dangling modifiers squared away?

Key takeaway: It's more important to know 'good' grammar than to use it slavishly. Have faith in your ear for language and your customer insight.

Funnily enough, the answer lies in two small organs placed diametrically opposite each other, either side of the brain. The ears. Unusually sensitive to claggy grammar *and* muddy meaning, they are the perfect sense detectors for picking your way through the minefield.

To paraphrase another sixties mantra: If it sounds good, do it.

Bad: As a regular saver, I am writing to you about our new deposit account.

Good: You're the sort of saver we like. So I wanted to let you know about our new deposit account.

Are you a poet or a killer?

The title of this section means, which matters more to you, selling or fine writing? It is also an indirect quote from David Ogilvy, master advertising craftsman of the 20th century. Funnily enough, Truman Capote, whom I would definitely place in the group called 'Knows how to write brilliantly' and whose thoughts on the 'rules' of writing begin this chapter, seems to suggest that they are there to be broken. So let's take a brief diversion in the form of a quiz.

It's a lighthearted attempt to explore your attitudes to the rules of English versus the commercial exigencies of copywriting. But it has a serious point. What matters to *you*?

You can be a good, great or even fantastic copywriter and never earn a disapproving look from a cane-swishing classics master. You will undoubtedly have to work harder than a copywriter with a more, shall we say, *relaxed* approach to the language. (I desperately wanted to say *laissez faire* there but that would kind of go against the grain of the book, wouldn't it.)

Be honest in your answers. I am not so naïve as to imagine you won't be able to see what the 'right' answers are, but by giving the true answers, as you feel them, you will reveal more of yourself, and that will help you in deciding how to write copy. So, the quiz.

Q1 **Which would you rather send:**

a) A sales letter riddled with punctuation and spelling errors that brings in £50,000 in revenue

b) A sales letter perfectly punctuated that brings in £45,000?

Q2 **When should you use clichés in your copy?**

a) Never

b) Occasionally

c) When it will deepen rapport with the reader

Q3 Sentences without verbs are:

a) Bad English

b) A useful tool for varying pace

c) Perfectly OK

Q4 **It's fine to end a sentence with a preposition if you:**

a) Know why you're doing it

b) Are using the passive voice

c) Don't care what harm you inflict on the English language

Key takeaway: If you're in business, the same rules apply to writing copy as to everything else. If it's making money and not hurting your brand, do it.

Q5 **The most important thing about writing copy is that:**

a) Your reader understands you

b) It's correct

c) Your reader does what you want them to

Q6 Beginning a sentence with 'And' is:

a) Never OK

b) Always OK

c) Sometimes OK

Q7 You can tell a piece of copy is bad if:

a) It doesn't bring in sales

b) It contains grammatical errors

c) It isn't on-brand

Q8 Copywriters who break the rules of grammar should be:

a) Ennobled

b) Whipped

c) Asked why

Q9 It's OK to split an infinitive provided you:

a) Follow it with a noun

b) Correct it straight away

c) Have a particular reason for doing so

Q10 If you want to be a good copywriter:

a) Learn to spell

b) Learn to sell

c) Learn to yell

Scoring

Q1 a) 5, b) 2
Q2 a) 1, b) 2, c) 3
Q3 a) 1, b) 3, c) 2
Q4 a) 3, b) 0, c) 1
Q5 a) 2, b) 1, c) 3
Q6 a) 0, b) 1, c) 2
Q7 a) 3, b) 1, c) 2
Q8 a) 2, b) 1, c) 3
Q9 a) 0, b) 1, c) 2
Q10 a) 1, b) 2, c) 0

How did you do?

> 10 or under: You are a hardcore pedant. Nothing gets past you, especially incremental sales. Lighten up and start selling. Or write a best seller on punctuation and laugh at me all the way to the bank.

> 11–17: English matters to you but so does making a living. You recognize the need to play by the rules but also the need to put results ahead of perfection.

> 18–25: You can write perfectly correct English, but this is about making money. As long as it doesn't cause a fight you'll do it.

> 26 and above: You are the copywriting equivalent of friendly fire, collateral damage and killzone rolled into one. You don't care who gets hurt so long as you hit your target.

Copywriting is a precarious way to sell. Face-to-face is much better. So using every weapon at your disposal is essential for maximum results.

That may, occasionally, mean breaking the rules – and the 'rules' – of English. Consider your brand, your reader and your own conscience before you do it. But don't be too timid. Your competitors aren't.

From theory to profit

I think you have to know what sort of copywriter you are. Do you play fast and loose with the rules of English or do you revere them? Or, in fact, do you revere them in the way one might revere an Old Master painting in an art gallery while preferring pop art in one's living room? Neither position is right or wrong, though each places constraints on you as a writer. Too much reverence can lead you into time-consuming and largely unnoticed efforts not to say something that will frighten the horses; too little can lead you to confuse, alienate or anger your reader. Neither of these sounds particularly effective as a commercial strategy. I think the best approach is threefold: firstly, ensure that your copy reads smoothly and with clear meaning; secondly, avoid doing anything your reader would notice and react badly to; thirdly, bear in mind that without acceptable results, your copy, and you, might come to be seen as dispensable by the finance director.

With that in mind, how are you going to persuade your colleagues that good copywriting matters more than 'perfect' grammar? Because this, I sense, is the bigger challenge. You are perfectly capable of writing grammatically when the occasion demands it, and ungrammatically when it demands that, too. The problem is promoting a culture of good writing with your organization *as a whole*. The person who ostentatiously points out split infinitives in marketing reports is almost certainly sending sloppily written emails to colleagues every day of the week. How about putting together a short training session on 'How to write well for emails'. I have found that to be a reliable attention-getter. In among your sensible and easy-to-implement advice on active voice and short sentences, you can gently expose the grammar myths for what they are and embed the truth in your colleagues' minds in such a way that they begin to repeat it to others.

Workshop

1 When is it OK to write, 'It's nothing me and the wife had ever thought about'?

   a) Never

   b) If you are writing in the character of an uneducated everyman

   b) If your CEO tells you to

2 The best organs for judging good grammar are the eyes. True or false?

3 Is it OK to start a sentence with But?

4 Verbs must always agree with their subjects. True or false?

5 The reference book on grammar I mentioned is called:

   a) *Fowler's Modern Usage*

   b) *Fowler's Modern Grammar*

   c) *Howler's Modern Usage*

6 Can you give an example of a spurious 'rule' of English?

7 Finance directors are more concerned with profits than grammar. True or false?

8 Arrange these three types of error in descending order of importance for clarity of meaning (so, most important first): spelling, grammar, punctuation.

9 Many of the rules governing English derive from those governing which language?

10 Who should be the final arbiter of what's acceptable in a piece of copy?

Putting it into action

Exercise 63: Spread the word

Ask a few colleagues to complete this quiz 'as a bit of fun'. Tabulate the results and see what you get – you may be surprised.

Exercise 64: The poster child for good grammar

Research a list of inviolable rules of English grammar. Have someone put them into a nice poster. Circulate the poster throughout your organization.

Exercise 65: And another thing

Imagine you are having a conversation with a customer. They mention in passing that they loved your last email except for the sentence starting with 'And'. Write down first what you would like to say, then what you think you ought to say.

Exercise 66: I ain't bothered about grammar

Write some copy, deliberately including grammatical errors, *that still sounds natural* when you read it out loud.

Exercise 67: All aboard the grammar train

Design a one-hour good writing workshop for colleagues. Promote it internally and run it as often as you have time for but at least every three months, especially for new starters. You will be seen as an expert and will have fewer people 'improving' your grammar.

Exercise 68: Spot the deliberate mistake

How many errors of grammar can you spot in the following paragraph?

> John gave the presentation to Sally and me. It was about good grammar. If we weren't good writers before we certainly are afterwards. Having listened to the questions he fired at Sally and I, we both agreed with him becoming head writer at the company.

Tweet: How are you doing? Tweet me @Andy_Maslen

Injecting life into your sales pitch: An age-old method

16

What one has not experienced, one will never understand in print.

ISADORA DUNCAN

Introduction

The techniques I present to you in this chapter involve the visual description we've already looked at, some of the storytelling approaches we've also explored and the use of actual images as opposed to words. We are going to look at how to dramatize and illustrate your product promise, benefits or USP. In a sense this goes beyond even 'show, don't tell'. Perhaps we can call it 'involve, don't show'. Our aim is to get our prospect to experience, as fully as possible, what life would be like if they'd already bought the product.

Ironically, the products for which it's easiest to employ dramatization may be those that really don't need it. If you are selling high-end diamond jewellery, you could fill pages with dramatic enactments of ambassadorial cocktail receptions or light glancing off ballroom chandeliers, but do you really need to? Your customer can pretty much do the job on their own. Just hire a really good photographer and forget it. Harley Davidson motorcycles? A photograph of Route 66 and a few lines from Jack Kerouac and you may not even need the bike in shot. Just a headline 'Born to be tame?' and those middle management types will be queuing up with their credit cards at the ready.

But, what if you are selling something less obviously dramatic? Like supply chain software or an electric depilator. Now you may want to draw the eye away from the foreground and towards the far horizon, where the CEO's office beckons, or silk scarves glide effortlessly over baby-smooth legs. B2B copywriting in particular is crying out for some new approaches, especially given that many companies still see focusing on benefits as a maverick approach.

*

I've touched on the idea of rhetoric here and there in this book. But those Ancient Greeks were also dab hands at drama. And while I'm not suggesting we have anybody putting their own eyes out or going on a sex-strike, the idea of dramatizing the way your product/idea helps your customer is a great one to play with.

Dramatizing an idea means bringing it vividly to life in your reader's mind. So this is more than just a static picture. But it's not necessarily as much as creating a complete story.

Let's take an example. Supposing you are marketing a new e-book. It's been a runaway success and half of all Kindle users have already bought a copy. You could write something like this:

As I write to you, 50% of Kindle users have already downloaded a copy.

Which is true, but hardly compelling.

Or, you could write something like this:

Imagine getting a bus to work one day. It's almost full, but there is one place left. You sit down and start flicking through emails on your smartphone. But then you notice something.

Everyone else on the bus is reading the same book on their Kindle. That's right. The whole bus is reading *Think Yourself Rich* by Cady McWilson. What do they know that you don't?

Now you've dramatized the statistic, brought it to life. Your reader can picture the bus and the mini-drama of boarding, sitting down and noticing the other passengers.

Six places where drama works in copywriting

There are plenty of things you can dramatize. Here are six to get you started:

1 **Low prices** – compare to an everyday purchase.

2 **High prices** – divide by 365 (days in the year) and then do the same as for low prices.

3 **Features** – 'it's not just waterproof – you could tie this to a rock, fling it off Tower Bridge, dredge it up a week later and it would *still* be working.'

4 **Guarantees** – 'if this doesn't do *exactly* what I promised you it would, *don't* send it back. If it's faulty I don't want it. Take the biggest, heaviest hammer you can find and *smash it to pieces*. Then email me to let me know you've done it and I'll send you a cheque by return.'

5 **Testimonials** – 'I didn't want you to have to rely on my words. So here's what I did. I phoned ten of our customers *at random* and asked them the same, simple question. 'Would you buy this again?' And you know what? They all said yes.'

6 **Calls to action** – 'To order, tear off this form and send it back to me at…'

Try this: Try to dramatize your most important product benefit. Use verbs to present it as action.

How to do it in three easy steps

At the heart of any drama is action. And I think the same applies to dramatizing your sales pitch. You need your reader to picture themselves (or somebody else) doing something.

Step 1: pick a verb. Make it a very powerful, concrete verb. Not thinking, but doing.

Here's a list of 100 verbs that would work well for many different pitches:

act	bleed	build
aim	blow	burn
ask	boil	charge
bash	break	chop

chuck	laugh	slash
clap	launch	slide
cough	lick	slip
crack	lie	smash
crouch	lift	smile
crunch	lug	sneak
cuddle	mend	sneeze
cut	peep	spin
dash	pick	sprint
drink	pitch	squeeze
drive	pluck	stand
drop	poke	stare
eat	prod	stroke
fall	pull	swallow
find	pump	swing
fix	punch	tear
flap	push	throw
fry	race	trip
gallop	relax	twirl
gawk	rip	twist
grapple	run	walk
grind	scream	watch
grip	shake	whip
hide	shimmy	whisper
hit	shout	wrench
jack	sigh	wrestle
jive	sing	yodel
jump	sit	zip
kick	skid	
kiss	skip	

Step 2: create a setting. In my example above it was a packed commuter bus. But it could be a classroom, the reader's own home – or a specific room within it – an office, shoeshine stand, fast-food joint, workshop, train station, concert hall, garage, supermarket, street corner, bed, cave, tree house, beach, hotel lobby... you get the picture, I'm sure.

The best settings are universal, so your reader doesn't have to work too hard to imagine it. Pick a biotechnology lab and you'd better be sure your reader knows a centrifuge from a carousel; pick a school playground or a beach and it's a safe bet your reader won't have any trouble.

Step 3: plonk your reader down, either with your product or something standing in for it, into the middle of the setting and have them 'do' the verb there.

CASE STUDY   Management briefing for Quintiq

Every business has its planning puzzles, some large, some complex, some seemingly impossible to solve. Quintiq's vision is to solve every one using a single software platform.

Content marketing is a major plank of Quintiq's marketing strategy. In this document – a management briefing for the retail industry – we wanted to strike up a rapport with the reader by showing we understood their pain through dramatic recreations of the demands made by customers.

Quintiq sums up its house style as SLAPP – 'speak like a professional person'. That means Plain English but with an appropriate vocabulary for a technical audience.

I'll give you another example, using one of the verbs and one of the settings above. I'm selling a new type of circular saw for hobbyists. Its unique selling point is that it stops when it comes into contact with skin so fast that you only get a tiny scratch if you get your finger in the way of the blade.

Customers are getting harder to please

Not so long ago you could satisfy customers with a day-long delivery slot. Now, many think two-hour slots are too long. They want to know where your driver is. Perhaps they want their parcels to be left with a neighbor or brought to the office instead of their homes.

Flexible delivery is part of customer service. If you can't give customers what they want, there are plenty of other vendors who will.

Whether you own your logistics resources or subcontract the services doesn't matter. Yours is the brand that will suffer – or shine – depending on how well you deliver.

Read on to discover the three critical things you can do to enhance the reputation of your brand by providing excellent customer experience.

By focusing on the increasingly specific demands of retail customers, we at once established rapport and dramatized the frustrations of the job for retail logistics managers.

in f t

Good: Now, here's the safety feature our competitors wish they'd thought of first. Suppose you're in the middle of a cut when the doorbell rings. For a second – and let's be honest, that's all it takes – your attention wanders. And in that split second, your free hand slips in front of the blade. With any other saw you're looking at a trip to A&E. With the SlipStop, you might need a plaster, but otherwise you're OK.

Try this: Dramatize your benefits and your prospect sees how you make their life easier without the need for a lecture.

In a way, this is yet more storytelling. The key is to take the feature or benefit you want to emphasize and, instead of just describing it, *you show 0it happening.*

Bad: The Acme WonderWidget is stronger than steel.

Good: Your bridesmaids will thank you for a dress they really can wear again. Another reason we love it? Discreet pockets keep little extras like lipstick close at hand. (From the J Crew US website)

When to use pictures instead of words

It may seem odd to talk about images in a book about writing. But as copywriters, we are, or should be, concerned primarily with modifying our reader's behaviour, not writing. As images become ever easier to procure and manipulate, there seems to be a vanishingly small reason for not considering them as part of our armoury – and not the exclusive preserve of our designer colleagues. In fact, there has always been a great deal of cross-fertilization between copywriters and art directors in the advertising world, graphic designers in direct response and web designers in the online/mobile space.

I believe that, as information designers, we should be thinking visually from the outset. With the exception of Google AdWords, plain text emails and a few other image-free zones, everything we write is destined for an environment where imagery can flourish. And think about it, it's a lovely way to exercise power without responsibility. You can just type [image of vintage jukebox morphing into cyborg], add your headline, and now some poor schmuck has to spend three days realizing your vision.

On a more serious note, getting together with colleagues to brainstorm ideas for signature images is often a great way to create something truly memorable. I once took part in just such a conversation with a data publisher and the idea we came up with, of a gold logo being revealed in a pan of water and grit, became a lasting hero image for the campaign.

Every image needs a caption

In any case, every image needs its accompanying copy. Pictures need captions, alt tags, 'handwritten' comments, download instructions and other bits of ultra-brief copy (covered in depth in Chapter 6). And guess who has to write those? Let's look at the way we can use imagery to enhance our selling message while saving ourselves some time and effort into the bargain.

Human beings are primarily visual creatures. Our sense of sight delivers massive evolutionary advantage in terms of avoiding predators, finding food and shelter, and securing a mate. So we are genetically programmed to look first and read second. That makes pictures a brilliant – and brilliantly simple – way of grabbing your reader's attention. This, I think, is their main purpose, with showing not telling a close second.

As it happens, I have said in the past that words are more important than pictures in marketing campaigns. But I was wrong. Or wrong in one particular case.

As you may know, I created an app called CopyWriter. The descriptive copy for the App Store says that it types copywriting tips for you. Which is what it does. Which is all it does. Nowhere does it say it's a working typewriter.

Yet every now and again, I receive an email complaining (or sometimes ranting) that 'this app sucks – i can't type on it' (or words to that effect).

I think what happens is people see the screen shot – which does, I admit, show a rather lovingly recreated 1970s portable typewriter – and think, 'Ooh, a typewriter, I'll have that'. Because it's free they just click 'install'.

They are buying the promise encapsulated in the picture and not even bothering to read the copy.

Key takeaway: In the absence of visual images, use graphic language to create pictures in your customer's head.

Seven places where pictures add value to copy

Which does prove the point. Pictures are brilliant for communicating. Here are a few instances where well-chosen pictures really amplify your selling message:

1. About us – staff biographies

I don't know about you, but when I am researching a company, perhaps on behalf of a client, I always click to the About Us page. Those that include staff biographies fall into two discrete categories – those with pictures and those without.

Those without pictures look odd to my eye. Almost as if the company is hiding its people from me. Although the text of the biographies is interesting, I need to see their faces. This is a basic human instinct. We are programmed to look for, and at, human faces, and especially the eyes.

2. Products for sale

Why not show your customer what you're proposing they buy from you? I know this sounds obvious – and I admit to having pressed the point in other books – but people want to see what they're getting for their money. If you are selling a service, show the person delivering the service. If you are selling something so intangible it doesn't even get delivered by a person, show a customer experiencing it.

Do not fall into the trap, referred to elsewhere in this book, of assuming that a) your product is boring (it isn't to your customer) or b) that, therefore, a picture would be equally boring. Remember, you're not selling to you.

3. Testimonials

Lots of companies use testimonials. But how many accompany the copy with a photograph of the customer giving the testimonial? Or, even better, turn the whole thing into a movie? As I mentioned above, we are wired to search out and respond to human faces.

4. Sign-up pages

If you have a sign-up form on your website, consider adding images, either of the free stuff your members will get if they sign up, or maybe a person looking straight out at the viewer.

For one campaign, I tested all kinds of images, including pack shots of the free content and then an A/B test of male vs female 'students' in a vaguely academic setting. The female student won the test convincingly, so there she stands, frozen in the act of pulling a folder from a shelf.

5. Order forms

Order forms are crucial, especially online, where the gossamer thread connecting your customer to your bank balance is stretched even thinner. If you are trying to reduce abandonment rates, consider using a picture right by the tick-box to place the order. This way, you can distract the customer from the thought of spending money by showing them the thing that's going to solve their problems.

6. Social media updates

I remember a time when most social media sites were virtually image-free zones. Now images are all over them like a rash. Even when a text-only update would be enough, canny social media users are adding images just to make the update itself look more interesting.

7. Sales letters

Everybody talks about the $2 billion sales letter. Written by freelance copywriter Martin Conroy in 1974 (and based, incidentally, on a much earlier letter written by a copywriter named Bruce Barton) this copy-only sales letter ran unbeaten by any test letter for 28 years, bringing in the aforesaid amount of money for the publishers of the *Wall Street Journal*.

When the control was eventually beaten, in 2002, by a copywriter called Mal Decker, he did two things worthy of note. First, he doubled the length of the letter, from two pages to four. Second, and the reason I'm including the example here, he added sample page images from the paper itself. So here are a couple of things to think about for your own marketing campaigns – on the App Store or elsewhere.

Download: You can download both versions of the letter by clicking on or typing the URL below into your browser.

The $2 billion sales letter

Three questions to ask yourself about images

1 If you are using an image, does it convey accurately the promise of the product? Or are the messages from picture and copy in conflict?

2 If you aren't using an image, why not? They are incredibly powerful and can, on their own, motivate people to act.

3 If you are using a picture that has nothing to do with your product, why? Illustrating your headline – pic of contortionist plus 'We bend over backwards to help you' for example – is not moving your reader closer to 'yes', just to 'I get it!'.

Engage: You don't have to use images, but as we're wired to respond to them, make sure you have a strong reason for avoiding them.

Use the power of the image to hook your reader, *then* drive the hook deeper with a great headline.

From theory to profit

Dramatization is less a standalone bit of linguistic trickery and more of a different approach to your overall sales pitch. You aren't selling the product, you are selling the experience of ownership. It's certainly more of a stretch than some of the other techniques I've put before you. So maybe you need to feel your way into it. Rather than overhauling your entire approach to writing copy, why not start small, by writing a passage of copy for your website or next sales campaign with a dramatic engine at its core? It could go on a landing page or a box within an HTML email or sales letter. The point is, with a catchy headline it will draw your reader's eye and will work fine on its own. Then, as your confidence grows, you can experiment with writing an entire pitch that revolves around dramatization.

Take a look around your organization. How are you using images at the moment? Do you have anything original and unique to your business, or are you drowning in a sea of library images? Who are the images for? The marketing department? The board of directors? Or your customers? An example: I was consulted by a large charity that was trying to engage farmers in its mission. In a workshop I stuck two rows of images along a wall. On the top row were images from the charity's marketing materials aimed at the farmers: 25 birds. On the bottom row were images from ads running in that week's edition of the magazine *Farmer's Weekly*: 25 tractors. Make sure that you select pictures in the same way that you select words: for their relevance to your customer and their usefulness in conveying your sales message.

Workshop

1 What part of speech do you need to use to dramatize a point?

a) A verb

b) A noun

c) An adjective

2 You dramatize your product benefits by using:

a) Motion

b) Action

c) Tension

3 Describe a technique for dramatizing high prices.

4 The Watkins Wonder Widget is 50 per cent stronger than our leading competitor. Dramatized or not?

5 Complete this dramatization mantra: _____, don't show.

6 Why are we so tuned in to images?

a) Because our eyes are capable of processing up to 30 million different colours

b) Because of shortened attention spans caused by the internet

c) Because it conferred evolutionary advantage

7 Name three ways a copywriter can enhance the power of an image.

8 What is the main purpose of an image?

9 When is it a good idea to use a library shot?

a) When you have neither the time nor the budget to commission original photography or illustration

b) When originality is not at a premium

c) To illustrate a blog post

10 You can't sell without using images. True or false?

Putting it into action

Exercise 69: One character in search of an author

Take one of your products. Pick its most important benefit. Using our three-step method above, write a passage of copy that dramatizes it.

Exercise 70: Dramatic headlines

Write a headline for the copy you wrote for the last exercise. Use a strong verb as the first word.

Exercise 71: Curtain calls

Write a call to action that continues whatever dramatic idea you are working with for this chapter's exercises. Do not use the word 'order'.

Exercise 72: From mind's eye to friend's eye

Write some descriptive copy that paints a detailed picture of a place, person or thing. Get a friend or colleague to read it and then describe or, preferably, draw, what they 'see'. How close were they to what you 'saw' in your mind's eye?

Exercise 73: Planning visually

The next time you are planning a piece of copy, don't start with the words. Start with the pictures. Block out the structure of your copy and then, before you type a single word, think about what images you will need to bring your copy to life. Product shots? Photos of people (always good)? Graphics? Start sourcing them at the same time as you start writing. Remember to write captions, Alt tags and the rest for each image you select.

Exercise 74: Image is everything

Look at all the images on your website. What are they there for? What are they doing? What do they say about you? Be honest.

Tweet: How are you doing? Tweet me @Andy_Maslen

AFTERWORD
The XYZ of copywriting

Picasso is supposed to have said that he spent 10 years learning to draw like an adult and the rest of his life learning to draw like a child. He meant, I think, that his formal, rules-based training equipped him to start his real artistic education: leaving the prescriptions of the academy behind to find a deeper truth. I have tried, in my own small way to follow his example. I learned, as a 20-something junior copywriter: a) the 'right' way to start a sales letter (Dear Client); b) the 'best' way to talk about benefits (a list of bullet points underneath a heading that read 'Benefits of buying X'); and c) the 'correct' ratio of references to reader and writer (3 to 1). I followed those prescriptions for a long time before I realized that there was more to persuading people than the ABC of copywriting.

From that point on, I began to explore other ways of writing copy, not always to universal acclaim from employer or client, I have to add. But, steadily, and with growing confidence (and, most importantly, with the results to back up my hunches), I started to assemble a new approach to my job. The XYZ of copywriting, if you like. As you know by now, it relies for its power not on grammatical punctilio, nor an encyclopaedic vocabulary, but on an understanding of, and feeling for, human nature.

One question I return to again and again, is why so many employers, clients and even marketeers seem so wary of exploring the approaches described in this book. Not all of them, by any means: some occupy the overlap of the copywriting Venn diagram, where one oval represents 'this is how "proper" copywriting sounds' and the other, 'this is the sort of language normal people respond to'. I feel the reluctance of the remainder is a combination of suspicion and anxiety. Suspicion that because they are unfamiliar or counter-intuitive, they won't work; and anxiety that trying something new might result in lost sales and, possibly, lost jobs. All completely understandable, of course.

The easiest method of pushing through this resistance without causing heart attacks or boardroom rows is the one I always return to when challenged. Test it. From the earliest days of advertising and the keyed press advertisement, through the golden age of direct mail, direct response advertising and scratch codes, to today's infinitely segmentable and measurable digital marketing, testing has been the copywriter's best friend. No need to bet the farm, just 5 per cent of it.

Seven core principles of copy testing

Here it's worth touching, just briefly, on the principles that underlie testing. When I talk about testing, I mean scientifically controlled testing. Seven core principles are:

1 Test a **hypothesis**. Before you start thrashing around writing alternative headlines, calls to action and landing page copy, decide what you are going to test and what you are hoping to achieve. For example, 'I believe that if we write a subtly different call to action copy on our landing page, we will get more sign-ups to our newsletter'.

2 Test alternative versions **simultaneously**. Mailing one version of an email on a Monday and the second on a Wednesday may reveal a difference in clickthroughs, but that could be due to the day of the week, not the different copy.

3 Test your hypothesis using a **sample** of your entire list. Do NOT divide your entire list in half. Should the test fail, you don't want to have used 50 per cent of your potential response to find out.

4 Use a test cell large enough to give **statistically significant** results. A result showing 12 clickthroughs from the test and 14 from the control from a list of 200 is unlikely to be significant.

5 Ensure the list is **split randomly**. The A/B test is so called because the recipients receive the test and the control in strict, alternating order: A, B, A, B, A, B...

6 Test **one thing at a time**. To do otherwise risks muddied waters and unclear conclusions about which factor being tested made the difference.

7 Test **big things before little things**. There is no point testing green buttons against red buttons until you have tested price, offer, copy length and guarantee terms.

Testing, incidentally, is not the same as trying. I still remember being told, over and over again by an older manager, when I suggested some new line of attack, 'We tried that 10 years ago and it doesn't work'. Trying something without controlling other variables is not a test.

The art and science of copywriting for the emotions

You may have noticed something strange about some of the ideas in this book. They contradict each other, and other advice in other books on copywriting – including mine. Or they appear to. The trouble is this.

Writing copy – writing anything – is not a science, it's an art. If you're born with a talent for it, your road is smoother than someone who's had to work at it. Whether you have that talent or not, what really matters are two related aspects of your writing. First, how it sounds. Second, the effect it has on your reader.

Most authorities on writing agree that how a piece of writing sounds is more important than how it looks. They will study the rules of English and more or less obey them. But they never let themselves become slaves to them.

A simple example. The use of 'shoulder' as a verb has been attributed to many different writers as far back as 1582. William Wordsworth, the poet, was allegedly rendered speechless with admiration when Samuel Taylor Coleridge used it in a poem. It is now in widespread use, yet many pedantic souls shudder when they spy somebody using a noun as a verb. Why?

This book is designed to help you become a better business writer. And what matters in business is results. If your writing achieves results it is because it changed your reader's behaviour. Your reader will not be swayed by 'perfect' English – if such a thing exists – but by the emotional power of what you say to them. Unlike a car engine, pump or electric motor, the power of a piece of writing is not determined by the creator but by the user.

If your reader feels no power, there *is* no power.

Please share this book with your friends

The tools, tips and techniques in this book have all proved immensely valuable to me as ways to bridge that gap between what I want and what my reader wants. I hope they help you in the same way.

Please feel free to quote from the book (while sticking to the copyright rules) – just attribute the quote to me.

And if you've enjoyed the book, as your final exercise, please contribute a review on Amazon.

Want to keep on improving the way you write?

Finally, if you would like more help with your writing, I publish a monthly newsletter, write two blogs and run regular open courses on copywriting. I also developed Breakthrough Copywriting – a video-based distance-learning programme **www.breakthrough-copywriting.com.**

Join my newsletter and find out more about my courses at: **www. copywritingacademy.co.uk.**

I do, still, write plenty of copy myself. Find out more about my copywriting agency and the ways we can help you sell more at: **www.sunfish.co.uk.**

GLOSSARY

A/B test   a way of discovering which of two pieces of copy or design works best

above-the-line   traditionally, marketing and advertising that does not include a response device such as an order form, website address or 0800 number – now increasingly blurred, as posters sprout Blippar codes, and press ads QR codes

active voice   form of sentence where the subject precedes the verb

advantage   the way in which a feature performs better than a rival or comparator

AIDCA   acronym for the planning structure: attention, interest, desire, conviction, action (itself derived from AIDA)

alliteration   literary technique where each word begins with the same letter (or occasionally sound)

alt tags   pieces of text 'behind' graphics on websites and emails that appear only if the user doesn't download the images

amygdala   small, almond-shaped organ in the limbic system

assonance   literary device where internal vowel sounds of words rhyme

assumptive close   a way of asking for the order where the fact of the sale is taken as a given

B2B   business-to-business (accountancy services, for example)

B2C   business-to-consumer (cosmetics, for example)

benefits   the ways a product or service make the buyer's life better

brain stem   portion of the brain between the spinal cord and the limbic system

bus-sides   advertisements pasted onto the sides of buses

call to action   the part of copy that asks for the order or required action from the reader

campaign   a marketing programme consisting of more than one element or execution

channel   any way of sending communications, eg TV, post, internet

Charlotte Street   street in the West End of London famous for advertising agencies in the 1980s, notably Saatchi & Saatchi

clickthrough   the action taken when a web user clicks on a link, especially one from an advertisement

clickthrough rate   the number of clickthroughs received as a percentage of the number of times an ad is shown

content marketing   form of marketing involving the provision of free information to build trust with potential customers

control in an A/B test, the best-performing copy so far, against which a new piece (the test) is compared

conversion rate the number of orders received as a percentage of the number of clickthroughs

digital natives people who know what a hashtag is but not a fax machine

direct mail letters sent by commercial organizations, charities and others to mailing lists soliciting custom, donations or support

direct marketing any form of marketing where messages are tailored and sent to individual people, whether consumers or business people

direct response essentially the same as direct marketing, applied to copy where the prospect is expected to take an action, eg send back a coupon or click on a link

empathy the ability to feel what another person is feeling

endorsement praise for a company, product or service from a well-known figure

feature marketing term for what a product or service is or what it contains

fMRI – functional magnetic resonance imaging a computerized scanning technique that displays brain activity in real time

hashtag a keyword with a # used on Twitter to categorize tweets

html acronym for hypertext markup language

hyperlink text or image on a web page or email that links to another web page

hypertext words or sentences on web pages or emails that act as hyperlinks

imperative mood the form of sentence giving an order or instruction, eg Order now.

infographic portmanteau word composed of information and graphics popular among content marketeers (formerly, diagram)

landing page web page with specific sales purpose reached by a link from an online or email advertising campaign or piece of content

library images also known as stock photos, commercially available images

limbic system area of the brain comprising a number of separate organs including the amygdala, hypothalamus and olfactory bulbs

logos the intellectual part of a rhetorical argument

Madison Avenue street in New York famous for its advertising agencies

Maslow's 'hierarchy of needs' pyramid diagram of human needs proposed by Abraham Maslow

metre rhythm of a sentence

multimedia all non-text-based information on a website, eg video, audio, animation, photographs

neural pathways   route taken by the electrical impulses that communicate between nerve cells in the brain

neurons   brain cells

NLP   quasi-scientific discipline standing for Neuro-Linguistic Programming

olfactory bulbs   small organs in the limbic system responsible for the sense of smell

orbito-frontal cortex (OFC)   the part of the brain responsible for driving decision-making

palaeomammalian   literally, 'old mammal'

passive voice   form of sentence in which the subject of the verb follows the verb

pathos   the emotional part of a rhetorical argument

pedant   small-minded individual who derives pleasure from pointing out the supposed errors of others

persona   pen-portrait of a company's typical customer

plasticity (brain)   the ability of the brain to relearn functions using different areas, sometimes seen in people who have suffered strokes or other brain injuries or diseases

point of pain   the thing that keeps a prospect awake at 3 am

pre-frontal cortex   the brain's 'grey matter' – responsible for high levels of thinking

prosody   the intonation, sounds and rise-and-fall of speech

register   the level of formality of a piece of writing

resonance   literary technique where one piece of writing borrows significance from an established story, idea, character or speech

salience   relative importance – in neuroscientific terms, the importance of a stimulus, used to direct limited cognitive and perceptual resources

scanning   reading strategy involving picking out headings and images

shibboleth   a sacred cow, something that marks people as members of a group (or outsiders)

spinal cord   part of the nervous system running inside the spine

staff turnover   percentage of employees leaving each year

statistically significant   a difference in results that cannot be attributed to random variation

strapline   a slogan or tagline

test   in an A/B test, a new piece of copy that is tested against the control

test cell   a portion of a mailing list used in an A/B test

UBC   ultra-brief copy, such as tweets, alt tags and picture captions

FURTHER READING

Barden, P (2013) *Decoded*, Wiley

Bird, D (1999) *Commonsense Direct Marketing*, Kogan Page, London

Bird, D (1994) *How to Write Sales Letters That Sell*, Kogan Page, London

Bly, R (2006) *The Copywriter's Handbook*, Henry Holt & Company, LLC, New York

Borg, J (2007) *Persuasion*, Pearson Education, Harlow

Burchfield, R W (2004) *Fowler's Modern English Usage*, Oxford University Press

Calne, D B (2000) *Within Reason*, Vintage, London

Caples, J (1998) *Tested Advertising Methods*, Prentice Hall, Parabus

Carey, G V (1971) *Mind the Stop*, Cambridge University Press

Chalker, S and Weiner, E (1994) *The Oxford Dictionary of English Grammar*, Oxford University Press

Cialdini, R (2000) *Influence*, HarperCollins, New York

Cochrane, J (2004) *Between You and I*, Icon Books, Cambridge

Crystal, D (2003) *The Cambridge Encyclopedia of the English Language*, Cambridge University Press

Crystal, D (2002) *The English Language*, Cambridge University Press

Damasio, A (2000) *Feeling of What Happens*, Vintage, London

The Economist Style Guide, Profile, London

Fraser-Robinson, J (1989) *The Secrets of Effective Direct Mail*, McGraw-Hill Book Company, Maidenhead

Gill, E (1993) *An Essay on Typography*, David R Godine, Boston

Gowers, E (1987) *The Complete Plain Words*, Penguin, London

Hopkins, C C (1998) *Scientific Advertising*, NTC Business Books, Lincolnwood

Humphrys, J (2011) *Lost for Words*, Hodder, London

King, G (2009) *Punctuation*, HarperCollins, Glasgow

King, S (2001) *On Writing*, Oxford University Press, Oxford

Knight, D (1997) *Creating Short Fiction*, St Martin's Griffin, New York

Knowles, E (1999) *The Oxford Dictionary of 20th Century Quotations*, Oxford University Press

Knowles, E (2009) *The Oxford Dictionary of Quotations*, Oxford University Press

Kobs, J (1992) *Profitable Direct Marketing*, NTC Business Books, Lincolnwood

Martin, S J, Goldstein, N J and Cialdini, R B (2014) *The Small Big*, Profile Books, London

Masterson, M and Forde, J (2011) *Great Leads*, American Writers and Artists, Inc, Delray Beach

McCorkell, G (1990) *Advertising That Pulls Response*, McGraw-Hill, Maidenhead

Ogilvy, D (2011) *Confessions of an Advertising Man*, Southbank, London

Ogilvy, D (2007) *Ogilvy on Advertising*, Prion, London

Ogilvy, D (1988) *The Unpublished David Ogilvy*, Sidgwick & Jackson, London

Partridge, E and Whitcut, J (1997) *Usage and Abusage*, Penguin, London

Room, A (1993) *Brewer's Dictionary of Phrase and Fable*, Cassell, London

Schwab, V (1985) *How to Write a Good Advertisement*, Harper & Row, New York

The Shorter Oxford English Dictionary (2002), Oxford University Press

Shotton, R (2018) *The Choice Factory*, Harriman House

Stein, S (1999) *Solutions for Writers*, Souvenir Press, London

Stone, B and Jacobs, R (2007) *Successful Direct Marketing Methods*, McGraw-Hill, New York

Strunk Jr, W and White, E B (1999) *The Elements of Style*, Allyn & Bacon, Needham Heights

Sugarman, J (2006) *The Adweek Copywriting Handbook*, John Wiley & Sons, Hoboken, New Jersey

Truss, L (2003) *Eats, Shoots and Leaves*, Profile, London

Waite, M (2004) *Oxford Thesaurus of English*, Oxford University Press

Weiner, E S C and Delahunty, A (1994) *The Oxford Guide to English Usage*, Oxford University Press

Weintz, W (1987) *Solid Gold Mailbox*, John Wiley & Sons, London

Wheildon, C (2005) *Type and Layout*, Prentice Hall, Paramus

Zyman, S (2002) *The End of Advertising As We Know It*, John Wiley & Sons, Hoboken, New Jersey

WORKSHOP ANSWERS

Chapter 5: Harnessing the power of emotional copywriting to persuade your prospects

1 The limbic system and the orbito-frontal cortex.

2 People make decisions solely on emotion then validate their decision using information.

3 Emotiona acts as a feedback mechanism in decision-making.

4 False. You can write emotionally without having strong feelings about the subject.

5 The emotion your prospect is feeling right now is called the steady state emotion.

6 Emotions are so important to humans because they conferred evolutionary advantage.

7 The six primary human emotions are happiness, sadness, disgust, anger, fear and surprise.

8 There are many secondary (social) emotions, including confidence, envy and guilt.

9 Egotism is not a tertiary (background) emotion.

10 False. ALL marketers need to worry about their customers' emotions.

Chapter 6: Three big ideas you should use for copy before highlighting the 'benefits'

1 False. Promises needn't explain in detail how the thing promised will be attained. The promise itself is the hook.

2 False. You must keep your promise.

3 Curiosity is triggered by the form of your promise.

4 Promises are part of the glue that binds societies together.

5 The style of writing where you give your reader an order is called the imperative mood.

6 Scarcity makes secrets inherently desirable.

7 The root of the word 'prurience' is 'itch'.

8 True. *She made it as a six-figure copywriter. But she's never going to tell you how* is a secrets headline.

9 DLS stands for Dirty Little Secrets.

10 Learning a secret feeds our need for belonging and social status.

11 Dialogue is not a key element of a story.

12 The limbic system responds when we hear a story.

13 You use the present tense for hypothetical stories.

14 Storytelling techniques include lean style, dialogue, surprise, the telling detail, character sketches, suspense and the present tense. There are others.

15 Action propels a story.

Chapter 7: A powerful process for developing customer empathy through copy

1 The Five Ps are Personal, Pleasant, Professional, Plain, Persuasive.

2 The character you have created is a persona.

3 True. You can personalize without being personal.

4 It is never OK to show your reader you are writing to more than one person.

5 You should use the word 'you' as often as you need to in a sentence.

6 John Caples headlined his hernia relief ad, 'HERNIA'.

7 People looking for the better mousetrap want a house free of mice.

8 Joseph Sugarman says the sole purpose of the headline is to make the reader read the next line.

9 The list of features is the approach you can't use in this style of copywriting.

10 Your prospect is most likely to be worrying about their problems at 3 am.

11 Questions your reader is asking you include:
- – Why did you want to see me?
- – What do you want to talk about?
- – How do I know I can trust you?
- – How are you going to make my life better?
- – Can you prove it will work?
- – Who else has it worked for?
- – How do I get hold of it?
- – What if I don't like it?

12 The word *amanuensis* means writer's assistant.

13 Both David Ogilvy and John Caples were fans of the 'what you say is more important than how you say it' school of copywriting.

14 You must find out what makes your reader tick.

15 The best place to discover more about horseracing enthusiasts is the track.

Chapter 8: Copywriting hacks: Flattery will get you everywhere

1 Flattery meets the human need for self-esteem. (And the esteem of others.)

2 The ideal place to use flattery is at the beginning.

3 True. Flattery only works if it's appropriate to the reader.

4 Benjamin Disraeli said that when it came to royalty you should apply flattery with a trowel.

5 Talking about 'liking', Robert Cialdini asserts that we are more likely to comply with people who do all three: make us laugh, pay us compliments and are physically attractive.

6 People like being offered upgrades because it makes them feel good about themselves.

7 Frequent Buyers' Club would not work as a luxury scheme name. Too obviously transactional.

8 Expensive things are worth the money; costly things aren't.

9 If your customer is moaning about price, you haven't shown them the value.

10 The best kind of product to work into a luxury deal is something that costs you a bit to produce and has a high price tag.

Chapter 9: The Ancient Greek secret of emotionally engaging copy

1 *Logos* refers to your argument.

2 The warrior-king advised by Aristotle was Alexander The Great.

3 'I have something I simply have to share with you' is based on emotion.

4 True. Advancing a logical argument enhances your character in the eyes of your reader.

5 If benefits are *pathos*, features are *logos*.

Chapter 10: Copywriting and connecting on social media

1 People love social media because they are social animals.

2 The golden rule of posting on social media sites is not to post anything you wouldn't want to see on a poster outside your office.

3 It's OK to post things that aren't strictly true if your followers can tell you're joking.

4 You should follow your organization's brand guidelines as closely as they say you should.

5 False. Because it's social media, the old rules of commerce don't apply. *They always apply.*

6 The ideal character limit to observe for email subject lines is 29–39.

7 In the author's experience of A/B subject line tests, including first names tends to increase the open rate.

8 The driving emotion behind clickbait headlines is curiosity.

9 The best punctuation mark to use in UBC is the full stop.

10 With its keywords at the beginning, length, question mark, storytelling approach, speech marks and promise, *Back pain? Try this 'ridiculous' cure* is the favourite.

Chapter 11: Creating calls to action: Top tips to bring home the bacon

1 Using 'if' in a call to action implies doubt in the writer's mind.

2 Yes, using emotion in a call to action is fine.

3 The best time to write your call to action is first.

4 True. The best way to write a call to action is from the perspective of the customer.

5 Buy is the odd one out: it is not an emotional word.

Chapter 12: Balancing pleasure and profit: Five techniques to write fantastic copy

1 Metre is the rhythm of your copy.

2 Alliteration is when two or more consecutive words share an initial consonant sound.

3 False. There is no need to limit all your sentences to between five and eight words.

4 True. Metaphors and similes are both forms of visual language.

5 'Sex' will get your reader's attention.

6 Accidental repetition is a bad thing because it distracts your reader.

7 The ideal number for a group of repetitions is three.

8 False. Repetition can work with individual words, sounds and initial letters as well as complete phrases.

9 When you deliberately repeat yourself your reader discerns a pattern.

10 The first people to consciously use repetition in argument were the Ancient Greeks.

11 Putting speech marks around figures of speech is a bad habit because it draws attention to your writing and away from your message.

12 The act of deleting passages of writing that make *us* happy is called murder your darlings.

13 It is OK to use humour in copywriting when you want to make your reader laugh.

14 The only person you should be writing for is your customer.

15 True. It is OK to say 'We're putting the cart before the proverbial horse'. It's just not necessary.

Chapter 13: How to engage your imagination and free your creativity

1 The tests you can use to prepare for some creative thinking are the playground test, the user test, the 'do I know what I am trying to say?' test and the planning test.

2 Techniques useful for creating new ideas are word association, word games and listing cultural references.

3 Until you have written an idea down you must never judge it.

4 You can stimulate new ideas by changing time, place or materials.

5 Using pencil and paper is an effective way of thinking more creatively because it frees you from the tyranny of the blank computer screen and because it uses more muscles than tapping keys. You can also scribble down ideas and images much faster and still see them if you cross them out.

6 Show, don't tell.

7 Adjectives are there to add information, not emphasis.

8 Anton Chekhov said 'Don't tell me it was night; show me the moon reflected in a shard of glass'.

9 False. You don't need to be emotional to convey emotion.

10 False. B2C and B2B copywriters can both benefit from trying their own products.

Chapter 14: Tone and technique in copy: Finding your voice (and that of others)

1 Different aspects of a writer's voice include sentence length, use of foreign words, use of long words, question tags, use of personal pronouns, use of old-fashioned terms, use of slang, use of jargon, use of punctuation, 'asides' to reader, mixing of register, literary references, wit/humour, deliberately poor grammar, childlike phrasing, reticence in place of boldness, boldness in place of reticence, attitude, surreality.

2 Trademark stylistic techniques are fine provided they are used in moderation.

3 You should avoid having a distinctive voice when you are supposed to be invisible.

4 Techniques that will make you sound educated include sentence length (long), use of punctuation (complex), use of foreign words, use of long words, literary references.

5 Playful techniques include question tags, use of slang, 'asides' to reader, mixing of register, wit/humour, deliberately poor grammar, childlike phrasing, surreality.

6 The easiest way to judge the tone of voice of a piece of writing is to read it aloud.

7 False. Only 7 per cent of your meaning is carried by the words you use when you are communicating feelings or attitudes.

8 False. Truthful is not a tone of voice.

9 Techniques that make your tone of voice sound friendly include using personal words, everyday words, 'polite' words and simple syntax.

10 Evoking is better than emoting.

Chapter 15: The definitive guide to when grammar matters in copywriting

1 It's OK to write, 'It's nothing me and the wife had ever thought about' if you are writing in the character of an uneducated everyman.

2 False. The best organs for judging good grammar are the ears.

3 Yes, it is OK to start a sentence with 'But'.

4 True. Verbs must always agree with their subjects.

5 The reference book on grammar I mentioned is called *Fowler's Modern Usage*.

6 'You mustn't split an infinitive,' is a spurious rule of English. As is, 'You mustn't end a sentence with a preposition'. As is, 'You mustn't start a sentence with And'.

7 True. Finance directors are more concerned with profits than grammar. But they still care about grammar.

8 In descending order of importance for clarity of meaning are errors of grammar, punctuation and spelling.

9 Many of the rules governing English derive from those governing Latin. Go figure.

10 The final arbiter of what's acceptable in a piece of copy should be your reader.

Chapter 16: Injecting life into your sales pitch: An age-old method

1 You dramatize points with verbs.

2 You dramatize your product benefits by using action.

3 A technique for dramatizing high prices is to divide by 365 (days of the year) then compare to the price of an everyday purchase.

4 *The Watkins Wonder Widget is 50 per cent stronger than our leading competitor.* Not dramatized. *The Watkins Wonder Widget can support six dray horses compared to only four for our nearest competitor* is better.

5 Involve, don't show.

6 We are so tuned in to images because they conferred evolutionary advantage in terms of being able to spot prey, predators and mates.

7 Copywriters can enhance the power of an image by adding captions, Alt tags, download instructions or handwritten comments.

8 The main purpose of an image is to grab attention.

9 It's a good idea to use a library shot in all three situations: when originality is not valued, when you don't have the time or budget to commission original imagery, or to illustrate a blog post.

10 False. You can sell without using images.

How did you do?

Add up all your correct answers. Be generous; give yourself a point if you believe your answer is better than, or equally as valid as, mine.

Divide the total by 125.
Multiply by 100.
That's your percentage score.
The higher the better.

Tweet: Why not tweet your score to me @Andy_Maslen using the hashtag #HeyAndy

The copy for the case studies featured in this book was written by either Andy Maslen or Jo Kelly at Sunfish, the author's writing agency, except for Quad and Inspire (pp 135 and 181 respectively), both of which were written by Natalie Mueller, a freelance copywriter in Chicago, United States; CareSuper (p 170), written by Dr Ryan Wallman, Head of Copy at Wellmark in South Yarra, Australia; and Lidl (p xviii), written by Jeremy Carr and team at TBWA\The Disruption Agency.

A NOTE ON THE TYPE

The body text in this book is set in Sabon. An old-style serif typeface, Sabon has often been described as a Garamond revival. It was designed by Jan Tschichold, the German designer and typographer, in 1964–1967. It was released jointly by the Stempel, Linotype and Monotype type foundries in 1967.

The headings are set in Milo Sans. This face was created by American designer and typographer Mike Abbink in 2000. Its compact design, with very low ascenders and descenders, makes it particularly suitable for magazine and newspaper work. The name comes from a species of sorghum, a cereal grass.

INDEX

CPSIA information can be obtained
at www.ICGtesting.com
Printed in the USA
LVHW070846191221
706633LV00006B/112